The Bible Speaks Today

Series Editors: J. A. Motyer (OT)
John R. W. Stott (NT)

The Message of 2 Peter & Jude

The promise of his coming

Titles in this series

The Message of 2 Peter & Jude

The promise of his coming

Dick Lucas
& Christopher Green

With Study Guide

Inter-Varsity Press
Leicester, England
Downers Grove, Illinois, U.S.A.

InterVarsity Press
P.O. Box 1400, Downers Grove, Illinois 60515, U.S.A.
38 De Montfort Street, Leicester LE1 7GP, England

InterVarsity Press®, U.S.A., is the book-publishing division of InterVarsity Christian Fellowship®, a student movement active on campus at hundreds of universities, colleges and schools of nursing in the United States of America, and a member movement of the International Fellowship of Evangelical Students. For information about local and regional activities, write Public Relations Dept., InterVarsity Christian Fellowship, 6400 Schroeder Rd., P.O. Box 7895, Madison, WI 53707-7895.

Inter-Varsity Press, England, is the book-publishing division of the Universities and Colleges Christian Fellowship (formerly the Inter-Varsity Fellowship), a student movement linking Christian Unions in universities and colleges throughout the United Kingdom and the Republic of Ireland, and a member movement of the International Fellowship of Evangelical Students. For information about local and national activities write to UCCF, 38 De Montfort Street, Leicester LE1 7GP.

USA ISBN 0-8308-1238-5
UK ISBN 0-85111-149-1

Typeset in Great Britain by Parker Typesetting Service, Leicester
Printed in the United States of America ∞

Library of Congress Cataloging-in-Publication Data

Lucas, R. C. (Richard Charles), 1925-
    The message of 2 Peter and Jude: the promise of His coming/R. C.
Lucas and Christopher Green.
        p.   cm.—(The Bible speaks today)
    Includes bibliographical references.
    ISBN 0-8308-1238-5 (paper: alk. paper)
    1. Bible. N.T. Peter, 2nd—Commentaries.   2. Bible. N.T. Jude—
Commentaries.   I. Green, Christopher, 1958-   . II. Series.
BS2795.3.L83   1995
227'.93077—dc20   95-43635
                                                              CIP

British Library Cataloguing in Publication Data

A catalogue record for this book is available from the British Library.

17	16	15	14	13	12	11	10	9	8	7	6	5	4	3
09	08	07	06	05	04	03	02							

General preface

The Bible Speaks Today describes a series of both Old Testament and New Testament expositions, which are characterized by a threefold ideal: to expound the biblical text with accuracy, to relate it to contemporary life, and to be readable.

These books are, therefore, not 'commentaries', for the commentary seeks rather to elucidate the text than to apply it, and tends to be a work rather of reference than of literature. Nor, on the other hand, do they contain the kind of 'sermons' which attempt to be contemporary and readable without taking Scripture seriously enough.

The contributors to this series are all united in their convictions that God still speaks through what he has spoken, and that nothing is more necessary for the life, health and growth of Christians than that they should hear what the Spirit is saying to them through his ancient – yet ever modern – Word.

J. A. MOTYER
J. R. W. STOTT
Series Editors

Authors' preface

'I confess there is no end of books. Pride and ambition may put many upon scribbling, and filling the world with chaff and vanity; so that there needeth a restraint rather than an incitement. Some merely blur paper, which is no small discouragement to modest and able men.' When the great Puritan commentator, Thomas Manton, wrote those words in his commentary on Jude,[1] he set up a warning that has been largely heeded; 2 Peter and Jude could lay claim to being the two least valued and noticed books of the New Testament. Their special contribution to Christian living lies unrecognized and unread at the back of most Bibles.

Rediscovering what these two writers have to say could well be a bracing exercise for today's churches. We may claim familiarity with most parts of the New Testament, but here we are in undeniably difficult and strange territory, and we are tempted to head back to more familiar landscapes. But when we find a part of the Bible that the churches ignore in public, and that Christians find irrelevant in private, then we may be sure that the enemy considers he has gained a major advantage. We must recover these letters, and learn again what these early Christian leaders risked their lives to teach. It is because of the unfamiliarity of these letters, as well as their difficulties, that this exposition is slightly longer than one would expect from the length of the basic material.

It might seem odd that two New Testament letters have been grouped together in one book, when they are not by the same author or written to the same readers. The reason will become clearer if the two letters are read side by side, for they share a large number of ideas and words, and 2 Peter contains what looks like the whole of Jude. They make a natural pair. We should not be fooled by their similarity, though, since they are two distinct and independent letters. This exposition has tried to mark out their different profiles and concerns.

Readers who are well versed in New Testament studies will know that the precise nature of the relationship between 2 Peter and Jude

[1] Manton, p. 99.

9

has been the subject of considerable debate, and even this non-technical exposition could hardly avoid the topic without being accused of ostrich-like tendencies. The discussion, however, is far too complex to include in the body of the text without holding up what Peter and Jude are saying. Readers who want to look at that subject (or, indeed, other matters that scholars debate) will therefore find that they are referred to the Appendix, 'The Authorship of 2 Peter and Jude'. The literature on 2 Peter and Jude has until fairly recently been comparatively meagre, but Richard Bauckham's magisterial commentary and subsequent book (see the Bibliography) have shown that these letters have a robust theology and a positive place in the New Testament.

The exposition itself is based on the New International Version, which is reproduced at the appropriate point in each section. In keeping with the aim of *The Bible Speaks Today* series, we have tried to produce an exposition which is aimed at any Christian who has a desire to understand God's Word better, and to live it out.

No doubt readers will sense the irony that a book about the work of two authors is itself the work of two authors. The two Introductions, which contain the core of our understanding of the letters, have been written by Dick Lucas, and the verse-by-verse exposition and Appendix by Christopher Green. Nevertheless, as we have worked together on the project it has become increasingly difficult to remember whose ideas were whose; and both of us have worked through the letters in the quiet of the study, the heat of the pulpit and the give-and-take of the lecture room.

The members of St Helen's, Bishopsgate, and various other churches around the country have listened to many talks and sermons on 2 Peter and Jude, and prayed with us that the book might be finished; we thank them for their support. Over some years, students of the Cornhill Training Course in London have not only heard the material but asked awkward questions about it. We hope those students will find that we have practised what we taught about exposition. The staff and readers of Inter-Varsity Press, and in particular Colin Duriez and Jo Bramwell, have been unfailingly helpful, patient and positive, and John Stott has shown great generosity in the time he has invested in the meticulous editorial skill with which he has helped this book reach its current state. Our debt to them is great, but none of them can be held to blame for mistakes which we may have made.

It is our desire that the message of these letters, so muted in our day and yet so greatly needed, will be taught from the pulpits and believed in the hearts of many Christians, and that they will steel those in positions of authority in the churches to take action in accord with their demands. As the God who speaks in these letters said to Isaiah, 'This is the one I esteem: he who is humble and contrite in spirit, and trembles at my word' (Is. 66:2).

CHRISTOPHER GREEN
DICK LUCAS

Chief abbreviations

ANF   *Ante-Nicene Fathers*, edited by A. Roberts and S. Donaldson, 10 vols. (Grand Rapids: Eerdmans, 1950–51; reissued Grand Rapids: Eerdmans; Edinburgh: T. and T. Clark, 1989).

AV   The Authorized (King James') Version of the Bible (1611).

BAGD   Walter Bauer, *A Greek–English Lexicon of the New Testament and Other Early Christian Literature*, translated and adapted by William F. Arndt and F. Wilbur Gingrich, second edition, revised and augmented by F. Wilbur Gingrich and Frederick W. Danker from Bauer's fifth (1958) edition (Chicago: University of Chicago Press, 1979).

DJG   *Dictionary of Jesus and the Gospels*, edited by J. B. Green, S. McKnight and I. H. Marshall (Leicester and Downers Grove: IVP, 1992).

GNB   The Good News Bible (NT, 1966, fourth edition 1976; OT, 1976; second edition of the complete Bible, 1992, 1994).

IBD   *The Illustrated Bible Dictionary*, edited by J. D. Douglas *et al.*, 3 vols. (Leicester: IVP; Wheaton: Tyndale House, 1980).

ISBE   *International Standard Bible Encyclopedia*, edited by James Orr, new edition edited by G. W. Bromiley, 5 vols. (Grand Rapids: Eerdmans, 1979–   ).

INT   *An Introduction to the New Testament*, by D. A. Carson, D. J. Moo and L. Morris (Grand Rapids: Zondervan; Leicester: Apollos, 1993).

JB   The Jerusalem Bible (1966).

JBP   *The New Testament in Modern English*, by J. B. Phillips (London: Collins, 1958).

JBL   *Journal of Biblical Literature*.

JSNT   *Journal for the Study of the New Testament*.

LB   The Living Bible (1962–70; British edition 1974).

LS   H. G. Liddell and R. Scott, *Greek–English Lexicon*, ninth edition, revised by H. S. Jones and R. McKenzie (Oxford: Oxford University Press, 1940).

LXX   The Old Testament in Greek according to the Septuagint, third century BC.

Moffatt   J. Moffatt, *A New Translation of the Bible* (London: Hodder and Stoughton, 1926, OT and NT in one volume; revised 1935).

MM   J. H. Moulton and G. Milligan (eds.), *The Vocabulary of the Greek Testament Illustrated from the Papyri and other Non-Literary Sources* (Grand Rapids: Eerdmans, 1914–30; London: Hodder and Stoughton, 1930).

NASB   The New American Standard Bible (1963).

NDT   *New Dictionary of Theology*, ed. S. B. Ferguson, D. F. Wright and J. I. Packer (Leicester and Downers Grove: IVP, 1988).

NEB   The New English Bible (NT, 1961, second edition, 1970; OT, 1970).

NIDNTT   *The New International Dictionary of New Testament Theology*, edited by C. Brown, 4 vols. (Exeter: Paternoster, 1975–78; revised edition, 1986).

NIV   The New International Version of the Bible (1973, 1978, 1984).

NKJV   The New King James Version of the Bible (1982).

NovTest   *Novum Testamentum.*

NPNF   *A Select Library of Nicene and Post-Nicene Fathers of the Christian Church*, second series, edited by H. Wace and P. Schaff, 14 vols. (1890–1900; repr. Grand Rapids: Eerdmans, 1975).

NRSV   The New Revised Standard Version of the Bible (1989).

NTI   *New Testament Introduction*, by Donald Guthrie (IVP, fourth edition, 1990).

NTS   *New Testament Studies.*

OTP   *Old Testament Pseudepigrapha*, vol. 1, edited by J. H. Charlesworth (London: Darton Longman and Todd; New York: Doubleday, 1983).

REB   The Revised English Bible (1989).

RSV   The Revised Standard Version of the Bible (NT, 1946, second edition, 1971; OT, 1952).

RV   The Revised Version of the Bible (1881–85).

TDNT   *Theological Dictionary of the New Testament*, edited by G. Kittel and G. Friedrich, translated by G. W. Bromiley, 10 vols. (Grand Rapids: Eerdmans, 1946–76).

Bibliography

Alford	H. Alford, *Alford's Greek Testament*, vol. IV, parts 1 and 2 (London: Rivingtons, 1859).
Barclay (*Jude*)	W. Barclay, *The Letters of John and Jude*, Daily Study Bible (Edinburgh: St Andrew Press; Louisville: Westminster John Knox Press, 1958).
Barclay (*Peter*)	W. Barclay, *The Letters of James and Peter*, *Daily Study Bible* (Edinburgh: St Andrew Press; Louisville: Westminster John Knox Press, 1958).
Bauckham (1983)	R. J. Bauckham, *Jude, 2 Peter, Word Biblical Commentary* (Waco: Word, 1983; Milton Keynes: Word UK, 1986).
Bauckham (1990)	R. J. Bauckham, *Jude and the Relatives of Jesus* (Edinburgh: T. and T. Clarke, 1990).
Bengel	J. A. Bengel, *Bengel's New Testament Commentary*, vol. 2 (1742; Grand Rapids: Kregel, 1981).
Bigg	C. Bigg, *A Critical and Exegetical Commentary on the Epistles of St Peter and St Jude, New International Critical Commentary* (Edinburgh: T. and T. Clark, 1901, repr. 1978).
Blum	E. A. Blum, '2 Peter' and 'Jude' in *The Expositor's Bible Commentary*, vol. 12 (Grand Rapids: Zondervan, 1981).
Boobyer	G. H. Boobyer, '2 Peter' and 'Jude' in *Peake's Commentary on the Bible* (rev. edn. [1962] reissued London: Routledge, 1991).
Brown	J. Brown, *2 Peter Chapter One* (1856; Edinburgh: Banner of Truth, 1980).
Calvin (*Jude*)	J. Calvin, *Harmony of the Gospels III, James and Jude, Calvin's New Testament Commentaries*, vol. 3 (Grand Rapids: Eerdmans, 1989).

Calvin (*Peter*)   J. Calvin, *Hebrews; 1 and 2 Peter, Calvin's New Testament Commentaries*, vol.12 (Grand Rapids: Eerdmans, 1989).

Charles (1990)   J. D. Charles, ' "Those" and "These": The Use of the Old Testament in the Epistle of Jude', *JSNT* 30 (1990), pp. 109–124.

Charles (1991)   J. D. Charles, 'Jude's Use of Pseudepigraphical Source-Material as Part of a Literary Strategy', *NTS* 37 (1991), pp. 130–145.

Clark   G. H. Clark, *2 Peter: A Short Commentary* (Phillipsburg: Presbyterian and Reformed, 1975).

Elliott   J. H. Elliott, *1–2 Peter and Jude, with James, Augsburg Commentary on the New Testament* (Minneapolis: Augsburg, 1982).

Ellis   E. E. Ellis, 'Prophecy and Hermeneutics in Jude', in *idem, Prophecy and Hermeneutics in Early Christianity: New Testament Essays* (Tübingen: Mohr, 1978; Grand Rapids: Baker, 1993).

Fornberg   T. Fornberg, *An Early Church in a Pluralistic Society: A Study of 2 Peter* (Lund, 1977).

Green (1961)   E. M. B. Green, *2 Peter Reconsidered* (London: Tyndale Press, 1961).

Green (1987)   E. M. B. Green, *2 Peter and Jude, Tyndale New Testament Commentaries* (Leicester: IVP; Grand Rapids: Eerdmans, rev. edn. 1987).

Hillyer   N. Hillyer, *First and Second Peter, Jude, New International Biblical Commentary*, vol. 16 (Peabody: Hendrikson, 1992).

Käsemann   E. Käsemann, *Essays on New Testament Themes* (London: SCM; Naperville: A. R. Allenson, 1964).

Kelly   J. N. D. Kelly, *A Commentary on the Epistles of Peter and Jude* (London: A. and C. Black, 1969; Peabody: Hendrikson, 1988).

Kistemaker   S. J. Kistemaker, *Expositions on the Epistles of Peter and Jude, New Testament Commentary* (Edinburgh: Banner of Truth; Grand Rapids: Baker, 1987).

Lenski   R. C. H. Lenski, *The Interpretation of the Epistles of St Peter, St John and St Jude* (Minneapolis: Augsburg, 1966).

Lloyd-Jones   D. M. Lloyd-Jones, *Expository Sermons on 2 Peter* (Edinburgh: Banner of Truth, 1983).

Luther	M. Luther, *Commentary on the Epistles of Peter and Jude* (1523; Grand Rapids: Kregel, 1982).
Manton	T. Manton, *Jude* (1658; Edinburgh: Banner of Truth, 1989).
Martin	R. P. Martin, *The Theology of the Letters of James, Peter and Jude*, New Testament Theology series (Cambridge: Cambridge University Press, 1994).
Moffatt (*Peter*)	J. Moffatt, *The General Epistles: Peter, James and Judas*, The Moffatt New Testament Commentary (London: Hodder and Stoughton; New York: Doubleday, 1928).
Nisbet	A. Nisbet, *1 and 2 Peter* (1658; Edinburgh: Banner of Truth, 1982).
Plummer	A. Plummer, *St James and St Jude*, The Expositor's Bible (London: Hodder and Stoughton, 1891).
Plumptre	E. H. Plumptre, *St Peter and St Jude*, Cambridge Bible for Schools and Colleges (Cambridge: Cambridge University Press, 1879).
Reike	B. Reike, *The Epistles of James, Peter and Jude* (New York: Doubleday, 1964).
Robinson	J. A. T. Robinson, *Redating the New Testament* (London: SCM; Philadelphia: Westminster Press, 1976).
Sidebottom	E. J. Sidebottom, *James, Jude and 2 Peter*, New Century Bible Commentary (London: Marshall, Morgan and Scott, 1967; Grand Rapids: Eerdmans, 1982).
Spicq	C. Spicq, *Les Epîtres de Saint Pierre* (Paris: Gabalda, 1966).
Thiede	C. P. Thiede, *Simon Peter, From Galilee to Rome* (Exeter: Paternoster, 1986).
Wand	J. W. C. Wand, *The General Epistles of St Peter and St Jude*, Westminster Commentaries (London: Methuen, 1934).
Watson	D. F. Watson, *Invention, Arrangement and Style: Rhetorical Criticism of Jude and 2 Peter*, Society of Biblical Literature Dissertation Series 104 (Atlanta: Scholars' Press, 1988).

Introduction to 2 Peter

At a recent preachers' conference, where local church leaders and pastors had met to stimulate one another in the work of teaching the Bible accurately and effectively, an outline on 2 Peter 3:18 was brought forward to be assessed by the group. This 'sermon skeleton' was a comprehensive one, using the fine exhortation to 'grow in the grace and knowledge of our Lord and Saviour' as a launching-pad for an overview of New Testament teaching on Christian growth in godliness, a notable theme of 2 Peter. Much excellent material had been gathered together on the necessity for spiritual maturity, and a practical application made to the effect that the watching world would hardly be impressed by Christian claims until confronted with believing people who had grown to their full stature as disciples of Jesus.

Naturally, this application was a truth no-one in the group was minded to deny. But by this time, as we studied 2 Peter together, it had emerged that the apostle's final exhortation had a very different thrust. Once the warning of 3:17 against false teachers was taken into account (an elementary example of context control), it became obvious that here, in this particular letter, 'growth in grace' was being urged as indispensable, not to impress the world but to rescue the young believers from spiritual disaster. The seductive influence of new and forceful teachers, recently at work in the congregations, was already destabilizing the faithful. These 'lawless men', unrestrained by apostolic authority, were attracting a numerous following through their high-sounding promises to bring the believers into a hitherto unknown 'freedom' of experience (2:19).

The purpose of 2 Peter is twofold: to expose such false guides for what they were (hence the colourful diatribe of chapter 2) and, more important still, to set before the churches the conditions of survival when doctrinal and moral perversions infiltrate their fellowships, appearing to carry all before them. So, in 3:17, the appeal to Peter's 'dear friends' is that they should be on their guard against error lest they 'fall from' their 'secure position'. Evidently the apostle values 'stability' very highly (1:12). Seeing the trouble-makers as essentially unstable people (3:16), he repeatedly urges the Christians to safeguard the security of their own position (1:10). Finally, in 3:18, the wisest way to do this is expounded in terms of steady growth in the favour of God, and in the knowledge of Christ.

2 Peter, then, is a homily on Christian growth, set in the context of threats to Christian stability from a type of destructive and heretical teaching (2:1–3) that is as common today as it was in apostolic times and that seems to hold out a perpetual attraction to some vigorous evangelical communities. In 1:1–11 we possess what is a classic New Testament exposition of this theme, including the brilliant little ladder of advance towards maturity, from faith to love, in verses 5–7. Arguments concerning the origin (whether Hellenistic or not) of such catalogues of virtues are of little interest compared with the fact that this 'programme for progress' has obviously been carefully edited to expose the manifest failures of the errorists. It is because these new spiritual guides patently lacked goodness, self-control and godliness (to name but three of the qualities) that Peter commends (perhaps 'commands' would be a more accurate word) to his readers a very different way of living.

A homily on spiritual growth, then, from the pen of the apostle Peter, lies before us. But growth in what? The answer to this question goes to the heart of 2 Peter and the apostolic concerns that led to the writing of this letter. What is at stake in the life of the young churches is nothing less than the true knowledge of God.

1. The knowledge of God

This emphasis on 'knowing' the Lord and 'knowing' the truth, repeatedly underscored, is characteristic of 2 Peter. There are two sides to this 'knowing'. First, there is that knowledge of God and of his Son Jesus Christ, which is the initial gift of free grace, constituting us true believers (1:2, 3, 8; the Greek word is *epignōsis*). There is no inequality here between Christian and Christian. Even more impressive, there is no inequality between the apostle (belonging to the first generation), and those of the second and third generations (1:1), so Peter's readers lack nothing of 'apostolicity' in their faith. No charge against them, on the score of the full validity of their spiritual standing or experience, can be sustained. This is the important assurance 2 Peter is intended to convey from the beginning.

The implication must be that the new teaching cast doubts on the proper standing as Christian people of Peter's readers. It is notoriously easy to 'seduce the unstable' (2:14; that is, the young

Christian) by exploiting easy dissatisfactions with spiritual progress, and longings for a deeper fellowship with the God who has made himself known. In 2 Peter 1:1 the apostle Peter gives these new converts the same assurance that Paul gives his readers in Ephesians 1:3: God 'has blessed us in the heavenly realms with every spiritual blessing in Christ'.

Secondly, there is that knowledge of the truth as it is in Jesus, which can be built up by application and endeavour only over a long period (*e.g.* 1:5, 6; *cf.* 3:18; the Greek word here is *gnōsis*). This distinction between the knowledge that is given, and a knowledge that is gained, is an important key to understanding apostolic Christianity.

2. The false teachers

What then of the new propagandists? It was as 'teachers' that they had come among the people (2:1, 3); but were they themselves possessors of a true knowledge of God? At first sight it seems as though they were. In 2:20–21 we are told three times of their knowledge (*epignōsis*) of Christ and his 'way'. At the same time, we are told of their comprehensive surrender to sensuality (2:19–20) as evidence of turning their backs on the authority of divine truth (2:21). Students of 2 Peter have been perplexed by these statements, especially since the striking proverb of 2:22 suggests, very starkly, that the essential natures of these men had never been changed. Experience of contemporary church life, however, presents us with similarly baffling examples of those whose early faith and ministry bore every sign of genuineness, yet who later denied the 'Lord who bought them' (2:1). Not infrequently, this has led to the practice of immorality of the most shameful kind (described in 2 Pet. 2).

2 Peter excels in conciseness, while putting before us a rounded picture. The apostolic tests of an authentic 'knowledge' of God centre on whether or not both 'the way of truth' (2:2) and 'the way of righteousness' (2:21) are followed. What is demanded of the Christian, and therefore of the Christian teacher, is not only pure (or wholesome) thinking (3:1) but also pure (or wholesome) living (3:14). No claims to special illumination should be countenanced by the people of God, especially when sound doctrine is repudiated and sound morality is rejected in word and deed. 2 Peter 2:1–10 combines both these aspects, but particularly the latter, as being 'especially true' (verse 10) of those responsible for the new teaching agitating the churches in Peter's time.

And what of their knowledge, in the sense of acquired understanding (*gnōsis*)? Here, chapter 3 seems unequivocal. Apparently, there was among them a deliberate ignorance of unpalatable truth

19

(3:5), as well as that instability that leads unbalanced enthusiasts to distort Scripture (3:16). It is intriguing to read that 'our dear brother Paul' (so Peter writes) was treated in just such cavalier fashion by his opponents.

It is not so much the familiar approach of a 'liberal theology' that easily dismisses what Paul writes as inappropriate in today's different cultural setting, as the unprincipled 'distortions' of Paul's teachings practised by those who feel bound to accept his authority. Their method is to twist the plain import of Paul's words and sentences in order to produce a very different meaning, one that will be more acceptable to their contemporaries.

In spelling out the 'ignorance' of the newcomers, Peter insists that, for their part, his readers must not 'forget' (we will return later to the importance of this concept) certain bedrock realities. With exceptional economy of words, these are beautifully set down in 3:8–10; they go to the heart of the difference between a genuine Christian outlook and its counterfeit.

Verse 8 will surely have reminded Peter's readers of Psalm 90, with its emphasis on the painful brevity of life, making this world wholly inadequate as a permanent home, or resting-place, for all who possess eternity in their hearts. Generations of believers have found in the eternal God alone a true refuge and satisfying dwelling-place. By contrast, the new teachers are entirely content with this world as their home, and look for no other. This is because they do not know the Lord, either in his anger[1] or in his compassion.[2]

Verse 9 famously spells out the glory of the divine patience: if the Lord delays his coming it is because of his longsuffering with sinners. But the new teachers were foolish enough to interpret mercy and forbearance as betraying divine impotence or negligence. Again, they did not know the Lord.[3]

Verse 10 is another splendid stroke. The force of the 'thief' analogy, as used by Christ, lies in the fact, now as then, that the burglar unerringly comes just when you do not expect him! But the new teachers had very clear notions about when the 'coming' should have taken place. It was they, not the orthodox believers, who insisted that Christ had promised an immediate return. Because this had not taken place, they no longer expected the realization of this promise. Ironically, this refusal of theirs any longer to expect the return of Christ fulfils the very conditions that will precede the Lord's return. But then they did not know the Lord or take seriously the demands of serving him.[4]

In all this, the false prophets of Peter's day, as in ours, revealed themselves as men of the world in contrast with the proper

---

[1] Ps. 90:11.   [2] Ps. 90:13.   [3] *Cf.* Ex. 34:6–7.   [4] *Cf.* Lk. 12:35–40.

otherworldliness of the true Christian (3:11–13). This has special application to Christians living at the end of the twentieth century, when the reigning orthodoxies of secularism are crumbling. In rejecting transcendence, a thorough-going materialism forces people to seek happiness solely in this world. It is now clear that in making sense of life and human hopes this is not working out. If fashionable theology follows secular trends (as it normally does a few years later), however, we can expect to find the popular preachers of the day rejecting the transcendent nature of the Bible message, and promising their listeners that spiritual hunger and heavenly aspirations can find complete satisfaction in the here and now. The result will be a consumer-orientated church suitable for a consumer-orientated society – and in the end, bitter disillusionment – but not before wave succeeds wave of 'special offers' and yet more exaggerated promises, each in turn to be laid aside in hopeless disappointment (*cf.* 2:17–19).

3. The apostolic eye-witnesses

What then can Peter put before the churches to counter the influence of the new voices being heard everywhere, especially when soon his own voice will be silent (1:14)? How can he secure for the believers a right understanding of the 'very great and precious promises' of the gospel (1:4), so that they know what is theirs to experience and achieve in this life, as well as what is to be theirs in the new heavens and new earth, glorious realities to be anticipated with eagerness (3:12–14)? The answer to such questions takes us right back to the origins of true prophecy in 1:12–21, perhaps the greatest single treasure within this letter.

The section 1:12–15 contains Peter's justification for writing. It is of primary importance in unlocking the message of 2 Peter, and is not to be downgraded as though it were merely a brief section in praise of repetition and memory work in the teaching ministry! Here Peter records a message, received from the risen Lord, that in a short while he is to depart from the earthly scene. It is a dramatic warning of little time left for his apostolic labours. It galvanizes Peter into making immediate arrangements so that gospel truth will be maintained when he is gone. True, the congregations are 'firmly established' in the truth they presently have (1:12). Nevertheless, the spread of the new lawlessness compels the apostle, while he still lives among them, continually to refresh their minds concerning their spiritual foundations. His efforts are to be concentrated on ensuring that the churches go on living under the rule of his apostolic testimony long after he has gone from the scene. Unless this happens, the post-apostolic church will, before long, forfeit its apostolicity in character and life.

The apostolic testimony of which Peter writes in 1:16–18 confirms the prophetic word (a contemporary description of the Old Testament as a whole), the foundational authority of which is described in 1:19–21. Through both apostolic testimony and prophetic word God speaks of 'the power and coming of Christ' (1:16), that climactic day of God when the world will be destroyed (3:10–12), from which final cataclysm God's people will escape to enter their new and eternal home (3:13). This terrible time of judgment that will see the 'destruction of ungodly men' (3:7) will also see the final demonstration of God's power to rescue the godly, a power anticipated in the present experience of Christian people whenever they are rescued from trials and temptations (e.g. 2:9).[5]

When Peter preached the coming of Christ to judge the world,[6] he was not charting or concocting imaginary descriptions of the future of planet Earth, as his rivals, the false teachers, may have accused him (or as they themselves practised for profit; 2:3). His message depended for its integrity on what he, and his fellow apostles, both saw (1:16) and heard (1:18). At the transfiguration they were, for a brief moment, eye-witnesses of the divine sovereignty of Christ, just as later they were eye-witnesses of his bodily resurrection.[7] In this unique, historical sense the apostles were witnesses of Christ's 'honour and glory'. As Peter reminds his readers in a telling little phrase, 'we were with him' (1:18).

But what could Peter and his friends make of so unexpected and awesome a sight? It is recorded elsewhere that, at the time, they woefully misunderstood its significance.[8] What they needed was an authoritative interpretation of the event they saw. And this, literally, was what was provided by the voice from heaven (twice, in verses 17 and 18, it is insisted that this voice was not of earthly origin). Intriguingly for us, the heavenly message was couched in Old Testament language, a God-given confirmation of the truth of the prophetic word; and it spoke of a messianic king[9] who was, at the same time, a Suffering Servant.[10] Thus, for Peter especially, was solved the agonizing question of how one who would suffer could conceivably be Messiah.[11]

4. The prophetic word

When the prophets proclaimed the coming of Christ to save all who believe,[12] they were not 'speaking visions from their own minds' as

---

[5] Cf. 2 Tim. 4:17–18.　　[6] Cf. Acts 10:42.　　[7] Jn. 20:8, 18, 20, 25–26.
[8] Mk. 9:5–6.　　[9] Cf. Ps. 2:7.　　[10] Cf. Is. 42:1.　　[11] Mk. 8:31–32.
[12] Cf. Acts 10:43.

false prophets in all times are wont to do.[13] Nor, like the false teachers described in 3:3, were they driven to say what they did because of their own strong personal desires or aspirations. It was the Spirit of God who, irresistibly, swept them along (1:21) in order to provide a God-given explanation, or interpretation, of the great saving acts of God in Israel's history (1:20). Just as it was of first importance to understand the evil desires that impelled the new teachers to mock the truth (3:3), so it was of first importance to recognize how different was the ultimate source of the true prophets' inspiration (1:20).

Since the prophetic word, as we have it, is an understanding of the Old Testament history of salvation given once for all by God to the prophets, both to speak to their contemporaries and to write down for the benefit of future generations, we are not to ascribe the teaching of the prophets to their own individual wisdom or insight. If their message had been like that of normal teachers, however gifted – limited by human fallibility and the inevitable prejudices of their times – we might well seek for help to reinterpret the Old Testament story according to our own modern lights.

But, insists our apostle, true prophecy never came by the 'will of man', that is by the prophet's own deliberate purpose or individual viewpoint. The Old Testament prophet was not volunteering his ideas or perceptions, only to be corrected by a more scholarly successor! 2 Peter 1:21, if taken with full seriousness, rules out completely any thought that we can treat the book of the prophet Isaiah (or any other Old Testament prophet, or indeed the Old Testament Scriptures as a whole) like any other book. If what Peter says is true, then the prophetic word remains for ever God's Word. It is not merely the prophet of long ago who speaks, but the living God himself. And if that is so, we shall be wise not to attempt to reinterpret what he says as though we were now in possession of some superior wisdom.

We are now in a position to grasp the enormous significance in 2 Peter of the repeated injunctions to remember or recall 'these things', that is, the authentic message of the apostles and prophets (1:12–15; 3:1–2). Words spoken in days past (3:2) can appear to lack the immediacy of words spoken in the present. There is a natural craving for a voice from heaven. That indeed has been given (1:18), but not to us. Unhappily, there are still those who trade, with some success, on the gullibility of unstable believers, and, by the use of bold claims and fictitious anecdotes (2:3), confuse the churches with claims that God's Spirit is speaking a fresh message through them.

The essential ministry of the pastor, therefore, is that which

[13] Je. 23:16.

23

recalls the work and words of Christ (hence the normal church furniture of table and pulpit). Just as the sermon loses its legitimacy if it does not make known 'the faith that was once for all entrusted to the saints',[14] so the supper likewise forfeits its legitimacy if it does not celebrate what Christ *has* done, once for all, by his sacrifice of himself on the cross. The moment we cease to be reminded of 'these things', the vacuum is likely to be filled by new 'prophets' and 'priests'. The churches, then unanchored to the Word of God and the work of Christ, cease to be truly 'apostolic', despite their claims.

These realities lie behind the powerful exhortation of 1:19. It is to this original 'prophetic word' that Christians would 'do well to pay attention', rather than to the showy new 'prophets'. For, as long as this world lasts, there never will be any divine light by which the churches may be guided other than the Scriptures. When Christ returns, and not until that day 'dawns', the morning star will arise in our hearts. This almost certainly refers to an inward illumination that will accompany the outward revelation, so that every believer on that day will be able to comprehend fully what then is so magnificently disclosed.[15] Very possibly, the new teachers were professing to have been given just such a personal enlightenment, enabling them to put aside the Scriptures as now superseded by the 'inner light', a claim frequently made in the history of the churches.

5. The authentic gospel

What then, according to this letter, is the genuine gospel message, against which we, like Peter's readers, can measure all fraudulent 'promises' made by new and popular teachers who echo the spirit of their times?

A fine description of Peter's gospel is given in 1:16. His preaching centred on 'the power and coming' of Christ (1:16). Particularly noteworthy is his concentration on Christ's *second* coming to judge, rather than upon his first coming to save, a prior emphasis that is noticeable elsewhere in Peter's teaching.[16] This difference should not be overstated, as though Peter had no message of present salvation. But it does mean that Peter's good news was primarily *eschatological*, as spelt out in chapter 3. Thus the ridicule heaped upon the idea of Christ's return by the new teachers (3:4) is not noted here by the apostle as an attack on one particular article of the faith, but as a rejection of the gospel as a whole.

By such an emphasis, Peter must be condemning the exaggerated promises made by the trouble-makers. Their message aroused intense excitement by claiming that the future expectations of the

---

[14] Jude 3.   [15] 1 Cor. 13:12.   [16] As in Acts 10:42–43.

Christian, linked in apostolic teaching with the world to come (note the 'looking forward' that occurs three times in 3:12–14), were to be expected *in this life* and experienced by all who followed their instruction and accepted their authority.

As so often happens, those who make such unreal claims are forced to live a lie (2:19). Even worse when heavenly aspirations are, in practice, disregarded, the appeal of such teachers must inevitably be to the passionate desires of the earthly nature, whether for prosperity, pleasure or any other form of self-seeking.[17]

But Peter, as always (and despite modern criticism of his plain speaking in chapter 2), does not over-react to error. For instance, it is true that righteousness (a notable theme in this letter) is at home only in the new heaven and new earth (3:13), so that justice will never be perfectly done in this world; yet the apostle demands that by lip (2:5) and life (2:7–8) righteousness should be the goal in this life of every Christian disciple. Or again, although God's power will be displayed to humankind in all its inevitable authority only when Christ returns in glory, nonetheless divine power *is* manifested and recognized now by (hardest of all tests) the transformation of human nature in its depravity (*cf.* 2:22) to godliness and genuine goodness (1:3–5). In the same way, while eventual rescue and escape from those evil desires that corrupt the whole world must await the final catastrophe (3:10–13), yet by participating in the divine nature, a real escape from those who live in error is our joyful experience now (2:18; *cf.* 1:4). The initial verses of 2 Peter provide us with a lovely picture of what is ours now to delight in, namely an apostolic faith, freshly minted as in the earliest days of pentecostal power, with grace and peace in abundance, while the third and concluding chapter delights to speak about the glories that will be ours only at Christ's return.

In 2 Peter the alarm bells are ringing. Churches may be attacked from without to the point of near destruction (as evidenced today in Iran, Sudan, and North Korea, to name only three examples of cruel oppression). But almost more deadly still is that self-destructive madness that operates within the churches as a direct consequence of ruinous heresies secretly introduced into the mainstream of church teaching (2:1). This letter is not the only apostolic warning about such matters. If the denunciations of chapter 2 are vehement in their ruthless exposure of evil men, Paul warned in similar fashion of 'savage wolves' among the flock.[18]

---

[17] *Cf.* 2 Tim. 3:1–5, with its exposure of a form of godliness where we profess to be lovers of God but are in reality lovers of ourselves.
[18] Acts 20: 29.

The western church of the twentieth century has seen many of its congregations dangerously depleted, indeed its buildings often emptied, by a rationalistic philosophy of religion that is not a genuine Christian theology at all. It is certain that the errors threatening the stability of the churches to which Peter writes included denials of orthodox beliefs. In particular, it is evident that the person of Christ was belittled in terms of his divine sovereignty and universal lordship. Why else the clear emphasis on his deity in the initial address (1:1)? The fine designation 'our Lord and Saviour (Jesus Christ)' appears in the New Testament only in 2 Peter, and here four times (1:11; 2:20; 3:2, 18). The final doxology is one of only two in the New Testament in which Christ alone is the object.[19] So clear is the apostle about Jesus as his 'Lord and God' that it is often impossible to be certain whether he is writing of God or of Jesus, as for example in 1:3.

Yet it is perhaps right to say that the lethal consequences of the newcomers lay even more in their sensuality and insatiable greed. Here the 'filthy lives of lawless men' were reminiscent of the cities of the plain (2:7). Openly shameless, they followed their own evil desires and taught others to do the same.[20] The combination of moral collapse following upon doctrinal declension is a familiar one in days of apostasy, and 2 Peter puts in our hands a powerful trumpet to sound when we find ourselves, like Noah, living in such times (2:5).

But Peter is a true pastor as well as a skilled polemicist. He warns the faithful, but not to the point where they lose their confidence in the sovereign control of the Lord over his church. It may seem that God is sleeping while wolves ravage the flock (2:3b). But from the very beginning, the condemnation of false guides has been pronounced and their doom is certain. God will not spare the ungodly of today, for he did not spare them in times past (2:4–10). A terrible prospect lies ahead for the spiritual manipulators and exploiters, for those who distort the Word of God,[21] and for apostate church leaders who sit loose to scriptural authority and faithlessly accommodate their message and moral standards to the spirit of the age. 'What is going to happen to the ungodly' (2:6), as expounded by Peter, is evidently intended to be terrifying, and we ought to be frightened by such warnings. 'If God did not spare angels' there can be no position of high privilege that offers any protection in the dreadful day of judgment. We who teach have been warned, and the people of God reassured. The lying teachers of Peter's day, as of ours, have 'long ago' had sentence passed on them by the Lord of the church. In the eternal world, their punishment continues to the

---

[19] Cf. 2 Tim. 4:18.   [20] Cf. Rom. 1:32.   [21] Cf. 2 Cor. 4:2.

present as they are kept for the day of final accountability. But for those who seek to make their 'calling and election sure' (1:10) there is, at life's end, an abundant entrance awaiting them into the eternal kingdom of Christ. If in 2 Peter there is an almost unimaginable severity for the apostate and the false prophet, there is also a vista, beyond our dreams, of unbounded joys for those who, never forgetful of what has been done for them (1:9), daily seek to increase, more and more, in the grace and knowledge of God.

2 Peter 1:1–2
1. The genuine article

Fakes are a nuisance. Fake artists make fools of collectors, fake financiers embezzle millions at the expense of honest investors, fake scientists inflate their own reputations by riding on the back of other people's hard research. In some other areas of life, though, fakes are not merely a nuisance but actually pose a serious threat. There is, for example, the potential damage caused by religious fakes. The obvious ones, those who are in it just for the money or the prestige, can be avoided without too much difficulty. Harder to uncover, but much more destructive in the end, are the well-meaning but muddled individuals who pass on a mixture of easy platitudes, biblical-sounding phrases and a view of life that is twisted out of any recognizable biblical shape. Such Christian con-men are the reason Peter wrote this letter. They not only prey on people's wallets or good nature; ultimately they can wreck our eternal destiny, since a false gospel tells lies about God.

Fakes lie at the heart of Peter's concern in this letter. He mentions false prophets and false teachers (2:1). They turn out to be false disciples (2:15), teaching stories they have made up (2:3). It is an alarming prospect, and we might be tempted to think that these words apply to darker days than our own. Peter is insistent, though, that 'there will be false teachers among you' (2:1), and he is writing this letter to 'stimulate you to wholesome thinking' (3:1). He is alerting his readers to the ever-present danger of being fooled by, or even becoming, Christian fakes. His urgency is caused by the nearness of his own death (1:13–15), which will mean an inevitable severing of one more link in the chain that bound the early church to the authentic message that Jesus taught. Peter's reason for writing is to enshrine that teaching decisively, so that after his death no group or faction can claim that he was the originator of their perverted gospel.

Simon Peter, a servant and apostle of Jesus Christ,

To those who through the righteousness of our God and Saviour Jesus Christ have received a faith as precious as ours:

²Grace and peace be yours in abundance through the knowledge of God and of Jesus our Lord.

These first two verses follow the standard opening to an ancient letter, but they also begin to crystallize Peter's concern. He wants us to ensure that the Christianity which we have received, believed, lived and passed on to others is the genuine article and not a substitute. Peter isolates four areas where we should check what we believe against what he believes: where our gospel came from; whether it is as good as the original; what difference it makes in real life; and the doctrine it teaches. In other words, we need first to check our gospel's origin, then its quality, thirdly its results, and fourthly its content.

1. The genuine apostle: the gospel's origin (1:1a)

Peter presents himself in the normal way at the start of the letter, and explains his credentials. From its first word, this letter claims to be the authentic writing of an apostolic eye-witness of Jesus' life, teaching, death and resurrection.[1] Jesus had called *Simon* (literally 'Simeon')[2] among his first disciples,[3] and made this rough-hewn individualistic fisherman into someone he could use as a leader, a 'fisher of men' who would 'feed my sheep'.[4] Simon took a long time to learn, and the gospels stare unblinkingly at his frequent misunderstandings of Jesus. But he still made sure that Mark wrote it all down to encourage every generation of slow-learning disciples.[5]

Jesus renamed him *Peter*, 'the rock', because he had acknowledged that Jesus was 'the Christ, the Son of the living God'. Jesus replied, 'Blessed are you, Simon son of Jonah, for this was not revealed to you by man, but by my Father in heaven. And I tell you

---

[1] See Appendix, 'The Authorship of 2 Peter and Jude'. Since this exposition will quote many others who do not accept Peter's authorship, it is only fair to them to recognize that when they use the name 'Peter' they mean 'the author of 2 Peter, represented as Peter'. Of the modern writers, Green, Thiede, Guthrie, Blum and Hillyer claim Peter as its author.

[2] The manuscripts are fairly balanced on the question of which reading is original, but it is more likely that Simeon would have been changed to Simon than *vice versa*. For some the name Simeon speaks of authenticity, for others of deliberate forgery! See Appendix. 'Simeon' is also used in 'the appropriate Jewish–Gentile setting of the Council of Jerusalem', Acts 15:14 (Hillyer, p. 157).

[3] Jn. 1:35–42.   [4] Mk. 1:16–18; Jn. 21:17.

[5] Mark is traditionally associated with Peter; see Eusebius, *Church History* 5.8. It is even more humbling therefore that it is this narrative which concentrates on Peter's inability to learn. See below on 1:15.

that you are Peter, and on this rock I will build my church, and the gates of Hades will not overcome it. I will give you the keys of heaven; whatever you bind on earth will be bound in heaven, and whatever you loose on earth will be loosed in heaven.'[6] Quite clearly, Peter was going to be significant in the history and authority of the church. He dominates the first half of Acts as strongly as Paul dominates the second, and he proved as vital to the racial spread of the gospel as Paul was to its geographical spread.[7] Peter took the initiative to include Samaritans and Gentiles as Christians, and although he never made those decisions alone, it is clear that his fellow apostles knew that Jesus had given him this door-opening responsibility. Significantly, once Gentiles believed and the Council of Jerusalem decided that it was possible to be a Christian without becoming a Jew, Peter had made his greatest speech and does not appear again in the book of Acts. He had discharged his role.

Simon Peter emerges as a man of enormous courage and tenacity, strengths he would need as he was repeatedly beaten and imprisoned for his faith. He left the church in Jerusalem under James's leadership so that he could evangelize in Corinth, Pontus-Bythinia and, less happily, Antioch.[8] By the time of 1 Peter he is in 'Babylon',[9] meaning the imperial capital Rome. The New Testament does not record his further work and death, but later Christian writers touch on it. Irenaeus[10] says that Paul and Peter founded the church in Rome together, although this is unlikely since Paul wrote to the church in Rome which he said he had not visited, and since Acts records Paul's first arrival in Rome to be greeted by existing Christians.[11] The early church historian Eusebius simply states that Paul and Peter cooperated in this period.[12] There is reasonable certainty that he was martyred with Paul under the Emperor Nero. The Roman historian Tacitus records Nero's ghastly pleasures. 'Derision accompanied [the Christians'] end: they were covered with wild beasts' skins and torn to death by dogs; or they were fastened on crosses, and, when daylight failed, were burned to serve as lamps by night.'[13] Babylon indeed. Our letter was written on the eve of Peter's death, 'because I know I will soon put [my body] aside, as our Lord Jesus has made clear to me. And I will make every effort to see that after my

---

[6] Mt. 16:16–19.   [7] Acts 2:14; 8:14; 10:1 – 11:18.
[8] 1 Cor. 1:12; 1 Pet. 1:1; Gal. 2:11–14.
[9] 1 Pet. 5:13.   [10] *Against Heresies* 3.1.1. (*ANF* 1, p. 414).
[11] Rom. 1:13; Acts 28:14–15.
[12] *Church History* 2.25.8, citing Dionysius (*NPNF* 1, p. 130).
[13] *Annals* 15.44 (Loeb edn., 1937, p. 285).

departure you will be able to remember these things' (1:14–15).[14]

Peter describes himself in two ways which define his position between God and the church: he is *a servant and apostle of Jesus Christ.*

a. Simon Peter the servant

In one sense, to describe himself as Jesus Christ's servant simply says that he is a willing disciple, as all Christians should be. Jesus has said that on the last day our only true self-description will be as 'unworthy servants',[15] because our best still falls below God's perfect requirement.

Yet Peter's focus here is less on his humility than on his God-given authority. In the Old Testament it was seen as a position of great honour to be owned by God as his slave, and Israel rightly took enormous pride in being called the servant of God.[16] So seriously did they take it that one Israelite could not sell another Israelite into slavery; both were already slaves, God's slaves.[17] Israel's leaders, judges, kings and prophets were all called God's servants because they did his will and must therefore be obeyed;[18] and even a pagan king, Nebuchadnezzar, could be called God's servant because he helped the Jews to return from exile.[19] Over the decades, though, Israel's leaders increasingly fell short of the ideal, and prophets began to speak of the one who would come in the future and be God's perfect Servant.[20]

When Peter calls himself *a servant ... of Jesus Christ*, he is claiming as special a role within the church as Isaiah, Jeremiah and even David had within Israel. Nor is Peter alone, for Paul and Timothy, James, John and Jude claimed the same title with the same power.[21] When Peter claims to be the servant of Jesus Christ, we must pay attention to his message.

b. Simon Peter the apostle

Secondly, Peter calls himself an *apostle of Jesus Christ*. Again, this

---

[14] There is a late and unlikely tradition that Peter was crucified head downwards, still preaching. It was probably written in the light of Jn. 21:18–19 to 'validate' Jesus' promise and show Peter in a humble (and evangelistic!) role to the end of his life. *Acts of Peter* XXXVII–XXXIX, in M. R. James (ed.), *The Apocryphal New Testament* (Oxford: Oxford University Press, 1924), pp. 334–336.

[15] Lk. 17:10. [16] Is. 41:8; 49:3. [17] Lv. 25:42.

[18] E.g. Gn. 32:10; Jdg. 2:8; Ps. 89:3; Je. 26:5; Am. 3:7.

[19] Je. 25:9; 27:6; 43:10. [20] E.g. Is. 49:1–7.

[21] E.g. Phil. 1:1; Jas. 1:1 Jude 1; Rev. 1:1. On the relationship between Jude 1 and 2 Pet. 1, see Appendix.

is a word with a wide range of meanings. The Greek word *apostolos* means a messenger commissioned to a task by a particular person. Uniquely, Jesus Christ is 'the apostle ... we confess',[22] because he was sent (literally, 'apostled')[23] by God to save us. In a much broader sense, Barnabas, Silas, Titus and Timothy are apostles,[24] and Andronicus and Junias are 'outstanding among the apostles',[25] who are 'those itinerant missionaries who were recognized by the churches as constituting a distinct group among the participants in the work of spreading the gospel'.[26] In that loose sense there are still 'apostles', or 'sent Christians', today, working as evangelists, missionaries and church-planters.

Normally in the New Testament, 'apostle' has a third meaning, referring only to a precise group of twelve among Jesus' followers, who had been commissioned by Jesus as his representatives.[27] When the decision was made to replace Judas, they looked for 'one of the men who have been with us the whole time the Lord Jesus went in and out among us, beginning from John's baptism to the time when Jesus was taken up from us. For one of these must become a witness with us of his resurrection.'[28] To be called an apostle, it was not enough merely to have seen the risen Jesus, for Paul mentions five hundred people in that category but does not call them apostles.[29] Paul himself could claim exceptional entrance only because of his personal commissioning by the risen Jesus on the Damascus road.[30] It was a group to which many people wanted to belong because of the prestige of being a named and commissioned delegate of the Lord Jesus.[31]

That unique group and its teaching are irreplaceable and authoritative, and they stand in the grand line of God's delegates and spokesmen. In the Old Testament there are five great commissioning scenes where God's agents are 'sent' to his people. God said

[22] Heb. 3:1.
[23] *E.g.* Jn. 3:17. It is an ordinary word for sending, but the importance lies in who does the sending.
[24] Acts 14:14; 1 Thes. 1:1; 2:6 (they work and write with Paul). In 2 Cor. 8:23 such workers are called, literally, 'apostles to the churches' (*apostoloi ekklēsiōn*), but translators recognize this as a non-technical use and translate the word as 'representatives' (NIV), 'messengers' (NRSV, JBP, RSV, NASB) or 'delegates' (JB, NEB).
[25] Rom. 16:7.
[26] C. E. B. Cranfield, *Romans* 2 (Edinburgh: T. and T. Clark, 1979), p. 789.
[27] Lk. 6:12–16.
[28] Acts 1:21–22. Matthias was chosen by lot so that Jesus, and not the apostles, chose him (Acts 1:24–26).
[29] 1 Cor. 15:6.
[30] 1 Cor. 15:1–11, where the Damascus road experience is listed as Jesus' last resurrection appearance.
[31] *E.g.* 2 Cor. 11:1–15.

to Moses, 'I am sending you to Pharaoh to bring my people the Israelites out of Egypt.' He said to Gideon, 'Go in the strength you have and save Israel out of Midian's hand. Am I not sending you?' He asked Isaiah, '"Whom shall I send? And who will go for us?" And I said, "Here am I. Send me!"' He commanded Jeremiah, 'You must go to everyone I send you to and say whatever I command you.' He warned Ezekiel, 'Son of man, I am sending you to the Israelites, to a rebellious nation that has rebelled against me.'[32] In that sense (God's directly commissioned delegates), God's apostles are an exclusive group. It is not surprising to find that the New Testament linked apostles and prophets in unique authority, the church being 'built on the foundation of the apostles and prophets'.[33]

Peter's self-description as an *apostle of Jesus Christ* is thus a second high claim. At a time when there were calls to replace, supplement or question the apostolic gospel, he writes as a direct source of that gospel, and he will use his letter to call the Christians back to it. He is claiming to be the New Testament equivalent of an Old Testament prophet. We face the same pressures today as Peter's readers did then. The gospel is seen by some as inadequate to meet the needs of modern men and women, and as requiring radical redrafting to be relevant. It will be important to acknowledge, along with Peter's first readers, that apostles in his tightly defined sense do not exist today, and to draw a sharp line between apostolic authority and our submission to that authority. We may call Christian leaders today 'apostolic' if they teach the message the apostles taught, but it is misleading to call them 'apostles'. Neither the questions of a secular society nor supposed new revelations from God permit us to alter the content of Peter's apostolic message.[34]

c. Simon Peter the servant and apostle of Jesus Christ

When Jesus washed his disciples' feet, he said, 'I tell you the truth, no servant is greater than his master, nor is a messenger (*apostolos*) greater than the one who sent him.'[35] The reason for Peter's importance and authority today lies not in his intellect or personality, but in the one who sent Peter to us as an apostle, the one of whom he is now a servant, Jesus Christ.

---

[32] Ex. 3:10; Jdg. 6:14; Is. 6:8; Je. 1:7; Ezk. 2:3. In LXX all five use *apostellō* or *exapostellō*, linked to the word 'apostle'.
[33] Eph. 2:20.   [34] *Cf.* Gal. 1:8–9.   [35] Jn. 13:16.

2. The genuine Christian: the gospel's quality (1:1b)

Peter and his fellow apostles, who actually knew and heard Jesus, undoubtedly benefited from that experience, and it was wonderful that those who had actually crucified Jesus could hear from Peter that they could be forgiven. We, however, live two thousand years from those events, and many people question their relevance. Distance seems to make the message less significant. Even Peter's first readers felt this, for he writes to reassure them that despite their remoteness from the gospel events, they (and we) are as privileged as the apostles. Peter does not identify his readers in either letter, and their open address to all Christians makes them timelessly relevant. This has led to their common title, 'catholic epistles'.[36]

a. You have received a faith . . .

How does someone become a Christian? One person might say, 'Because I believe,' and another, 'Because God chose me.' According to Peter, both ways of stating it are correct. On the one hand, we believe. It is a fundamental definition of a Christian that he or she is a 'believe-er'; that he or she 'has *faith*' (the two words have the same root in the Greek). By 'faith' here, Peter could mean the objective facts of 'the faith', but it is more likely that he means to stress the subjective 'faith' in Jesus Christ that is the inward reality of every live Christian.[37] But Peter also knows that it is not our feeble faith that holds us close to God. It is God who does all the holding, and that is the reality behind the word *received*. The Greek word *lanchanō* comes from politics, and was used of the appointment of government officials, 'of persons who have a post assigned to them by lot'.[38] Here it implies that the fact that any Christian believes at all is evidence of 'the sheer fairness'[39] of God. Christians who survive a lifetime of trouble are not evidence of their own resilience and toughness; rather, they see increasingly clearly that any progress has been God's doing, and not their own.

---

[36] According to Jerome, Peter 'wrote two epistles which are called Catholic, the second of which, on account of its difference from the first in style, is considered by many not to be by him' (quoted in *INT*, p. 440).
[37] *Pace* Boobyer, p. 1032, who draws the meaning from Jude 3.
[38] LS, p. 1022. *Cf.* Acts 1:17.
[39] D. H. Wheaton in *New Bible Commentary* (Downers Grove and Leicester: IVP, 3rd edn., 1970), p. 1252.

b. ... as precious as ours ...

Marvellously, Peter says that this faith was the same experience that the first Christians had, and that everything they found precious in the gospel these Christians find *as precious* too. The superficial differences are vast. Above all, he writes as one of the apostles (indicated by *ours*) to non-apostles. But he also writes as a Jew to Gentiles, and as a first-generation Christian to those who will be alive long after his death; in fact, to people like us. Yet the youngest Gentile Christian has *received a faith as precious as ours*, first-century Jews and apostles though they were. Can anything speak of God's wonderful impartiality more than the truth that we stand in the same relation to him as did all the generations of believers in the past? They may be giants and inspiring examples, but how gracious of God to fling open the doors of his heaven so wide as to include absolutely anyone who has faith!

c. ... through the righteousness of our God and Saviour

One word Peter uses sums up everything he has said so far – *righteousness*. He is using the word slightly differently from the way Paul uses it. This is not the righteous declaration God speaks over his people; it is the righteousness which God is in himself, his character, his moral uprightness and utter impartiality. 'As in 1 Peter (2:24; 3:12, 14, 18; 4:18), so in this Epistle (2:5, 7–8, 21; 3:13) the word has the ethical associations which we find given to it in the Old Testament.'[40] Peter says that this fairness of God guarantees that what he received and believed is what his first readers later received and believed, and indeed, what we receive and believe. God's righteousness ensures that men and women, Jew and Gentile, first-century and twentieth, all receive the same message and offer from God.

3. The genuine experience: the gospel's results (1:2)

The third area Peter wants his readers to check is the difference genuine Christianity makes. He says that it gives *grace and peace ... through the knowledge of God and of Jesus our Lord.*

---

[40] Green (1987), p. 68. This requires that *en* + dative be translated 'by the righteousness of God' rather than 'in the righteousness of God', but *pace* Clark this is well attested; *cf.* BAGD, p. 260, III; LS, p. 552, III.

a. Grace and peace

New Testament writers frequently started their letters by taking over the standard secular way of opening a letter.[41] *Grace (charis)* normally meant no more than 'hello', but they coupled it with the usual Hebrew greeting, *peace (šālôm,* shalom; both greetings are still used today in Greece and Israel respectively) to produce a new and beautiful idea. It acknowledged that the church in a particular place would contain both converted Jews and converted Gentiles. Peter employs this greeting to show from the outset that grace and peace are at the heart of what he believes and what the Christians are slipping away from. They are what Peter longs and prays for them to experience.

Grace means the generous heart of God who determines to treat sinful men and women as he lovingly wishes rather than as they actually deserve. It is God the Father's sovereign good pleasure, totally unmerited by us, which raises us from the ash-heap to a throne of glory. It is the servant-like manner of God the Son who became a man, lived, taught, died, rose again and reigns for us. It is the humble work of God the Holy Spirit who equips us to love and serve him now with his grace-gifts *(charismata)*, and who is the down-payment for the day when we shall be changed into the likeness of Jesus Christ himself. The gospel is grace, God's good pleasure to delight in people who do not deserve it.

The immediate result of God's grace is that his rightful anger at our disobedience is appeased, and that we have *peace* with him. That is achieved through the death of *our God and Saviour Jesus Christ.* Ever since Adam and Eve were banished from Eden after their attempt at moral autonomy, humans and God have not been at peace; Jesus said we have been in a state of barely disguised hostility.[42] Yet the hope of peace with God runs through the Old Testament,[43] and was won by the cross, as the risen Jesus demonstrated. 'On the evening of that first day of the week, when the disciples were together, with the doors locked for fear of the Jews, Jesus came and stood among them and said, "Peace be with you!" After he said this, he showed them his hands and side. The disciples were overjoyed when they saw the Lord. Again Jesus said, "Peace be with you!"'[44] That becomes Peter's message in Acts: 'the message God sent to the people of Israel, telling the good news of peace

---

[41] Peter started his first letter this way (1 Pet. 1:2), but see also Rom. 1:7; 1 Cor. 1:3; 2 Cor. 1:2; Gal. 1:3; Eph. 1:2; Phil. 1:2; Col. 1:2; 1 Thes. 1:1; 2 Thes. 1:2; 1 Tim. 1:2; 2 Tim. 1:2 (both with 'mercy'); Tit. 1:4; Phm. 3; 2 Jn. 3 (with 'mercy').
[42] Mt. 21:33–46.
[43] *E.g.* the high point of Aaron's blessing of the Israelites in Nu. 6:22–26.
[44] Jn. 20:19–21.

through Jesus Christ, who is Lord of all'.[45] As a result of being reconciled to God by the death of Jesus on the cross, we have peace with God. But we also have peace with one another. Peter spoke those words to the Gentile Cornelius as the gospel was suddenly extended to those who were outside the racial Jewish fold. Peter and the other apostles thus extend this greeting to all Christians, including us, for if we are Christians the gospel is doing its work and God is re-creating his people under his rule. If we slip away from the message of grace, we forfeit peace with God and face only his anger.

b. Knowledge

Peter says this grace and peace come *through the knowledge of God and of Jesus our Lord*. *Knowledge* is another important term in his letter.[46] It is possible that Peter means the knowledge that God has of us, but in view of the way the word-group is used later (1:5, 8, 16, 20; 2:20–21; 3:3, 17–18), it is much more likely that he means the knowledge we have of God. Peter uses two related but distinct Greek words for 'knowledge'.[47] *Gnōsis* is the word he uses for 'information knowledge' (1:5–6; 3:18; and as a verb in 1:20; 3:3). As he makes clear, that is the kind of knowledge which we can add to or grow in by being better informed about God and his Word. We can have that kind of knowledge by understanding Bible passages, reading good books and being well taught. But it is dangerously easy to be a well-informed non-Christian who misses the key ingredient, which is Peter's other word for 'knowledge', *epignōsis*.[48] It has the sense of 'personal knowledge', the knowledge of a husband or wife or good friend that goes beyond knowing things *about* them and actually knows *them*. Knowing God is so momentous that Peter uses the word almost with the meaning of being converted (1:2, 3, 8; 2:20; in 2:21 twice as a verb). This is an essential foundation, for if we do not know Christ himself then it is empty to know about him. Peter is not making any point about intelligence or stupidity, because this is a knowledge that God gives. Such an amazing gift of grace and peace can come only through a personal knowledge of God himself, face to face and person to person; and that genuine personal knowledge of God is guaranteed only if we remain within the authentic gospel. Our deadly danger,

---

[45] Acts 10:36.   [46] See Introduction above, pp. 18–19.
[47] At least, they are distinct in this letter if not elsewhere. See Bauckham (1983), p. 169.
[48] Formed by adding the prefix *epi-* to *gnōsis*. Sometimes this makes no difference to the meaning of a word, although it usually intensifies the meaning.

as Peter is going to tell us, is that we might prefer to exchange that truth for a lie.

4. The genuine Christ: the gospel's content (1:1b–2)

Just as water flowing from a pure mountain spring can be polluted by a chemical works downstream, so an initially pure gospel can be polluted by muddled teaching – and a polluted gospel is a powerless gospel. In these verses Peter makes four extraordinary statements about Jesus, the man he knew as a close friend, and he designs them as indicators of the purity of our message's content.

a. Jesus is the Saviour

Our *Saviour Jesus Christ* is a frequent phrase on the lips of Christians. But it is awesome in its meaning, as we can see by turning the phrase on its head and asking, 'What is it that Jesus saves us from?' Peter gives clues in his use of this surprisingly rare New Testament term.[49] He calls Jesus 'Saviour' five times (1:1, 11; 2:20; 3:2, 18) and talks of 'salvation' once (3:15). These highlight the three tenses of salvation: past, present and future. Of the past, Peter says we have 'been cleansed from [our] past sins' (1:9), and he attributes that work to our *Saviour Jesus Christ* (1:1). Of the present, he says that genuine Christians 'have escaped the corruption of the world by knowing our Lord and Saviour Jesus Christ' (2:20). Of the future, he writes that Christians need not be concerned about the apparent delay of the second coming, because 'our Lord's patience means salvation' (3:15). We can say, then, that Jesus Christ has saved us, because those sins which defiled us in God's sight have been cleansed away. We can say that he is saving us, because he protects us from the influences in the world which pull us away from him. And we can say that he will save us, because on the day of judgment the only safe place to hide will be behind the cross. Of those three meanings, it is that third sense of ultimate salvation which will dominate Peter's letter.

b. Jesus is God

Peter goes further than saying Jesus is Saviour – he says he is *our God and Saviour Jesus Christ*. Some find these words too strong to be simply about Jesus Christ, and say that Peter is distinguishing between two persons of the Godhead: God and Jesus Christ. Most

---

[49] See E. M. B. Green, *The Meaning of Salvation* (London: Hodder and Stoughton; Philadelphia: Westminster Press, 1965), pp. 194–197.

scholars today think this unlikely.[50] Peter attributes full deity to Jesus. Yet there is subtlety in his position, for only a few words later he makes another distinction, *the knowledge of God and of Jesus our Lord*. Just as it is clear in the first case that Peter is speaking of one person, there it is equally obvious that he is speaking of two: God the Father and Jesus Christ. Quite clearly, Peter is articulating in an early form what later became recognized as orthodox Christianity: 'the Father is God, the Son is God and the Holy Ghost [Spirit] is God, and yet there are not three Gods but one God'.[51]

It is quite right for us to affirm that Jesus Christ is God, and quite right for us to affirm that Jesus Christ is not all there is to God. In his lifetime on earth he accepted and described himself with Old Testament titles for God, such as 'shepherd', 'bridegroom', 'rock' and 'vinedresser'; his teaching had an authoritative note which had not been heard since God spoke at Sinai; he spoke, acted and promised as only the God of Israel could.[52] Yet he submitted himself to the will of 'the Father', he prayed to 'the Father' and spoke of going to 'my Father'.[53] The balance was striking at the end of his life on earth, when he said, 'I am returning to my Father and your Father, to my God and your God', but did not quibble when Thomas recognized him as 'my Lord and my God'.[54] As the first Christians read their Old Testaments in the light of what had happened, they saw that they lived at the time of ' "Immanuel" – which means, "God with us" '.[55] Peter shares this clarity, for he will call Jesus 'God', but he will not call God 'Jesus'. Peter does not directly mention Jesus' humanity here, but the truth that God the Son really became a man who was a first-century Jewish carpenter called Jesus still breathes through his letter. He mentions Jesus by name nine times, as he had been used to doing to his face for three years; and as he remembers what happened in that time (2:16–18), and

---

[50] The discussion has three strands. First, on the grounds of grammar: the translation requires one subject not two, as in the parallel construction in 1 Pet. 1:3 where 'the God and Father of our Lord Jesus Christ' is one person, God and Father, not two. Second, on the grounds of context: when Peter uses the word 'Saviour' in this letter (1:11; 2:20; 3:2, 18) he always links it with another noun referring to the same person. Third, on the grounds of theology: 'there is no improbability in 2 Peter's use of *theos* ("God") for Jesus, nor does the usage require a second century date for the letter'. Bauckham (1983), p. 169.

[51] The Athanasian Creed.

[52] *E.g.* shepherd: Ps. 23; Ezk. 34:1–31; *cf.* Jn. 10:1–21. Bridgegroom: Is. 62:5; Ezk. 16:1–63; *cf.* Mt. 9:15; 25:1–13. Rock: Dt. 32:1–43; 1 Sa. 2:2; 2 Sa. 22:2–3; Pss. 19:14; 31:3; Dn. 2:1–45; *cf.* Mt. 21:42 (and see 1 Cor. 10:1–5). Vine: Is. 5:1–7; Ezk. 15; *cf.* Jn. 15:1–8. For Jesus' authoritative teaching, see Jn. 8:58; *cf.* Ex. 3:14; Mt. 5:1–7:29; Mk. 2:1–28.

[53] Jn. 13:31 – 17:26.   [54] Jn. 20:17, 28.   [55] Mt. 1:23.

what Jesus said (*e.g.* 3:10, alluding to Lk. 12:39). One of the most remarkable features of the titles Peter gives Jesus is that he writes about one of his closest friends, and yet recognizes him as God.

c. Jesus is the Christ

This combination, 'Jesus' and 'Christ', is so normal that it is difficult to recapture how radical it must have seemed to Peter and the other first Christians as they used it in their teaching and praying. *Christ* (Greek *christos*, literally, 'anointed one'; in Hebrew, *māšîaḥ*, 'Messiah') was the name used for the one who would fulfil all the Old Testament hopes. Prophets, priests and kings were anointed with oil to show that they were dedicated to God as his servants,[56] but *the* Servant would be *the* Messiah, the one above all others who would fulfil God's plan. When Peter first dared to breathe the phrase, 'You are the Christ, the Son of the living God',[57] he was breaking wholly new ground in Israel's dealings with God by identifying this man as the fulfilment of God's plan for humankind. Of course, Peter did not fully understand what he was saying; and when Jesus immediately explained that he must suffer as the Christ, Peter rebuked him, thinking that the Christ should be a glorious king. Jesus insisted that death was his destiny, and after his resurrection it was that sense of inevitability that began to control the first Christians' thinking. It became the heart of Peter's message to the crowd on the day of Pentecost: 'This man was handed over to you by God's set purpose and foreknowledge; and you, with the help of wicked men, put him to death by nailing him to the cross. But God raised him from the dead, freeing him from the agony of death, because it was impossible for death to keep its hold on him . . . God has raised this Jesus to life, and we are all witnesses of the fact . . . God has made this Jesus, whom you crucified, both Lord and Christ.'[58] The risen Jesus is the glorious, lordly Christ precisely because he went the way of the cross, and it is that to which Peter and the other apostles are witnesses.

d. Jesus is the Lord

Lord (*kyrios*) was the standard translation in the Septuagint (the Greek version of the Old Testament) for the Hebrew name of God, Yahweh. To call Jesus *Lord* among people who knew their Old Testaments, then, was to say that Jesus was present all the way through the history of Israel as their covenant Lord. Whenever Christians read that the Lord did such and such, they were to

---

[56] Ex 28:41; Ps. 105:15.   [57] Mt. 16:16.   [58] Acts 2:23–24, 32, 36.

understand Jesus as acting there. How else could they explain Jesus' thinking through Psalm 23, 'The LORD is my shepherd', and coming to the conclusion, 'I am the good shepherd'?[59]

They would also be aware that the titles 'Saviour', 'Lord' and 'God' were used in contemporary religious groups and political circles as titles for the Emperor. To use them of Jesus was therefore to make a decisive stand against all the other claimants for Jesus' crown. This would have sounded ludicrous to non-Christians, because the cross of Christ does not resonate with apparent heavenly glory, any more than his whipped body wearing a fool's crown and robe resonates with political glory. But such is the wisdom of God that it turns such apparent foolishness into wisdom, and such apparent weakness into glory.[60]

This fourfold description of Jesus is important because it puts him at the focal point of human history. As *God*, he guarantees that his words and his works cannot be replaced or revoked; as *Christ*, he fulfils all the Old Testament promises; as *Saviour*, he died on the cross for our salvation in the past, present and future; and as *Lord* he claims the right to our individual love and obedience – notice how Peter calls him *our* Lord.

There is a constant temptation to separate these four titles. Michael Green writes that 2 Peter 'was written to people who claim Jesus as Saviour but do not obey him as Lord. That appears to be the reason why the writer significantly combines the roles of Lord and Saviour'[61] (1:11; 2:20; 3:2; 3:18). These two titles go together. It is only because Jesus is the Lord that he can be the Saviour; and if he is the Saviour then he owns those he has saved, and he has the right to be their Lord. The words are inseparable. The reason this is so central to Peter's letter is that the false teachers are denying the future coming of Jesus Christ. Peter reminds the Christians that the Judge on judgment day will be Jesus, and the Saviour on judgment day will be Jesus. On that day Jesus will be, visibly and finally, both Lord and Saviour. As a result, we should live in gratitude for his salvation and in obedience to his lordship. He is 'the source of eternal salvation for all who obey him'.[62]

This description of Jesus is the wonder of the message Peter spoke on the day of Pentecost, where themes of Saviour, Lord, God and Christ emerge and intertwine.

'Let all Israel be assured of this: God has made this Jesus, whom you crucified, both Lord and Christ.'

---

[59] Jn. 10:11. See also Ezk. 34.   [60] 1 Cor. 1:17–25.
[61] E. M. B. Green, *op. cit.*, p. 195.   [62] Heb. 5:9.

... The people ... were cut to the heart and said to Peter and the other apostles, 'Brothers, what shall we do?'

Peter replied, 'Repent and be baptised, every one of you, in the name of Jesus Christ for the forgiveness of your sins. And you will receive the gift of the Holy Spirit. The promise is for you and your children and for all who are far off – for all whom the Lord our God will call.'

With many other words he warned them; and he pleaded with them, 'Save yourselves from this corrupt generation.'[63]

---

[63] Acts 2:36–40.

2 Peter 1:3–4
2. The power and the promises

In this section, Peter gives some of the most thrilling promises of any in the Bible. As Bengel says, 'There is a wonderful cheerfulness in this opening.'[1] But Peter is also alert to the danger of taking shortcuts to heaven, and behaving as if God had magically so transformed us that the categories of 'sin' and 'obedience' have become irrelevant. He does not want us to forget that Christians talk of Jesus as their Lord as well as their Saviour.

> *His divine power has given us everything we need for life and godliness through our knowledge of him who called us by his own glory and goodness. ⁴Through these he has given us his very great and precious promises, so that through them you may participate in the divine nature and escape the corruption in the world caused by evil desires.*

In private, Christians will often admit to envying non-Christian friends in their free-wheeling lifestyles and morality. They see other people, who sometimes call themselves more 'liberated' Christians, enjoying things which the Bible clearly forbids. They might feel sure that such behaviour is wrong, but secretly wish they could join in. They are paralysed into indecision, sometimes wishing they had the courage to enjoy a fully committed Christianity, and at other times wishing they had the courage to forget it and enjoy being utterly pagan. Peter warns that obedient Christians are not killjoys or repressed, and that a Christianity which wants to have the best of both worlds will actually have the best of neither. This present world is being 'kept for the day of judgment and destruction of ungodly men' (3:7), and the future world will be a 'home of righteousness' (3:13). We face a choice, and to choose a home in one world will mean not having a home in the other.

There is a fine division of responsibility as we live in this world in

[1] Bengel, p. 761.

the hope of a future home. Jesus Christ has the power and makes the promises (verses 3–4), but we need to add to our faith consistent changes in character in order to be effective, productive, clear-sighted Christians (verses 5–11). Peter's letter is constructed around Jesus Christ's power (chapter 2) and promises (chapter 3), and this section introduces the main ideas in miniature.

Peter's timescale is central to his thinking. He says that Jesus Christ has given us two massive resources. To equip us in the present, Jesus *has given us everything we need for life and godliness.* To direct us to the future, *he has given us his very great and precious promises.* Those two resources make up the great gift of the 'faith' we 'have received' (1:1), but we shall need to keep a strong hold on each of them individually, and not confuse them. Peter has a clear perspective on the practical results of being a disciple today, but he says that such a committed life will make sense only if we have a deeper perspective on God's future plans for the universe. 2 Peter is one of the most explicitly future-oriented books in the New Testament, and Peter will demonstrate the everyday implications of that future goal. The 'now' of the power and the 'then' of the promises go inextricably together, and he will show that there are awful consequences if they are uncoupled.

Peter wrote one sentence which extends from verse 1 to verse 11 in the Greek, but that makes such hard reading in English that modern versions start a new paragraph here at verse 3. There is an important connection between verse 2 and verse 3, though,[2] and it lies in that *knowledge* that Christians have of Jesus Christ (verse 2), in which they must grow (verses 3 and 8).

Peter makes a number of startling assertions about Jesus and his work in this section. They are phrased in the language and form of Greek philosophy and religion, and some have accused him of uncritically absorbing the secular spirit of his age.[3] But Peter's background remains so thoroughly Jewish, and his ideas so thoroughly Christian, that we have to account for his odd vocabulary in another way.[4] As he begins his exposure of the problem, he

---

[2] *Hōs* with the genitive absolute meaning 'assuming that' or 'seeing that'. The connection is there, but it is not as strong as between verses 4 and 5. The NIV is probably wise to omit a translation.

[3] Of course, many go further and say that this Greek philosophical and religious language is more proof that Peter is not the author. See below.

[4] Bigg warns of the danger of overemphasizing the occurrence of these words, and shows that they were in common, non-philosophical use at the time. Bauckham has wisely pointed out that although the vocabulary may come from non-Christian sources, the ideas and shape of the section certainly come from Jewish writings. Green has taken it further by showing how Peter has deliberately adopted the vocabulary of the religious world in order to confront the false teachers on their own ground. Bigg, p. 254; Bauckham (1983), p. 182; Green (1987), p. 73.

'answers a fool according to his folly,[5] by showing up the worldly nature of the error and using secular language to do it. It can be a risky tactic to adopt,[6] but here it warns the Christians of the danger of the position they were about to fall into, which was that of becoming utterly indistinguishable from surrounding paganism, and aping non-Christian concerns.

1. The power of Jesus Christ (1:3)

This is one of the relatively few occasions on which the New Testament actually calls Jesus divine,[7] and it is for a reason. Even people with no religious commitment may speak of their religious experiences, and some church people affirm these as genuine encounters with God. Peter will not rest with such diplomatic generalizations, because he wants to anchor everything to Jesus Christ, who uniquely has *divine power*. The idea of God's power is a frequent one in the Bible, covering every major stage in the history of God's people. Peter wants to make that link between Jesus and the great acts of God in the past, and to remind us of the power that accompanied Jesus' ministry. But two clues show that he is also working within a secular environment. First, although the phrase 'divine power' does not echo any particular phrase in the Bible, it was very frequent in contemporary secular writing. Secondly, although the word 'divine' is confined in the New Testament to this letter and Paul's speech in Athens,[8] it was common currency outside.[9] It is repeated in verse 4 in the phrase *divine nature*, and the two phrases form a bracket around this paragraph. The word, *theios*, could be used by the apostles either in order to put their thoughts into words that non-Christians would understand or, as here, to show how some of the Christians' ideas were shading off into paganism.

For the first time the question is becoming clear, and it is one that is not confined to Peter's time. Is the power of Jesus Christ sufficient on its own to strengthen the resolve of anxious and tempted Christians in a tough and attractively pagan world? Peter's answer is that Jesus' power is more than adequate, for Jesus not only sets the highest standards for Christians to live up to, he also gives the resources to meet those standards, and in the end he will defeat the forces who oppose him. Everything hangs on that last point, for if Jesus does not have the ultimate power to enforce his rightful rule,

[5] Pr. 26:5.   [6] See Pr. 26:4!
[7] Although Peter could be talking about God the Father here, it would be odd to talk about God's *divine power*. The nearest name in the Greek is Jesus Christ, and he is the subject of this entire paragraph. For other NT passages on Jesus' divinity see Jn. 1:1; 20:28; Rom. 9:5 (probably); Tit. 2:13; Heb. 1:8.
[8] Acts 17:22–31.   [9] See Bauckham (1983), p. 177, for details.

then it is really no power at all. People look back to Jesus' remarkable teaching and miracles, and rightly think that they see there the great power of God. But Peter sees a greater working of Jesus' *divine power* in the seemingly unimpressive reality of men and women able to live lives that honour Jesus. People look back to the Jewish carpenter friend of Peter, whose dreams led to the cross in weakness; but Peter looked forward as well, to Jesus' mighty return as King and Judge. 'The *dunamis*, power and authority of Christ, is the sword which St Peter holds over the head of the false teachers.'[10]

a. *Jesus Christ sets the challenge for us*

Jesus Christ sets high standards in *life and godliness*, which are best thought of not as two things but one, a 'godly life'.[11] Those high standards were apparent throughout his life and teaching, and nowhere more clearly than in the Sermon on the Mount. There he said that 'unless your righteousness surpasses that of the Pharisees and the teachers of the law, you will certainly not enter the kingdom of heaven'.[12] We are so used to hearing Jesus' religious contemporaries marked low for their standards that it comes as something of a shock to realize that Jesus meant this as an awesome warning. The people to whom he spoke assumed that the Pharisees and teachers of the law were the very model of scrupulous perfection, and to be required to exceed that standard was breathtakingly ambitious and radical. Jesus had shown that those Pharisees who were spiritually open enough to want to learn from him had to go further. The Pharisee Nicodemus had to be 'born again', and the teacher of the law who agreed with Jesus on God's standards was told only that he was 'not far from the kingdom of God'.[13] Jesus taught that the Pharisees' perfection was inadequate because it was built on reconstructing the law so as to demand the least of themselves. He reconstructed it to demand the most, and he made that standard irrevocable. That level of positive perfection is the godly life.

Such a standard seems hopelessly naïve, because ordinary human beings are not necessarily noble or altruistic. Some suggest a lower standard that more people can reach. But in the Sermon on the Mount, Jesus is not setting out a new and more demanding code of ethics that only a few disciplined ascetics can achieve. Rather, he is redefining the people of God. They are the people who recognize him as their lawgiver, who come to him not on the basis of their

---

[10] Bigg, p. 253.   [11] So Bauckham (1983), p. 178.   [12] Mt. 5:20.
[13] Jn. 3:7; Mk. 12:34.

perfection or strength but in their imperfection and weakness. They are men and women who ask for forgiveness, not approval,[14] and their perfection is not interior and invisible, but worked out in everyday life.

The word translated *godliness* is *eusebeia*, the word ordinary non-Christians would use to describe what they would hope to be the results of their religious practices in observable holiness. It spoke of decency, honesty, trust and integrity, and could mean something that a religious person has earned or deserved. Peter had encountered that misunderstanding in the first few months of Christian leadership, when a man's miraculous healing was causing a stir. The people were thinking that Peter must be a very good man, since God used him in this way. Instead, Peter directs them to Jesus. 'Why do you stare at us as if by our own power (*dynamis*) or godliness (*eusebeia*) we had made this man walk?'[15] Because it has this overtone of man-made piety, it is a word the New Testament normally avoids;[16] but it has a sharp significance in an environment where non-Christians were becoming scandalized at the immorality of church leaders (2:2). The ordinary Christian, faced with a battle against sin, could easily give in to despair. Are we to follow those who claim to be our leaders but clearly lead us into sin? Are they right in teaching us that fighting sin is an outdated battle? Peter says that the quality of a Christian's discipleship should be so evident that non-Christians should be able to watch us reaching, and even surpassing, their highest standards of life and godliness.

b. Jesus Christ meets the challenge for us

If the high expectations of the New Testament are not watered down, the average Christian is left feeling massively daunted. Peter's answer to that inadequacy is that Jesus Christ *has given us everything we need for life and godliness*. This is a slight under-translation, because *has given* renders *dōreomai*, which can mean a generous imperial gift, or even volunteering for service.[17] It

[14] Mt. 5:3–10. See D. A. Carson, 'Matthew', in F. E. Gabelein (ed.), *The Expositor's Bible Commentary* 8 (Grand Rapids: Zondervan, 1984), pp. 122–194.

[15] Acts 3:12. 'It is yet another example of Peter's being consistent in his spiritual and exegetical thinking over a period of more than thirty years.' Thiede, p. 117.

[16] Outside this letter, Acts 3:12 and the pastoral epistles: 1 Tim. 2:2; 3:16; 4:7–8; 6:3, 5–6, 11; 2 Tim. 3:5; Tit. 1:1 Gordon Fee puts those letters in a context similar to 2 Peter and says such language 'has to do with behaviour that can be seen'. He also says that 'Most likely this is the [false teachers'] word, being used by Paul to counteract them'. G. D. Fee, *1 and 2 Timothy, Titus*, New International Biblical Commentary (Peabody: Hendrickson, 1984), p. 63.

[17] MM, p. 174. Bauckham translates it 'has bestowed', saying that the word denotes 'royal . . . official . . . or divine . . . bounty'. Bauckham (1983), p. 178.

underlines the graciousness and generosity of the giver. Jesus Christ has generously given all that could ever be required to be godly. Merely by being Christians, we are in touch with everything we need to live a godly life. That supremely important word 'everything' is both a tremendous encouragement and a tremendous warning.

It is encouragement because it means that there is nothing extra to find out or gain access to than we have already obtained just through being Christians. The gospel is sufficient for us to meet God's requirements. If there is a major scientific, artistic, moral or philosophical question, or even a matter of personal decision-making, which the Bible does not address, then we have to assume that although it may be intriguing and important from a human perspective, it is irrelevant to the quest for a godly life. God has made his directions for life perfectly clear and sufficient, for *he has given us everything we need*, and that provides a clear view on what is centrally important in his plan and what is relatively trivial.

There will always be people who want to supplement the work of Christ with extra teaching, and convince us that we are living less than Christian lives, while their particular form of teaching is the ingredient missing from traditional Christianity. It takes different forms: Christ plus healing, Christ plus success, Christ plus prosperity, Christ plus counselling, Christ plus an overwhelming experience. Anxious Christians may spend many years going through these, searching for an assurance that is already theirs in Christ. Simply by being Christians we have access to everything we need to live a life that pleases God. Those who want to add to that are false teachers.

That sufficiency of Christ is good news. But the tremendous warning these words contain is that we have to face up to our accountability to him. We cannot blame God for not making us godly enough or not making his will clear enough, for we already have *everything we need*. A godly life is not something that only a few super-saints are destined to achieve, for Peter says it is well within the reach of the ordinary Christian. There is no point in seeking a special secret of sanctification that will transform us into godly people in a faster way than ordinary Christian obedience. There is no other way. If there were, it would mean that the death of Christ is sufficient to save but insufficient to sanctify. Peter will lay out later how to live a godly life (verses 5–11), and it will be a matter of hard submission to God's Word. The Christian who is not godly has only one person to blame.

We gain access to the remarkable resource that will enable us to meet this daunting challenge *through our knowledge of him who called us by his own glory and goodness*. This is again the knowledge of Jesus Christ that comes when we are converted (*'epignōsis* knowledge'), and which is the birthright of every Christian. We are not to look for the source of that knowledge in our experience of conversion, however, for Peter ties it back to the ministry of Jesus. All the apostles had an especially clear memory of being *called* by Jesus,[18] but the *we* and *us* must mean that Peter remembered a moment when Jesus called all Christians.[19] Perhaps he recollected the occasion on which Jesus gave the invitation, 'Come to me, all you who are weary and burdened, and I will give you rest. Take my yoke upon you and learn from me, for I am gentle and humble in heart, and you will find rest for your souls. For my yoke is easy and my burden is light.'[20] We may remember having responded to that invitation at a particular time, but it would be wrong to identify that event with the moment we were called. We have a vital link with the historical Jesus.

Peter underlines that truth by saying that the way Jesus called us was *by his own glory and goodness* (and perhaps again it is right to combine the two words and talk of Jesus' 'glorious goodness').[21] What has attracted men and women to Jesus Christ for nearly two thousand years is his unique ability to reflect the glory and goodness of the invisible God[22] into our visible and fallen world. Goodness, *aretē*, is another common word from Greek religion, which also makes Old Testament appearances, partnered, as it is here, by the word *glory*.[23] The two words could be merely synonyms. But 'goodness' here probably means 'a manifestation of divine power, [a] miracle'.[24] Peter does not want to focus on Jesus' goodness in the abstract, but in the reality of what God has done and achieved. That forces us back to Jesus' life, teaching, example and miracles, and to his transfiguration, which will be so central to this letter. Above all, it forces us back to the great manifestation of God's power in Jesus' death and resurrection.[25] In other words, people may seem to become Christians because they find Jesus' ministry deeply attractive, but underneath that, Peter says, is the saving work of Christ

---

[18] Mk. 1:14–20.

[19] *Kalesantos*, 'called', is an aorist participle, referring to something which happens once but has lasting implications.

[20] Mt. 11:28–30. The contrast is with the heavy burden of the Pharisees, seen in the next story (their criticism of the hungry disciples on the Sabbath, 12:1–18).

[21] The Greek is ambiguous, and it is possible to translate the phrase as if the glory and the goodness were the destiny to which Christ is calling us; but the word for *his own*, *idia*, makes the NIV translation *by* certain.

[22] *Aretē* (goodness) is also found in Greek religion, but as Green says, 'It is not without significance that these two words, *aretē* and *doxa*, belong to God in the Old Testament.' Green (1987), p. 72.

[23] Is. 42:8, 12, LXX.   [24] BAGD, p. 106.   [25] 1 Cor. 1:18; 6:14.

which has called us into fellowship with the Father, and it is only through the cross that we have knowledge of him.[26]

c. Who fails the challenge?

The false teachers threatening the churches to which Peter is writing found this idea of high standards an unnecessary burden. They collected followers by 'appealing to the lustful desires of sinful human nature' instead (2:18). The reason, which will become clearer in chapter 2, is that they denied that Jesus Christ has any power to judge, in which case there is no reason to live up to his exacting standards. They saw non-Christians all around them living a life which was the total opposite of Jesus' standards and yet thoroughly enjoying themselves, and that made them feel privately envious. They began to wish that Christians did not have to stand out from the crowd. They had started to argue that Christian theology and morality should develop and grow over time, and that it should lose some of what they might have called its primitive judgmentalism. Peter is firm in reply. No, he says, the Jesus who will return to judge will measure us by the standards he has left us and which he has equipped us to fulfil.

2. The promises of Jesus Christ (1:4)

Jesus Christ's glorious goodness is demonstrated in the second great resource he makes available to us: *he has given us his very great and precious promises*. The theme of 'promise' runs throughout the Bible, stemming from the promise God made in the garden of Eden, that the disastrous fall would not determine humanity's destiny irrevocably.[27] Chapter 2 of this letter focuses on the promises that God made to Noah and Lot, that they would not be destroyed in the judgment played out in the flood and the end of Sodom and Gomorrah. Of all the biblical promises, Peter has in mind the particular group to do with God's decisive role at the end of history, 'the promise of his coming' (3:4, AV). These are the promises that the false teachers question (3:4), and that Peter defends (3:9). In fact, the heart of Peter's reply to the false teachers is that Jesus Christ will return to reign, visibly and unchallenged. The false teachers have decided that this is not the case, and so what Peter sees as future

---

[26] That should be how 1 Pet. 2:9 is understood too: 'we declare the praises (*aretas*) who called us out of darkness into his wonderful light', means declaring 'God's praiseworthy *deeds*'. J. R. Michaels, *1 Peter, Word Biblical Commentary* (Waco: Word; Milton Keynes: Word UK, 1988), p. 110.

[27] Gn. 3:15.

(such as being morally perfect) the errorists have to bring into the present. Because they cannot pretend to be perfect, they have to decide that such standards are unnecessary. They too make a promise, for they 'promise . . . freedom', but they are in no state to fulfil it, for they are still 'slaves of depravity' (2:19).

a. The promise of glory

In one breathtaking phrase Peter brings into view the ultimate content of the promises of Jesus Christ, that we shall *participate in the divine nature*. It is a claim without equal in the New Testament, and Sidebottom calls it 'the strikingly original note in 2 Peter'.[28] Some writers dislike it intensely and imply that it is semi-pagan. 'It would be hard to find in the whole New Testament a sentence which, in its expression, its individual motifs and its whole trend, more clearly marks the relapse of Christianity into Hellenistic dualism.'[29] Yet although it is a unique phrase in the New Testament, it is not a unique idea. Peter wrote in his first letter that Christians 'will share in the glory to be revealed',[30] and Paul wrote of our 'adoption as sons', that we might be 'conformed to the likeness of his Son'.[31] And of course Paul's key phrases 'in Christ' and 'with Christ' locate our destiny within the destiny of Jesus himself.[32]

At this high point of the New Testament, we must not play down the wonder of what Peter says. There is a long tradition, beginning with Clement of Alexandria (c. 150–c. 215), that places more weight on this verse than it can fairly carry,[33] and we must preserve the awesome distance between the creator God and everything and everyone he makes. To say that we are God, or become God, would be a shocking misinterpretation of Peter. Nevertheless, we should still marvel with Calvin that 'it is the purpose of the gospel to make us sooner or later like God; indeed it is, so to speak, a kind of deification'.[34] Peter is able to promise far more than the false teachers can ever do, because he is pinning his faith on the promises of God.

This participation in the divine nature is solely an act of God's graciousness, his undeserved generosity, in order that we might

---

[28] Sidebottom, p. 106; but this is not Peter's only original contribution to the New Testament.

[29] Käsemann, pp. 179–180.   [30] 1 Pet. 5:1.   [31] Rom. 8:23, 29.

[32] *E.g.* Rom. 6:1–14; Eph. 1:20; 2:6.

[33] See P. E. Hughes, *The True Image* (Grand Rapids: Eerdmans; Leicester: IVP, 1989), pp. 281–286, for a helpful historical survey.

[34] Calvin (*Peter*), p. 330. For a different approach and translation see A. Wolters, '"Partners of the Deity", A Covenantal Reading of 2 Peter 1:4', *Calvin Theological Journal* 25 (1990), pp. 28–44.

escape the corruption in the world caused by evil desires. Peter will make a major theme of the rightness of God's judgment on the world, and how there is only one route of escape (3:10–12). Either we share the character of those who are being judged, or we share the character of the one who does the judging. Peter has put the gospel into a form of words appropriate to a society 'haunted by the conception of *phthora, corruption*',[35] because he wants to create a hunger in the lives of his readers for the highest promise that God makes. Any other promise seems insipid and irrelevant beside that.

b. The promise of escape

Peter will explain in his letter what it is that Christians can expect here and now, and what should be expected only in the future. To use the technical word, what is at issue is eschatology, the doctrine of the last days.

Attitudes to the last days can take two forms, which are sometimes called 'under-realized' and 'over-realized' eschatology. 'Under-realized' eschatology does not take into account the tremendous difference in the relationship between humankind and God that has been effected by the life, death and resurrection of Jesus. It approaches God as if the Old Testament model were still appropriate. Even though there are no more animal sacrifices, it will design awesome buildings, and perform mystical music and uplifting spectacle, conveying a sense of mystery and dread. Such an approach can leave a Christian feeling that God is still as unapproachable as ever, except for a tiny spiritual élite; and that the way to please this distant God is to follow a strict regimen of rules as if to appease the God who was not fully appeased by the death of his Son.

'Over-realized' eschatology is an opposite error, which is to think that everything Jesus promised for the time after his death must be true for us now. His resurrection inaugurated the new age, and so every blessing promised for the new age must be fully available now. The elements of truth in this cannot conceal its weakness. A compassionate view of the real world shows us that even the most Christ-like Christian still sins or falls sick. A further version of this view says that those promises will not in fact be kept, and that people have to do the best they can, living with impossible Christian ideals in a far from perfect world.

The answer to both errors is to understand God's timing. These are the 'in-between' times, in between Christ's coming as servant and his coming as Lord. One day we shall have resurrection bodies

[35] Green (1987), p. 73.

like Christ's, but in the meantime Christians die; one day we shall
have a perfect desire to please God, but in the meantime we still
sin. We do not have to pretend that God has kept promises which
he says will be fulfilled only in the future, but we do have to
believe them and not water them down.

Peter is concerned because he sees a highly liberal 'over-realized'
eschatology in the churches to which he writes. The false teachers
denied any future element in Christianity at all. They were
sophisticated 'scoffers' (3:3) who thought that the ideas of Jesus'
return and judgment were too crude and simplistic (3:4), and that
they were metaphors that had to be reinterpreted and adjusted to
meet the questions of modern people. Jesus' standards, they
argued, had to be interpreted in a new way to be acceptable to
modern lifestyles.

Peter is quite clear about what this means, and in order to
counter it he restates basic Christian truth in a fresh way. Unlike
some Greek philosophers, and modern New Agers, the Bible
teaches that we are humans, not gods. We were made by God,
according to Genesis 1:26. We are created rather than creators. We
fell, not from godliness in heaven, but from full humanity on
earth. Nor is it our automatic destiny (as again some Greek and
modern religions teach) to be absorbed into the Godhead as we
evolve (either spiritually or scientifically) into greater or better
humans. The Bible treats our rebellion against God as a deep
tragedy, and the fall was not a growth point or step upwards.
Some will always see the physical world as base and bad, and the
spiritual world as elevated and true. They say that the way to find
God is to escape the physical realm in a mystical experience. But
Peter is clear that the *corruption* we are to flee is not our physical
bodies, but sin. In 2 Peter, the 'world' (*kosmos*) is always
rebellious human society which is under judgment and which will
be destroyed (1:4; 2:5, 20; 3:6).[36] The appropriate Christian
reaction is to run away from those things which cause God's anger
(2:18, 20). God does not call us to seek him on a higher,
non-material plane by out-of-the-body experiences, transcendental
meditation or visions, shaking off the supposed limitations of our
bodies. Being human in human society is a right and good thing.
Having understood this, though, we are not to be so identified
with God's world that we cease to flee the corruption in it, which
is in rebellion against him, and which he will destroy.[37]

---

[36] The NIV is helpfully consistent in this by translating *kosmos* as 'world', which
means the corrupt human society, while translating *gē* as 'earth', the physical globe.
In that way the flood in chapter 2 can destroy the world (*kosmos*) without destroying
the earth (*gē*).

[37] Because *apophygontes* is a second aorist, it is said that it has a backward

Peter calls Christians to live out the new relationship with Jesus Christ in practical obedience today while still keeping hold of the fact that much, much more remains in store. We do not pretend to be perfect, which would make his promises unnecessary; or say that we do not need to be perfect, and so make his promises cheap and tawdry. Instead, we can say that we *will be* perfect, and that makes them *very great*[38] *and precious promises*. God will do all that he has promised to bring us to a position of deep intimacy with him.

These words immensely influenced the young John Wesley in the middle of his spiritual crisis early in the morning of 24 May 1730. Looking back on that crucial day, he wrote in his diary for 4 June, 'All these days I scarce remember to have opened the New Testament, but upon some great and precious promise. And I saw, more than ever, that the gospel is in truth but one great promise, from the beginning of it to the end.'[39] He had grasped Peter's massive time-scale, and understood that the full evidence of Jesus' power will be seen only in the future when he keeps his promise. That truth frees us from having to pretend to be perfectly whole people today. We are Christians who are gripped by God's promises for the future, thrilled by them, and motivated to live godly lives now in his power.

---

reference point to our conversion. But the aorist means that the event is a point in time, not necessarily a point in the past, and, *pace* Green (1987), p. 73, the NIV's future-tense translation is fair. See D. A. Carson, *Exegetical Fallacies* (Grand Rapids: Baker, 1984), pp. 69–74.

[38] *Megista*, 'an adjective in the superlative degree'. Kistemaker, p. 250.

[39] Quoted in Moffatt (*Peter*), p. 179.

2 Peter 1:5–11
3. The productive Christian

James Hogg, a nineteenth-century Scottish writer, wrote an extra-ordinary novel called *Private Memoirs and Confessions of a Justified Sinner*. The central character is so absolutely convinced of the certainty of his salvation, and sure that he is a member of 'the elect', that he commits a series of increasingly gross and self-indulgent acts. He is so secure in the belief that his behaviour will not affect his eternal destiny that he feels completely freed from any restraint, even to the point of murder. The book was written as a sharp parody of an extreme position, and we should be grateful that very few Christians have had the foolishness and wickedness to go so far.

Even so, we frequently come across a false understanding of Christian freedom which says that if we are justified by God's irrevocable grace, we enjoy a new kind of relationship with God where ideas of law and obedience are inappropriate. Those from a conservative position suddenly feel free to do things that earlier generations of Christians judged wrong. Television loves to expose those Christian leaders whose sense of spiritual security is so strong that they feel free to enjoy various forbidden fruits. More radically minded people wonder what to do with those parts of the New Testament which forbid some behaviour in an apparently legalistic way. Should they be seen as hangovers from Old Testament think-ing, the New Testament writer having failed to absorb the full implications of the gospel? Should Paul's requirement for sex to be contained within heterosexual marriage be deleted as firmly as he deleted the requirement for circumcision? Anxious Christians think they lack the key to Christian growth and certainty, and move from guru to guru seeking the touch of God to change them. Some even claim to have had an experience that makes it impossible for them to sin, and therefore the battles Peter writes about are not ones that need concern them.

When such thinking occurs, the connection between private, internalized 'faith' and public, observable 'obedience' has been severed. People say that provided they believe as the early Christians believed, they need not behave as the early Christians behaved. A convenient contrast is drawn between the supposedly simple, liberating message and ethics of Jesus and the supposedly complicated, restricting theology of the later New Testament, which is usually blamed on Paul. Permission is thus given to reinterpret the requirements of the New Testament by saying that whether or not they were correct expressions of Christian obedience then, they are hardly so today. On a less sophisticated level, the gospel might be reduced to a few simplistic phrases and slogans, and the more demanding parts of the New Testament neatly avoided.

Such positions are fundamentally wrong. They set up a wholly false division between Jesus, who most certainly did teach a very complex theology,[1] and the first Christians. They open the way for a destructive liberalism, for if the first Christians had not sufficiently thought through their ethics, it is inevitable that they had not thought through their doctrine either. If the one is not binding on us, neither is the other. Most importantly for 2 Peter, such positions do not see that the first Christians could not divide belief from behaviour precisely because they could not teach theology apart from ethics.[2] Peter would say that if we believe what he believes, then we must behave as he behaves. If we do not see that need, and if we do not follow his prescription, we demonstrate that we actually believe something different, a false gospel.

One of the major concerns of Peter's letter is that Christian faith which is firmly rooted must make a radical difference to the way we behave. We will want to please Jesus Christ more, rather than presume upon his love. In this section, he shows that our faith, if it is genuine, sets up a chain of deep, internal, and experiential changes that will meet our hunger for God's reality.

1. The effective Christian (1:5–9)

For this very reason, make every effort to add to your faith goodness; and to goodness, knowledge; [6]and to knowledge, self-control; and to self-control, perseverance; and to perseverance, godliness; [7]and to godliness, brotherly kindness; and to brotherly kindness, love. [8]For if you possess these qualities in increasing

---

[1] See, for example, R. T. France, 'Mark and the Teaching of Jesus', *Gospel Perspectives* 1 (JSOT Press, 1980), pp. 101–136.

[2] They learned that lesson from the Old Testament, where the Ten Commandments (*i.e.* ethics) opens with theology: 'I am the LORD your God, who brought you out of Egypt, out of the land of slavery. You shall have no other gods before me' (Ex. 20:2–3; Dt. 5:6–7).

measure, they will keep you from being ineffective and unproductive in your knowledge of our Lord Jesus Christ. ⁹But if anyone does not have them, he is short-sighted and blind, and has forgotten that he has been cleansed from his past sins.

a. Adding to our faith

If Peter was talking about 'the faith', he would be saying something very odd here. He would be teaching that we need to add new doctrines to the faith, which is the false teachers' mistake. He would also be contradicting what he has just said about already having been given 'everything we need for life and godliness' (1:3). He is, however, still talking about *faith* as he meant it in verse 1, the individual belief of the Christian.

There is beautiful balance in what Peter writes, echoed in other New Testament writers.[3] Having said that it is the faith which is God's gift that puts us right with him, now he writes that personal and private assent to Jesus' lordship, if it is authentic, must work itself out in public and practical ways. Faith is to be both foundational and functional. Peter still has the great future picture in mind too, and this is above all the *reason* for Christians to *make every effort* to live a life here and now which is consistent with what God promises.

Christians are to *add to* their *faith*, and the word translated *add to* is *epichorēgeō*. Originally, the word was a theatrical term, used for a theatrical 'angel', a *chorēgos*, who provided some of the money for staging a production. The word came to be used of any generous city benefactor, and by the time Peter was writing it simply meant an extremely generous giver. We are to cooperate with God, working with him without thinking of the price. Peter emphasizes the cooperation by making the verb an imperative here and by repeating it in verse 11, in the word translated 'you will receive' (literally, 'you will be provided with'). There, God is the benefactor, and this emphasizes the price that Jesus paid to be our Saviour. The two uses of *epichorēgeō* form a bracket around verses 5–11.[4]

b. The Christian's character

Peter gives us a list of Christian virtues in which we are to grow. Such lists were common at that time, and there are several in the New Testament.[5] Once again, Peter uses common words from the

---

[3] 2 Thes. 3:11–13; Jas. 2:5.
[4] *Cf.* 1 Pet. 4:11, 'the strength God provides', *chorēgeō*.
[5] Rom. 5:3–5; 2 Cor. 6:4–10; Gal. 5:22–23; Col. 3:12–14; 1 Tim. 4:12; 6:11; 2 Tim.

surrounding culture, but gives them a distinctively Christian twist by starting with *faith* and ending with *love*. Within that frame he presents a series of Christian character sketches that are designed to be disturbingly familiar to the minds of his readers. It is difficult to spot any particular order in the virtues he describes, and attempts to detect a logical flow are often very ingenious but not too convincing. That is not to say that his selection is random; far from it. Each virtue is chosen for its sharpness in pinpointing the errors of the new teachers whom Peter's readers were encountering. Rather than thinking of Peter moving logically from step to step in this list, it might be better to think of him drawing a rounded description of a Christian character. None of the Christian virtues is logically dependent on its place in the chain to exist, so we cannot say, 'You must not expect me to persevere, because I have not yet achieved self-control.' Instead, Peter would say that a Christian without perseverance is missing a vital ingredient.

i. Add to your faith goodness . . .
Faith is the starting-point for the Christian, who then wants to become like the master he or she believes in; and so it leads automatically to Christ-like *goodness* (verse 3). Apparently, goodness was a matter of great concern to thinking non-Christians of the time. What is it that makes a person good or excellent at being a human? Peter's answer is not a particularly philosophical one: the ideal person is Jesus Christ, and Christians will find their excellence in imitating him. Since his goodness was shown by what he did, our faith will show itself to others in our active goodness.

The false teachers do not believe this, because they have 'turned their backs on the sacred command' (2:21). Far from having fled the corruption in the world, they are 'entangled in it and overcome' (2:20). 'They talked a great deal about faith, but exhibited in their lives none of that practical goodness which is indispensable to genuine Christian discipleship.'[6] If Christians are supposed to be the kind of people non-Christians admire for their genuine goodness, it should not surprise us that the visible immorality of the new teachers will 'bring the way of truth into disrepute' (2:2). It is still a frequent obstacle for many non-Christians that publicly recognized Christian leaders advocate standards that non-Christians find unprincipled.

2:22; 3:10. For parallels in secular and Jewish writings, together with comparisons of form, content and language, see Bauckham (1983), pp. 174–176.
   [6] Green (1987), p. 77.

ii. ... knowledge ...

By *knowledge* Peter no longer means the *epignōsis*, saving knowledge, of verses 2 and 3, for he has removed the prefix *epi-*. He means information about Jesus Christ and what pleases him. It is the kind of knowledge that comes from reading, thinking and discussing as a Christian. If we want to grow in Christ-like goodness we shall have a hunger and desire to grow in our knowledge of Christ.[7] The nineteenth-century Scottish preacher John Brown, whose commentary covers only this chapter, said that this knowledge means 'making a distinction not only between what is true and what is false but also between what is right and wrong – what is becoming and unbecoming – what is advantageous and hurtful'.[8] The false teachers, of course, claimed to have a newer knowledge offering 'freedom' (2:19), but Peter says it is based on 'stories they have made up' and 'empty, boastful words' (2:3, 18). They may appear highly intelligent and intellectually respectable, for nothing here says that Christians automatically have high intelligence and that people who teach error are idiots. Peter does believe, though, that the most intellectually feeble Christians have knowledge, but that the most intellectually gifted heretics 'blaspheme in matters they do not understand' (2:12).

iii. ... self-control ...

If we know God's view of us and our world, we are able to live in accordance with that knowledge. John Brown wisely said that 'the Christian does not consider the wealth, the honours, and the privileges of the world, as things altogether destitute of value; but he sees that that value is by no means as great as the deluded worshippers of Mammon suppose it to be ... The views which, as a believer, he has obtained, lead him to look on the prosperities of life with some measure of alarm.'[9] This is the complete opposite of the lifestyle adopted and taught by the false teachers, who feel under no obligation to control themselves or to obey Jesus Christ. Instead, they are found 'denying the sovereign Lord who bought them' (2:1), and at ease in 'following their own evil desires' (3:3).

iv. ... perseverance ...

Just as self-control is moderation with regard to good things, so *perseverance* is the willingness to put up with tough times because of the promise of better times ahead. A Christian will therefore persevere, even though it may be distressing to stand out in a society opposed to God. A Christian trusts that 'the Lord knows how to rescue godly men from trials' (2:9). The reason Christians are to

---

[7] *Cf.* Eph. 5:17; Phil. 1:9; Heb. 5:14.   [8] Brown, pp. 75–76.   [9] Brown, p. 81.

persevere is that history has its goal in the return of Christ, and, 'since you are looking forward to this', you are to 'make every effort to be found spotless, blameless and at peace with him' (3:14). Perseverance means keeping going until the very end. The false teachers, who have ceased to believe in the ability of God to intervene in his world, are reduced to scoffing: 'Where is this "coming" he promised?' (3:4). It is not primarily the tough times or hardship that, Peter fears, will cause Christians to stop persevering, but the insidious enticements of those who have ceased to believe that there is any point to biblical Christian behaviour once we remove the return of Christ. They are, of course, quite right. Christianity without the return of Christ is an irrational nonsense.

v. . . . godliness . . .
Godliness has already occurred in verse 3 as a catch-all word for 'a very practical awareness of God in every aspect of life'.[10] Perhaps Peter lists it here because he has now explained what is a Christian attitude to both good times and bad. Once again, there is a sharp contrast with the false teachers, who are 'ungodly' (2:6; 3:7). Peter makes his point with a pun, because 'godliness' (*eusebeia*) is a word similar to 'ungodliness' (*asebeia*). He uses word-plays frequently in his letter, probably because it would be read publicly rather than privately, and such attention-grabbing devices would enable the audience clearly to grasp his main points at a first hearing.

vi. . . . brotherly kindness . . .
Christian faith covers our attitude not only to problems but also to people, and Peter turns first to our relationships with other Christians. Two English words, *brotherly kindness*, translate one Greek word, *philadelphia*, a common term for relationships within a family unit; the New Testament is the only place where the word has been found outside the context of a home.[11] A first-century reader would therefore come across it here with a sense of shock; Peter really does mean that Christians should have a quality of relationships which is demonstrably different and satisfying, demanding a high and new loyalty.[12] For us, the metaphor is dimmed through familiarity, but we must not lose the reality of the fact that when Peter calls the Christians 'my brothers' (1:10) he

---

[10] Green (1987), p. 79.
[11] Peter uses it strongly (1 Pet. 1:22; 3:8), but see too Rom. 12:10; 1 Thes. 4:9; Heb. 13:1.
[12] Mk. 3:31–35.

means it. By contrast, the false teachers show no love for God's family. They do not show brotherly love, but do 'harm' (2:13), and 'entice people' (2:18). In the end they destroy God's people (2:1).

vii. ... love

The final ingredient is the need to *love, agapē*. Although this word is usually explained as uniquely Christian love, this is not necessarily the case.[13] Here it seems to mean not so much the love a Christian has for a fellow Christian (which was *philadelphia*), as love for anyone, Christian or not.

Peter's list may not have a logical sequence running through it, but there is an undoubted sense of climax as he presents *agapē* as the highest Christian characteristic.[14] It is marked by its indiscriminate and deliberate habit of loving not just brothers but those outside the family circle too. Nothing could be further from the false teachers' attitude of self-centredness and exploitation (2:3).

c. Producing the results

No Christian can ever claim to have arrived as a model believer; indeed, one of the hallmarks of Christian maturity is a growing dissatisfaction with our level of godliness. That should not produce despair, but make us aim to *possess these qualities in increasing measure* and become even more self-controlled, persevering and loving. Peter insists that this growth is our own responsibility – not that we are to 'let go and let God', as some Christians say. The verb translated *possess (hyparchō)* is an estate agent's word, the related noun meaning 'property which one fully possesses and which is therefore fully at one's disposal'.[15]

Peter is convinced that true Christian *knowledge* is not irrelevant book-learning, but that it changes the Christian and then impacts the world. Once again (verses 2–3), he is talking about full, personal, conversion-knowledge (*epignōsis*), but by now he has made the point that we are not to focus on that at the expense of either human society or the church. Such an attitude would have the twin results of making us *ineffective and unproductive*, which was the disastrous effect that Peter's false teachers were having, with neither work nor fruit to show for themselves. Instead, Peter wants Christians to be the opposite, both effective and productive. As we transform ourselves and our churches into the likeness of Jesus

---

[13] See D. A. Carson, *Exegetical Fallacies* (Grand Rapids: Baker, 1984), pp. 51–54. His argument is that there is too much overlap between *agapē* and *phileō* to make a hard distinction.

[14] As at 1 Cor. 8:1; 13:13; Col. 3:14.   [15] Kelly, p. 307.

Christ, we will learn to see the world through the eyes of its Saviour and its Judge. If we believe that Jesus Christ will return as Lord and Judge, that will not only prevent us from sinking into the kind of sloth demonstrated by the false teachers as they felt free to follow 'their own evil desires' (3:3); it will spur us on to *make every effort* (1:5; 3:14), and to produce work that will stand and fruit that will last.[16]

By contrast, a Christian who does not have *these qualities in increasing measure* is spiritually sick with short-sightedness, blindness and amnesia. The first two words appear a bit of a puzzle; literally, Peter puts *blind* before *short-sighted*, and the NIV is not alone in feeling the anticlimax and reversing the order. Others translate the word for *blind* as the squint caused by looking for too long at the sun.

Perhaps the simplest solution is to take the words in their original order, with their normal meaning, and ask what it is that each disability prevents. Someone who is blind cannot see at all, someone who is short-sighted cannot see what lies ahead in the distance, and someone who has forgotten cannot remember what lies behind him. This fits the problem of the false teachers and the peril of their victims. An inability to see the present will lead to a failure to understand God's verdict on the corrupt world (1:4) and the way of salvation (1:10); an inability to see into the future will leave them morally and religiously independent of God the Saviour (3:3–4); and an inability to see the past will mean failure to perceive how they can be *cleansed from* their *past sins*.[17] In their blindness, short-sightedness and forgetfulness they no longer understand their past sins, their present rebellion or their future condemnation. Peter's fear is that the Christians will come under the influence of these blind guides; and, as Jesus himself had said to Peter, 'If a blind man leads a blind man, both will fall into a pit.'[18] A clear-sighted Christian, by contrast, will take great care to avoid the misleading directions and useless advice of someone who cannot see where he is going.

2. The eternal Christian (1:10–11)

Therefore, my brothers, be all the more eager to make your calling and election sure. For if you do these things, you will never fall, [11]and you will receive a rich welcome into the eternal king-dom of our Lord Jesus Christ.

[16] 1 Cor. 3:12–15; Jn. 15:16.
[17] It is not as clear as most commentators would wish that the word 'cleansed' means that Peter has baptism in mind.
[18] Mt. 15:14.

Peter has already written in verse 5 that we are to 'make every effort' as Christians, but since then he has listed eight areas in which growth is required. Now he reinforces his argument: *be all the more eager*. He even echoes the same Greek word (*spoudē*, the noun, in verse 5; *spoudazō*, the verb, in verse 11), but he underlines it twice by adding *therefore* and *be all the more*. His serious concern is that we take the responsibility to continue to the end of our Christian lives more deeply grounded within the same hope with which we started.

Two words describe the content of our hope: *calling* and *election*. Both come with a long biblical pedigree. Our *election* is God's sovereign choice of us in Christ from before time. Paul said that God 'chose us in [Christ] before the creation of the world,'[19] and as Peter has said in verse 3, our *calling* is anchored in Jesus' call to follow him. Peter is expressing himself with his usual care, for just as God's sovereignty once more occupies centre stage (1:3–4), so does our responsibility. We are to *be all the more eager to make* our *calling and election sure*. Without contributing anything to our salvation, the acid test of the genuineness of our faith is that either we make costly life changes on the basis of it, or we treat sin and judgment as irrelevant to a Christian. The word *make (poieisthai)* is in a form[20] which emphasizes our responsibility in this activity. It is as if Peter were saying, 'you, for your part, make sure . . .' The word *sure (bebaios)* has a legal flavour, suggesting 'ratified'. So the wonderful truth that Christians have been eternally called and chosen is not an abstract matter of irrelevant theology which requires no response apart from an intellectual assent. Rather, the evidence that we have been called and chosen will be the energy that we put in to making our calling and election sure.

If we do 'make every effort', Peter assures us of blessings that will last for eternity. First, we *will never fall*. That does not mean that we will never sin, because the Bible never promises us that kind of perfection outside heaven.[21] Nor is it a rigid guarantee of salvation that frees us from activity and responsibility. Instead, it means that we will never 'suffer a reverse',[22] because God will never change his mind about how to get people into heaven, and will never send us back because we are not good enough. Specifically, it means that a Christian who is permanently devoted to following Jesus will never fall into the kind of error the false teachers had blundered into because of their blindness and short-sightedness. They had failed to take seriously their responsibility to live Christianly. The attitude that takes hold of Christ by faith and then lives a life of obedience to

[19] Eph. 1:4. The words for 'election' and 'chose' are from the same Greek root.
[20] The middle voice.   [21] Jas. 3:2.   [22] *TDNT* 6, p. 884.

him is the one that proves that our salvation will last.

The second blessing that will last for an eternity is that Christians *will receive a rich welcome into the eternal kingdom of our Lord and Saviour Jesus Christ*. *You will receive* is the passive form of the verb *epichorēgeō*, 'provide', translated 'add to' in verse 5. Here it means 'you will be provided with', and it is Jesus Christ who takes the responsibility for paying the price. Michael Green paints a picture of a victorious marathon runner being welcomed to the finishing-tape by a delighted home crowd.[23] The *welcome* will be *rich*, not because God is repaying a price to the Christian, but because he is lavishly meeting our needs for an eternity of serving him as our King. Throughout the gospels, the idea of Christ's *kingdom* has both a present and a future aspect, where what is true and available today is put alongside what is true and available only to those who believe the promise. When Christ returns as *Lord and Saviour*, though, it will all be present. As Lord he will rule his kingdom, visibly and eternally, and as Saviour he will be able both to condemn sin and to save sinners.

[23] Green (1987), p. 84.

2 Peter 1:12–15
4. Remember, remember

Amnesia is distressing. Sufferers forget what they have done, what they were doing before being interrupted, and what they were about to do. Everyone has mild memory lapses, but clinically severe lapses cause crises of identity. Patients can even cease to know who, what and where they are. In his letter, Peter challenges his readers with having appallingly bad memories. They are forgetting what they have been told about the past and the future, and that is attacking the very root of their identity as Christians in the present. Before they can hear this message, he has to convince them that their memory, or rather their lack of memory, is a problem.

So I will always remind you of these things, even though you know them and are firmly established in the truth you now have. ¹³*I think it is right to refresh your memory as long as I live in the tent of this body,* ¹⁴*because I know that I will soon put it aside, as our Lord Jesus Christ has made clear to me. And I will make every effort to see that after my departure you will always be able to remember these things.*

Peter's main point in this section can be inferred from the frequency with which he underlines his responsibility in making sure that Christians do not forget their basic message. The NIV happily translates their three tasks with words that begin with the same letter: *remind* (verse 12), *refresh your memory* (verse 13) and *remember* (verse 15). This theme is set in a particular sequence of circumstances: first, Peter's life (*as long as I live,* verse 13); then his death (*I will soon put [my body] aside,* verse 14); and thirdly what happens to the Christians alive *after my departure* (verse 15). They must not forget when Peter has gone from them.

1. Reminding (1:12)

Peter announces the major theme of his letter as he explains why he is writing this letter as a matter of great urgency. He is worried in case the Christians forget *these things*, the doctrines he has been explaining so far. He uses the same Greek word term in verses 8, 9 and 10.[1] The future tense of *will always remind you* causes considerable difficulties to the scholars, because technically Peter should have used the present tense if he was referring to what he was actually writing, and the future tense would normally imply that he intended to send another letter.[2] But the word *always* modifies that sense, and Peter is almost certainly referring to this letter. He wants to make sure it will have an effect 'up to and after the apostle's death'.[3]

To understand Peter properly, we have to appreciate that the corporate memory within Israel plays an important teaching role. The weekly sabbath was given them by God so that they would 'remember that you were slaves in Egypt and that the LORD your God brought you out of there with a mighty hand and an outstretched arm. Therefore the LORD your God has commanded you to observe the Sabbath day.'[4] There was no danger of the story being lost for ever, of course, but it was a weekly duty to bring it to mind so that they would always think about what it meant to be saved. The same was true for the passover meal: the Israelites were to celebrate it annually 'so that all the days of your life you may remember the time of your departure from Egypt'.[5] It was important to go back and teach one another the basic truths of their deliverance.

Paul also says that his apostolic ministry is 'to remind you of the gospel I preached to you, which you received and on which you have taken your stand'.[6] The answer to the Corinthian heresy was not new teaching but a correct understanding of the old teaching. Similarly, Timothy's ministry, when he is faced with error, is first to 'remember Jesus Christ, raised from the dead', and then to 'keep reminding them of these things'.[7]

Peter tells his readers he is going to *remind* them now, and to 'make every effort to see that after my departure' they 'will always be able to remember these things'. Later on, he says that he has written two letters 'as reminders,' and that he wants us 'to recall'

---

[1] But *cf.* verse 15, where the topic changes. See p. 71 below.
[2] In fact it is even more complex, and Kistemaker rightly refers to 'a double future' (p. 260). The commentaries give more information, but see below on 1:15.
[3] Bauckham (1983), p. 196. Bauckham, with many others, takes this section, 12–15, as the clear demonstration to first-century readers that the letter was *not* by Peter himself but fell into the category of a testament. See Appendix, below.
[4] Dt. 5:15.   [5] Dt. 16:3.   [6] 1 Cor. 15:1.   [7] 2 Tim. 2:8, 14.

(3:1–2) the message that has come through the apostles and prophets. In addressing his readers in this way, he is laying out his continuing ministry to all Christians through his letter. This is the safeguard, ensuring that they will not be 'carried away by the error of lawless men' (3:17). We should always be wary, then, of people who arrive with a new or different Christian message, and look out for the danger sign that Peter's basic lesson is being sidetracked in favour of a more attractive or 'relevant' message. Those who teach the Bible have a great responsibility here, because there will always be a temptation to hold people's attention with something new. We have to be humble enough to recognize that we are not creators of the Christian message. The task – the vital task – is to keep reminding people of it.

This is the message that Peter calls *the truth*. Ever since the publication of an influential essay by Ernst Käsemann,[8] it has frequently been said that this dogmatism is a sign of 'early Catholicism'. That is, this letter betrays a hardening of Christianity away from its charismatic first leaders, their spoken messages and simple gospel, to a second-century, written, codified doctrine – in Jude's phrase, taken to be late, 'the faith'.[9] But references to a body of teaching are not limited to these two letters. Paul wrote about 'the word of truth, the gospel', Peter of 'the truth', and Luke of 'the apostles' teaching'; and John's gospel records Jesus' promise that we shall 'know the truth, and the truth will set [us] free'.[10] Unless we take a position of extreme scepticism and consign all such strands, and the traditions behind them, to a very late date, we have to say that it is not necessarily a sign of a declension into second-generation Christianity when Peter talks of *the truth*.[11] It is instead a sign of great certainty on Peter's part. His fear is not that the second generation will codify and fossilize the truth, but rather that they will become so careless about it that they will forget it altogether.

That *truth* is a teaching that they *now have*. An unlikely, though attractive, option is that Peter means his first letter,[12] but it is much more likely that he means the gospel that Paul had preached to these Gentile readers.[13] Whether they had heard from Paul or read from

---

[8] Käsemann, pp. 169–195.   [9] Jude 3.
[10] Col. 1:5; 1 Pet. 1:22; Acts 2:42; Jn. 8:32.
[11] We must disagree with R. P. Martin's extraordinary comment that '2 Peter represents a Christianity that is on the road to becoming tradition-bound, authoritarian and inward-looking. The next steps will be along the road to fossilization and fixation, with no room to change or receive new light' (Martin, p. 163). The false teachers would have presented themselves as the proponents of new light and change, and doubtless called Peter an authoritarian old fossil!
[12] *Pace* Plumptre, p. 169.   [13] Gal. 2:7.

Peter, though, they had adequate teaching to 'make' their 'calling and election sure' (1:10).

Peter identifies three phases in these Christians' growth. First, they came to *know*, then they came to be *firmly established*, and now Peter has to *remind* them. Are they especially flawed as Christians to have come so far only to need to be reminded? Not at all! Returning continually to the core truths of Christianity is part of a growing Christian self-understanding. This is poignantly underlined in Peter's own growth as a disciple. He promised faithfully that he would follow Jesus to prison and to death. But Jesus knew him better, and said that even he would find it impossible to stay loyal when the Roman troops came. Jesus said that he had prayed for Peter, however, and promised that when the nightmare was over Peter was to 'strengthen' the other disciples.[14] The word translated 'strengthen' in the gospel is the word translated *firmly established* here (*stērizō*). So, as Peter wrote, he was fulfilling the command Jesus had given him many years before. To show that he had not forgotten that his stability had lain in Jesus' praying for him, there is the reassurance in his first letter that 'the God of all grace, who called you to his eternal glory in Christ, after you have suffered a little while, will himself restore you and make you strong (*stērizō*), firm and steadfast'.[15]

The lesson Peter is applying from his own experience is this: no matter how close to the Lord we have been as Christians, or how long-standing our Christian commitment, or how central our position in the fellowship, that danger of wobbling still remains, and we should check ourselves constantly for the tell-tale signs. The only way to be sure of not wobbling is to remember. There is possibly one of Peter's subtle puns here; whereas the Christians are *firmly established* (*estērigmenous*), the false teachers 'seduce the unstable' (*astēriktous*) (2:14). Such 'unstable people distort' (3:16) the Bible itself. So perhaps the Christians here are less stable than they think, which means that we too are probably less stable than we think.

2. Refreshing (1:13–14)

Peter knew his death was imminent. The description of it which Jesus had given him ensured that he would recognize the times, for 'when you are old you will stretch out your hands, and someone else will dress you and lead you where you do not want to go'.[16] The mixture of timing ('when you are old') and compulsion ('where you do not want to go') now fitted the horrific circumstances in

---

[14] Lk. 22:32.   [15] 1 Pet. 5:10.   [16] Jn. 21:18.

Rome when Nero used the Christians as scapegoats. Peter has a definite moment of revelation in mind here, as the aorist tense of *has made clear to me* bears witness, and the passage at the end of John fits neatly. Jesus had told him how he would die, but not when, and Peter could now see both coming. The word for *soon*, *tachinos*, might be better translated *swiftly* (*cf.* 2:1), because what alerted Peter was the way the violence of the times matched the description Jesus gave.

Clement, the first bishop of Rome and a colleague of both Peter and Paul,[17] wrote a letter towards the end of the first century from the church in Rome to the church in Corinth. He mentions the vicious persecution under Nero: 'Peter, through unrighteous envy, endured not one or two, but numerous labours; and when he had at length suffered martyrdom, departed to the place of glory due to him.'[18] We can be no more specific than that: Peter died at the hand of Nero, and thus before 9 June of the year AD 68, when Nero took his own life. All the earliest records say that Peter was crucified, and Origen says he was crucified upside down.[19] He received a simple and secret burial on the Vatican Hill in Rome.[20]

Given the grisly nature of what he was about to endure, his attitude to his approaching death is remarkable. Like Paul,[21] he saw his body as a *tent* which he must soon *put . . . aside*. It is a mixed metaphor which speaks powerfully about the way these men, who knew they faced painful and humiliating deaths, saw themselves as striking camp and moving on, or taking off a set of clothes. 'How calmly does he speak of putting off his tabernacle . . . The old, worn-out apostle is one of the happiest men out of heaven.'[22]

Knowing that his death was imminent, Peter wanted to make the best use of the time left to him. Strikingly, he has no new teaching to impart to the Christians. Instead, he simply has to *refresh* their *memory*. He had told them certain things in a previous letter[23] which he wishes to ensure they do not forget. His teaching in this letter will be preventative, to stop the new teaching from so flooding their minds with novelties and wonders that they lose their critical faculties and become victims of a brainwash.

---

[17] Possibly the Clement of Phil. 4:3.   [18] *1 Clement* 5 (*ANF* 1, p. 6).
[19] See Thiede, p. 190, for references.
[20] The consistent witness to knowing the position of Peter's tomb is impressive – see Thiede, pp. 192–193 – although the claims of some archaeologists to have found his bones are still treated with scepticism by most.
[21] 2 Cor. 5:1.   [22] Brown, p. 170.
[23] 2 Pet. 3:1. This might be 1 Peter, but the content of the two is not so similar that 2 Peter could justifiably be called a reminder of it.

3. Remembering (1:15)

While he was still with them, of course, he could continue that work in person and by letters. With his death looming, however, Peter must provide for what will happen *after my departure* so that they will still *remember these things*.

He gives 'a solemn pledge'[24] that he will *make every effort* in this provision. It is a word-group he has already used to spur the Christians on to 'make every effort' and to 'be all the more eager' (1:5, 10). So what is the result of the effort?

There are several options. Blum thinks that Peter is referring to the continuing effects of his ministry, and that 'no specific writings are in view',[25] but this seems unlikely in that Peter is writing expressly to areas where he has not ministered in person ('your apostles', 3:2). If Peter is referring to a written record, it is just possible that the documents were either lost or never written; but that again is unlikely, given the value that Peter places on them here. He is clear about his intention to write instructions, and about the care with which the readers are to take note of them when they arrive. Some commentators point out that the later apocryphal letters and *Acts of Peter* might have been written to fill the perceived gap.

There are two frequently offered and more plausible explanations, neither of which is easy. One is that Peter is referring to this letter itself. The other centres on the tradition that Peter's memories of Jesus were written down in the gospel of Mark. Most modern commentators prefer the first of these options, even though the verb's future tense is 'difficult'.[26] Most recently, Bauckham makes this an important stage in his argument that 2 Peter fits into the literary genre of 'testament', a work written after the death of an important figure, and in his name.[27]

Some modern writers (such as Green, Hillyer and Thiede), along with most older writers, take the second option and assume that this word points outside the letter to another document which actually was written. 'Certainly no document would redeem the apostle's promise so well as a gospel, and if a gospel is meant, the reference can hardly be to any other than that of St Mark.'[28] The links between Peter and Mark's gospel have always been impressive, and now there is some fascinating, if ambiguous, archaeological

---

[24] Kistemaker, p. 262. The word is *spoudazō*.   [25] Blum, p. 273.
[26] Kelly, p. 315. There is another future verb in verse 12, but contextually that seems to refer to the letter much more easily than this future tense, which seems to refer beyond the letter.
[27] See Appendix.   [28] Bigg, p. 265.

evidence[29] that might back up the connection. But even its most enthusiastic supporters admit that it is a tentative suggestion.

Neither of these solutions is without its problems, but if we take our eyes off the scholars we can see that it actually makes very little difference to the danger Peter saw invading the churches. Whatever he wrote, and whether or not he actually wrote what he intended, his acute analysis of the problem is still accurate. He is worried that after the first generation of Christians dies, the second generation will fail to carry the torch of *these things*. Now Peter's focus begins to change. In addition to the general Christian truths he has been teaching (the 'these qualities', 'them' and 'these things' of verses 8, 9, 10 and 12; in the Greek the word is the same in each case), he has some quite specific points to bring to their attention.[30]

4. The danger of spiritual absent-mindedness

Peter is far from being a bitter old man who resents the abilities and energies of the next generation of Christian leaders and does everything in his power to thwart them. His plan is for the Christians to 'grow in the grace and knowledge of our Lord and Saviour Jesus Christ' (3:18), and his fear is that their growth will be stunted. The relevance of his fear becomes clearer as we look at the grand sweep of church history as well as the history of individual churches. The temptation is for each generation to model itself on the previous one, reacting to the mistakes they can see and compounding the errors they cannot. That is the inevitable way to guarantee a wobbling church leadership, always controlled by the weakness of its parents. Peter calls us to go back to the original model, time and again. Although two thousand years of church history have elapsed, there is a sense in which every generation of Christians is only the second generation. We do not have the direct knowledge and experiences of the first generation (which is why Peter takes such care to pass his experiences on to us), but neither are we at such a distance from the apostles that we need other teachers and interpreters. Martyn Lloyd-Jones said that 'the business of the church and of preaching is not to present us with new and interesting ideas, it is rather to go on reminding us of certain fundamental and eternal truths.'[31] Peter's fear for his readers is precisely his fear for us. We too live without the living presence of

---

[29] See Green (1987), pp. 89–91.

[30] 'The "these things" of 1:15, with the explanatory clause of the following verse, is a verbal combination that points forward rather than backward. Naturally, this does not exclude the earlier exhortations, but it seems to emphasise the contents from 16–21.' Clark, p. 21.

[31] Lloyd-Jones, p. 56.

the apostles; we too have only their written teaching to rely on. Will we act to make sure we remember what they said, or will we listen to some other voice?

1:16–21
5. The witnesses

One of these days, perhaps, the cold bright light of science and reason will shine through the cathedral windows and we shall go out into the fields to seek God for ourselves. The great laws of nature will be understood – our destiny and our past will be clear. We shall then be able to dispense with the religious toys that have agreeably fostered the development of mankind. Until then, anyone who deprives us of our illusions – our pleasant, hopeful illusions – is a wicked man and should (I quote my Plato) 'be refused a chorus'.[1]

So wrote the young Winston Churchill, and many others would echo his sentiment. Christianity, they say, is a pleasant but illusory tool for social control. Churchill seemed willing to wait for Christianity to die when it was no longer needed; but others were, and are, keener to kill the illusion before it does greater damage.

It is no new ambition. The false teachers whom Peter opposes claim that his message is a restrictive and demeaning lie. Instead, they offer 'pleasure' and 'freedom' (2:13, 19) without the bother of his narrow doctrine (2:3). Peter has to defend the authenticity of what he says against an undeniably attractive opposition, and to do that he needs two sets of witnesses in the dock. He calls the New Testament apostles (verses 16–18) and the Old Testament prophets (verses 19–21), and requires them to give first-hand evidence about what they saw and heard.

1. The apostles' evidence (1:16–18)

We did not follow cleverly invented stories when we told you about the power and coming of our Lord Jesus Christ, but we

---

[1] Quoted in Martin Gilbert, *Churchill: A Life* (London: Heinemann; New York: Henry Holt and Co., 1991), p. 68.

were eye-witnesses of his majesty. [17]For he received honour and glory from God the Father when the voice came to him from the Majestic Glory, saying, 'This is my Son, whom I love; with him I am well pleased.' [18]We ourselves heard this voice that came from heaven when we were with him on the sacred mountain.

Peter and his fellow apostles are being accused of serving up *cleverly invented stories.*[2] The emphasis in the Greek is on the common human tendency to manufacture and embroider helpful religious myths.[3] Such 'slyly invented'[4] nonsense, the false teachers say, is not credible to modern men and women, and must be demythologized and replaced. In particular, they accuse Peter of fabricating the doctrine of the second coming of Christ. *The power and coming of our Lord Jesus Christ*[5] were teachings that Peter concocted when he *told*[6] them the gospel.

Although Peter defends his position from within his memories of the earthly life of Jesus, these people were not attacking the idea that Jesus had existed. The problem lay deeper, in their understanding of *why* he had existed.

The Old Testament looked forward to the day of the 'coming' of God, when he would reveal himself in all his glory, judge the wicked and redeem his people.[7] There was also a strand of messianic promises, referring to someone who 'comes in the name of the LORD'.[8] Jesus was so close to what was promised that John the Baptist's disciples asked him, 'Are you the one who was to come, or should we expect someone else?'[9] Their dilemma was caused by Jesus' manifest willingness to say that he was God's agent in the world, alongside his refusal to fulfil the Old Testament promises about judging people. He put such duties firmly in the future, with himself at the centre. Geerhardus Vos has written that 'perhaps no more sweeping and, in its effects, more momentous transfer of an Old Testament concept and its reincarnation, as it were, in the New Testament frame of thought can be imagined'.[10] The Christians learned to look forward to a second coming of Christ, as glorious

---

[2] *Cf.* the reaction to Ezekiel, Ezk. 20:49.
[3] Hillyer, p. 177, says that 'cleverly invented' 'was a term applied to the claims of quack doctors'.
[4] Reicke, p. 156.
[5] Another hendiadys – 'the powerful coming'. *Cf.* GNB. Bigg (p. 266) was probably the first to suggest that Jesus' power is the theme of chapter 2 and his coming the theme of chapter 3.
[6] *Gnōrizō* is 'almost technical in the NT for imparting a divine mystery' (*e.g.* Lk. 2:15; Jn. 15:15; 17:26; Rom. 16:26; Eph. 6:19; Col. 1:27). Kelly, pp. 316–317.
[7] Pss. 50:3; 58; 59; Zc. 14:5; Mal. 3:1; 4:6.   [8] Ps. 118:26.   [9] Lk. 7:19.
[10] G. Vos, *The Pauline Eschatology* (repr. Phillipsburg: Presbyterian and Reformed, 1991, p. 73).

Lord who saves and judges. This second coming was often called the *parousia*, a Greek word for the splendid arrival of a dignitary or king. It came to acquire a technical status for Christians.[11] The false teachers are therefore being quite blatant when they mock this teaching by asking, 'Where is this "coming" he promised?' (3:4). 'Peter and the other apostles have deluded you', they seem to say, 'by encouraging you to believe this silly nonsense. Instead of looking to a fairy-tale future, look to the present and enjoy the freedom of being a Christian.' Rather like the men Paul encountered, 'they say that the resurrection has already taken place',[12] or as much of it as was going to happen, and that there was no future element to the gospel. Paul called their teaching gangrenous; Peter calls it destructive (2:1).

He attacks the error by retelling the story of Jesus' transfiguration. No doubt part of Peter's reason in choosing this event was that it was the most supernatural event in the life of Jesus, and so would offend the anti-supernatural bias of the false teachers. But there were other issues, closer to Peter's line of thinking, which made him choose it. It was something of which he and others were *eyewitnesses*,[13] which pointed forward to the future *coming of our Lord Jesus Christ*, and to which God the Father gave his verbal approval and explanation. This moves into the centre Peter's major concern, which is that these men dare to question the very Word of God, denying and distorting it (3:4, 16).

a. What the apostles saw: Jesus' majesty (1:16)

Three gospels recount the events on the mountain when Peter, James and John saw Jesus in his true glory.[14] Even though the story is not in John's gospel, the experience is clearly there, for John wrote that 'we have seen his glory, the glory of the One and Only, who came from the Father, full of grace and truth'.[15] Peter's account here differs from the three accounts in subtle ways. He is closest to Matthew's version, but his major change is to omit the phrase, 'Listen to him.'[16] Peter wants to focus on what God said at that

[11] *E.g.* Mt. 24:3, 27, 37, 39; Mk. 13:26; 1 Cor. 15:23; 1 Thes. 3:13; 4:15; Jas. 5:7–8; 1 Jn. 2:28. 1 Peter uses the term *apokalypsis* (1:7, 13). That does not prove different authorship, for both terms are used by Paul. The earliest consistent use of *parousia* referring to Christ's first coming seems to be by the second-century writer Justin Martyr, *First Apology* 48 (*ANF* 1, p. 179).
[12] 2 Tim. 2:18.
[13] *Cf.* 1 Pet. 2:12; 3:2 – the only two other NT occurrences of a word with an (over-stressed) background in pagan religious initiation – and 1 Pet. 5:1.
[14] Mt. 17:1–8; Mk. 9:2–8; Lk. 9:28–36.
[15] Jn. 1:14; *cf.* 2:11; 17:24. John uses this as evidence, 1 Jn. 1:1–3.
[16] Mt. 17:5; Mk. 9:7; Lk. 9:35.

precise moment, rather than on the subsequent teaching ministry of Jesus.

What they saw was a breathtaking display of Jesus' *majesty* (*megaleiotētos*). That is a remarkable word of very high honour, speaking of divine rather than human majesty.[17] Luke uses the word in the story that immediately follows the transfiguration. While Jesus was on the mountain with his three closest disciples, the other nine were unable to cast a demon out of a boy. Jesus was able to heal the lad, and Luke records that 'they were all amazed at the greatness (*megaleiotētos*) of God'.[18] All the disciples saw the results of Jesus' 'majesty', but they still misunderstood him. Luke records that when Jesus immediately explained that it was his destiny and desire to die in Jerusalem, 'they did not grasp it'.[19] Even though Peter and the others were *eye-witnesses of his majesty*, they still did not understand the meaning of what they had seen. What they lacked was the explanation to go with the event. They needed to be ear-witnesses (if there is such a word!) as well as eye-witnesses. They needed God to speak.

b. What the apostles heard: God's voice (1:17–18)

God did indeed speak. He spoke from the *Majestic Glory*, which is Peter's phrase for the 'cloud' that Matthew reports,[20] the awesome sign of the presence of God from the Old Testament.[21] This is the glory that Jesus shares with his Father. Jesus received this *when the voice came to him*, so what Peter and the others heard when the voice spoke is just as important as what they saw. God said, *This is my Son, whom I love; with him I am well pleased.* Jesus publicly received God's own commissioning *honour and glory*[22] for the work which lay ahead of him. Unlike the gospel accounts, Peter uses the word *my* twice, to stress this: literally, God says, 'This is my Son, my beloved.' To question Peter's explanation of Jesus'

---

[17] Dt. 33:26; Pss. 21:5; 145:5. All three verses use this word in LXX. It is the word the Ephesian silversmiths used of the Greek goddess Diana, speaking of her 'divine majesty' (Acts 19:27).
[18] Lk. 9:43.　　[19] Lk. 9:45.　　[20] Mt. 17:5.
[21] Grammatically, the sentence from now on should be in parentheses, lacking a main verb; but Peter does not close the bracket and verse 19 carries on with the thought.
[22] The OT background seems to be Ps. 8:5 and Dn. 7:14. When God says, 'You are my son,' we must take care to understand him. 'Son of God' was a title to be given to Messiah, with overtones of royalty. Thus Jesus is appointed 'Son of God' (*cf.* Rom. 1:4). However, that is not describing what the Trinity is like. 'God the Son' describes what Jesus always has been and always will be. In that way we could say that Jesus' baptism was the moment when God the Son took on the messianic title of 'Son of God'. Heb. 1 reflects both titles.

life-work is to question God's explanation of Jesus' life-work.

In all the transfiguration accounts there are explicit echoes of Psalm 2:

> Why do the nations conspire
>   and the peoples plot in vain?
> The kings of the earth take their stand
>   and the rulers gather together against the LORD
>   and against his Anointed One.
> 'Let us break their chains,' they say,
>   'and throw off their fetters.'
>
> The One enthroned in heaven laughs;
>   the Lord scoffs at them.
> Then he rebukes them in his anger
>   and terrifies them in his wrath, saying,
> 'I have installed my King
>   on Zion, my holy hill.'
>
> I will proclaim the decree of the LORD:
>
> He said to me, 'You are my Son;
>   today I have become your Father.
> Ask of me,
>   and I will make the nations your inheritance,
>   the ends of the earth your possession.
> You will rule them with an iron sceptre;
>   you will dash them to pieces like pottery.'
>
> Therefore, you kings, be wise;
>   be warned, you rulers of the earth.
> Serve the LORD with fear
>   and rejoice with trembling.
> Kiss the Son, lest he be angry
>   and you be destroyed in your way,
> for his wrath can flare up in a moment.
>   Blessed are all who take refuge in him.

This psalm may have been written for a coronation in Jerusalem, but its claims are so extravagant that the discrepancy between what it promised and the reality of the kings of Israel and Judah would have been embarrassing. Even Solomon did not rule over such a kingdom, and later kings ruled over little more than a divided and occupied state. Like all such Old Testament promises, this psalm was written to make its readers hungry for the way God intended to fulfil his word through Jesus.

We may note, first, that this psalm presents a *family scene* between the 'Father' and the 'Son', in which the 'Son' is promised his 'inheritance'. It will be global, encompassing all 'nations' and their lands to 'the ends of the earth'. No king of Israel or Judah had such subjects or lands, but Peter was given a glimpse of the universal responsibility of Jesus.

Secondly, this is a *royal scene* between 'the One enthroned in heaven' and one on earth whom he calls 'my King', presumably because he rules in God's place on earth. His authority is awesome, for he 'will rule them with an iron sceptre', and 'will dash them to pieces like pottery'. People of Jesus' day saw him as a carpenter and preacher, but Peter now knows who it is who walked willingly to that cross, because Peter saw Jesus' majesty.

Thirdly, this is a *conflict scene* with 'the nations', 'peoples', 'kings of the earth' and 'rulers' opposing 'the LORD' and 'his Anointed One' (literally, 'his Messiah'). Jesus' universal right to rule will not be universally accepted, and there is a desire to escape his jurisdiction in the shout, 'Let us break their chains . . . and throw off their fetters.' Jesus was rejected throughout his three-year ministry, and Peter saw it happening again in the church, with people 'denying the sovereign Lord who bought them' (2:1). Just as in the psalm, Peter warns such people to make peace with the Son before he comes as Judge.

In verse 18 Peter explains that this psalm was written about what he and the disciples had seen when *we ourselves . . . were with him*. The word *we* is emphatic, because he personally can vouch that they heard a voice that came from heaven, and that it was God who had spoken to them *on the sacred* (or holy) *mountain*. When God had given the law at Sinai, Moses had called the place 'holy';[23] in the psalm, God spoke again on a mountain, this time on the 'holy hill' called Zion, the foundation rock for Jerusalem.[24] Here, Peter elevates to the same high level the place where he stood with his friends and saw this amazing scene, calling it *the sacred mountain*. It would not have been that impressive or holy to anyone else, but to that group it was the place where God had spoken, and therefore it stood in that holy line.

One other Old Testament scene lies behind this one. On another hill, another father had stood with his son, but it was not a royal coronation. It was a sacrifice, and Abraham was about to kill Isaac in response to God's command: 'Take your son, your only son, Isaac, whom you love, and go to the region of Moriah. Sacrifice him there as a burnt offering on one of the mountains I will tell you about.'[25] It was a supreme moment of testing for Abraham, for God had told him that his line of descendants was going to come through Isaac. Abraham believed that God could raise Isaac from the dead if

---

[23] Ex. 19:23.   [24] See Pss. 43:3; 48:1; 87:1; 99:9.   [25] Gn. 22:2.

necessary,[26] but in the end God provided a substitute sacrifice for Abraham's beloved son. Those words are echoed here in God's words to Jesus, *This is my Son, whom I love*, but this time there was to be no substitute. This Son would die as a substitute for others, believing that God would raise the dead.

Both Psalm 2 and Abraham's obedience thus point to 'the power and coming of our Lord Jesus Christ' (verse 16). It is as though that moment on a hilltop had burned into Peter's mind such an indelible image of Jesus Christ in his true glory that it had left him hungering for more. Not even his personal, face-to-face encounters with the risen Jesus had sated that hunger, and decades later he still looked forward to the day 'when his glory is revealed'.[27] The resurrection was a second partial glimpse of glory,[28] but there still remains more, much more, to come. That is true of each of the gospel accounts of the transfiguration; the setting in all three is a discussion about what will happen when 'the Son of Man ... comes in his glory and in the glory of the Father and of the holy angels'.[29]

The authority of the apostles is being defended[30] precisely on the issue of whether they spoke about God accurately and authoritatively; hence Peter's emphasis that they both saw and heard. He said the same to the Jewish council; the apostles 'cannot help speaking about what we have seen and heard'.[31] Today we have to accept that same double authority. It is not simply their testimony to a series of encounters with Jesus that is important and decisive. They claim to have the right to give the only true interpretation, the unique meaning, of those events, because they heard that interpretation from the mouth of God himself. The Bible is not the subjective record of a religious quest that we can supplement or challenge with our own experiences. God has spoken.

2. The prophets' evidence (1:19–21)

And we have the word of the prophets made more certain, and you will do well to pay attention to it, as to a light shining in a dark place, until the day dawns and the morning star rises in your hearts. [20]Above all, you must understand that no prophecy of Scripture ever came about by the prophet's own interpretation.

---

[26] Gn. 22:5 (note '*we* will come back'); Heb. 11:17–19.   [27] 1 Pet. 4:13.
[28] Mt. 17:9; Mk. 9:9; Lk. 9:31 (the word 'departure' is *exodos*, Peter's word for his own death in 2 Pet. 1:15).
[29] Lk. 9:26, *cf.* 23–27; Mt. 16:24–28; Mk. 8:34 – 9:1.   [30] *Pace* Bauckham.
[31] Acts 4:20; *cf.* 1 Jn. 1:1–3.

²¹*For prophecy never had its origin in the will of man, but men spoke from God as they were carried along by the Holy Spirit.*

Peter's second witnesses are the *prophets*, or specifically *the word of the prophets*, which was a standard way of referring to the Old Testament.³²

This section is surrounded by exegetical difficulties, and even comparing Bible translations will reveal the two greatest problems.³³ Readers who want to concentrate on the flow of Peter's thought can skip the following explanatory notes and pass on to the section headed 'What the prophets saw: the light in the darkness'.

Explanatory note 1: 'more certain'
The word translated *made* in verse 19 is not present in the Greek, which reads literally, 'and we have more certain the prophetic word'. What has to be decided is whether the *word of the prophets* has been *made* more certain by the transfiguration in verses 16–18, which is the NIV's understanding,³⁴ or whether the Old Testament is more certain than the transfiguration. The NEB, for example, says, 'All this only confirms to us the message of the prophets.'³⁵

The difference is important: Peter is saying either that the New Testament message needs the stronger support which the Old Testament provides, or that the Old Testament points to Christ's second coming but that the promise has been underlined by the transfiguration. On the whole, despite the weight of tradition, the latter seems stronger in its context (see below), and most modern scholars³⁶ support the NIV's interpretation. Calvin's balanced comment is wise: 'The authority of the Word of God is the same as it was in the beginning, and then it was given further confirmation than before by the advent of Christ.'³⁷

Explanatory note 2: 'the prophet's own interpretation'
The NIV's words *the prophet's* in verse 20 are not present in the

³² Literally, 'the prophetic word'. 'The term is virtually synonymous with "Scripture" . . . In the current Jewish understanding all inspired Scripture was prophecy.' Bauckham (1983), p. 224.
³³ See Green (1987) and Bauckham (1983) for the range of problems and their different solutions.
³⁴ See also RSV, NRSV, GNB.
³⁵ See also AV, NKJV, REB, JB. The NASB makes the ambiguity clear and leaves the reader to decide.
³⁶ Green (1987), p. 97, goes for the former and Bauckham (1983), p. 223, the latter, but he reduces the sense of comparison between OT and NT. Hillyer, p. 179, says that no comparison is intended, but that Peter 'is expressing complete confidence'. The word could mean that, but the comparative meaning is still the normal one.
³⁷ Calvin (*Peter*), p. 340.

Greek, and the nuance of the word *idios* is 'one's own'. So the question here is: is Peter assuring us of the Holy Spirit's guidance of the original prophet's interpretation, or of the contemporary reader's interpretation?

In support of the latter are the facts that the word 'prophet' (strictly, 'prophetic') has not appeared since the beginning of verse 19, which is a long was to carry a meaning; that the word translated *interpretation* can be used of an exposition of the Old Testament;[38] and that the criticism would fit the false teachers, who do exercise their own interpretation of Scripture in that they 'deliberately forget' it and 'distort' it (3:5, 16). Most contemporary scholars find these arguments, and particularly the third one, so convincing that they translate the verse with William Barclay, 'no prophecy in Scripture permits of private judgment'.[39] On this interpretation, men and women were deviating from the official church's line and had to be told to teach only what the church believed. Clearly, this would fit with a late, even second-century, setting for the letter.

Bauckham and Green reject this position with an impressive battery of arguments. *Idios* was a standard way of referring to the author's intentions and not the reader's; verse 21 builds on verse 20; and contextually it makes more sense if Peter is defending the origin and not the explanation of prophecy. The word *interpretation* does not need to be translated in any other way, though, because 'the Holy Spirit of God inspired not only the prophets' dreams and visions, but also their interpretations of them, so that when they spoke the prophecies recorded in Scripture they were spokesmen for God himself'.[40]

The arguments are finely balanced. Although the majority of past scholarship would disagree, it would seem that Green's and Bauckham's most recent and thorough scholarship is right, and the NIV's explanation again makes most sense.

a. What the prophets saw: the light in the darkness (1:19)

Peter's experience on the hilltop confirmed all the Old Testament prophecies about Jesus Christ and made Peter look forward to Christ's return. He is now convinced that *we* apostles *have the word of the prophets made more certain.* That had been his testimony on the day of Pentecost, in his subsequent teaching and in his first letter.[41] He is not replacing the Old Testament with his experience, for chapter 2 depends on the Old Testament; but

---

[38] In the verb form, Mk. 4:34; Acts 18:19.   [39] Barclay (*Peter*), p. 367.
[40] Bauckham (1983), p. 235; *cf.* Green (1987), p. 101.
[41] Acts 2:16–21; 3:16–21; 1 Pet. 1:10–12.

neither is he putting the Old Testament in a different league from his experience, which would undermine his whole case that it was God who spoke on the hilltop. Rather, he is saying that God has spoken again, confirming what he said before and giving a partial fulfilment of it, increasing Peter's expectation of the next stage in God's plan. He had seen how the prophets had spoken not just about a glorious king, but about a suffering king; and, as a witness to the suffering, he had become even more certain about the glory.[42]

The right reaction, then, is to go back to the Old Testament as a matter of priority and to *pay attention to it*. Peter gives us two reasons for reading the Old Testament.

First, it is *a light shining in a dark place*. The idea of the Bible as a light is a common one,[43] as is the darkness of the world.[44] But Peter has used a particularly unusual and strong word (*auchmēros*), meaning 'thirsty, sunburnt and so squalid', or even 'the squalor and gloom of a dungeon'.[45] Into this 'murky' (NEB) world comes a *light shining*.[46] If we are not to lose our way, the word of the prophets is our only sure guide in the world.

Secondly, the Old Testament is our only guide out of the world, *until the day dawns and the morning star rises in* our *hearts*. The *day* refers to the great Old Testament expectation of judgment, the 'great and dreadful day of the Lord',[47] which the Christians learned to look forward to as a day of salvation as well as judgment.[48] The *morning star* (*phōsphoros*) is Venus, which catches the sun's rays just before dawn and is a promise of daytime. It reflects yet another Old Testament picture: 'A star will come out of Jacob; a sceptre will rise out of Israel.'[49] That was regarded by Jewish teachers of Peter's time as a promise of the coming Messiah, and the Christians naturally took it up gladly and applied it to Jesus and his second coming.[50] But Peter says that the morning star rises in our *hearts*.[51] Some older scholars took the phrases to mean that the light shining in darkness is the Old Testament period, the day dawning is the preaching of the gospel, and the morning star rising in our hearts is conversion.[52] But that view founders on Peter's use of 'day' to

---

[42] Cf. 1 Pet. 1:10–12, which argues in the same way.

[43] E.g. Ps. 119:105. [44] E.g. Jn. 1:5; Eph. 6:12; 1 Thes. 5:4; 1 Jn. 2:8.

[45] Wand, p. 161; Plumptre, p. 174.

[46] In the Greek, Jesus uses the same words of the last great prophet, John the Baptist; Jn. 5:35.

[47] Mal. 4:5. [48] E.g. Rom. 13:11–14; Heb. 10:25; 1 Pet. 2:12.

[49] Nu. 24:17, a true prophecy from Balaam (cf. 2 Pet. 2:15–16!).

[50] Lk. 1:78–79; Rev. 2:28; 22:16.

[51] The text is difficult, but the meaning is clear. See Green (1987), p. 99.

[52] Most significantly, J. B. Mayor, *The Epistle of Jude and the Second Epistle of Peter* (1907), *ad loc.*

mean the second coming (3:10). Instead, we should probably understand him to say that the return of Christ will marry the objective promises of God with our subjective belief in them. As Paul said, 'then I shall know fully, even as I am fully known'.[53] Until that day, we have to believe with our hearts despite the evidence of our eyes, and the Old Testament remains the permanently valid voice of God until the end of human history.

b. What the prophets heard: the voice in the silence (1:20–21)

What Peter is saying is crucially important, and, having just told us to 'pay attention' to the prophets, he now has something for us to grasp *above all*.[54] We *must understand that no prophecy of Scripture came about by the prophet's own interpretation.* Assuming that this translation is right (see the explanatory notes above), Peter's point is that the person who wrote the prophecy had not only the experience but the interpretation to go with it. For instance, not only did Jeremiah see an almond branch and a boiling pot, but God told him what those two visions meant.[55]

To intensify his case, Peter repeats the negative before he states the positive. *Prophecy never had its origin in the will of man*, or, as Clark puts it, 'Isaiah did not get out of bed one morning and say, "I have decided to write some prophecies today."'[56] Instead, *men spoke from God as they were carried along by the Holy Spirit.*[57] The prophets were gripped by God as he spoke to them and gave them a message to communicate,[58] and the New Testament writers unambiguously and consistently supported the prophets' claims.[59] Notice how Peter balances the human authorship (*men spoke*) with God's authorship (*from God*), even though he is aware that such a partnership is not the work of equals, but that the humans were *carried along by the Holy Spirit.*[60]

So Peter leaves us in no doubt about the authority of his second

---

[53] 1 Cor. 13:12.
[54] Literally, he says 'This first', *touto prōton*, but the phrase seems to have lost that precise numerical force (*cf.* 3:3, where no 'secondly' was even intended).
[55] Je. 1:11–14. *Cf.* Ezekiel's experience in Skeleton Valley (Ezk. 37:1–14), and the repeated questions and answers in Zc. 1:18 – 2:2; 4:2 – 6:8.
[56] Clark, p. 28.
[57] The translation 'holy men' (AV, NKJV) has strong manuscript support, but most scholars omit it, as it is easier to account for its later pious addition than for some scribes omitting such a key phrase.
[58] *E.g.* 2 Sa. 23:2; 1 Ch. 28:11–12, 19; Je. 1:7–9; and even Je. 20:7–10!
[59] *E.g.* Mk. 12:26; Acts 3:21; 2 Tim. 3:16; Heb. 1:1.
[60] Luke uses the word translated 'carried along' of a ship being driven before a strong wind; Acts 27:15, 17.

group of witnesses to the promises of God. God spoke to them and through them.

The striking parallel between the apostles and the prophets has been underlined throughout verses 17–21 in three ways. First, Peter has illustrated the coming of the Lord with the language of sight: *glory* (17), *light, day, morning star* (19). Secondly, he has illustrated the equal authority of the prophets and apostles with the language of sound: *voice* (17), *word* (19) and *spoke* (21). And thirdly, he has linked them by the verb *pherō*, to 'carry along' or 'move'. God's voice *came to* Jesus (17), and the apostles heard that voice which *came from heaven* (18). Now Peter has underlined that no prophecy *had its origin* in mankind's ingenuity, but only as the prophets were *carried along by the Holy Spirit.* Quite clearly, Peter puts on an equally divine and authoritative footing the message of the New Testament apostles and the message of the Old Testament prophets (*cf.* 3:2, 16). God spoke to both groups, giving them his once-for-all and irrevocable explanation of his actions. So certain is Peter of this parallel that he will even call Paul's letters by the awesome word *graphē*, 'Scripture' (3:16; *cf.* 1:20). How dare we think we can replace that?

2 Peter 2:1–3
6. The fifth column

During the Spanish Civil War, General Emilio Mola marched on a city. He was asked how many columns of men he had. 'Five,' he is said to have replied. 'Four at my back and a fifth column inside the walls.' His reference to the partisans ready to fight for him inside the siege gave rise to a powerful image of betrayal and enmity: the fifth column. Peter's contention is that although the church is buffeted from outside, her greatest weakness comes from the enemy within, her own fifth column.

> *But there were also false prophets among the people, just as there will be false teachers among you. They will secretly introduce destructive heresies, even denying the sovereign Lord who bought them – bringing swift destruction on themselves.* ²*Many will follow their shameful ways and will bring the way of truth into disrepute.* ³*In their greed these teachers will exploit you with stories they have made up. Their condemnation has long been hanging over them, and their destruction has not been sleeping.*

This section is closely tied with what has gone before, and is carefully constructed. Having explained that we have true teachers, the apostles (1:16–18), and that the Old Testament was written by true prophets (1:19–21), Peter now warns that just as there *were also false prophets* then, so there *will be false teachers* today. The reality of the threat makes him change from a general warning in the future tense (*there will be*) to the present tense at the end of verse 3 as he announces their doom.[1] There is a frame around this longer section, for Peter begins by saying that the apostles 'did not follow cleverly invented stories' (1:16) and ends by contrasting the false teachers' *stories they have made up* (2:3).

¹ The Greek verbs are in the present tense. Paul similarly moves from future to present (1 Tim. 4:1–11; 2 Tim. 3:1–6). Most commentators see this as a slip in pseudo-Peter's mask, but *cf.* Green (1987), p. 104.

1. The ever-present danger (2:1a)

Peter has argued for the continuing relevance of Old Testament prophecy, but he now has to warn of a second continuing phenomenon, that *there were also false prophets among the people* (a standard title for Israel, in both Old and New Testaments). Peter had played a key role in engineering the amazing understanding that Gentiles who believed in God could be members of God's people too.[2] Hence the warning to a church to beware the same group that did so much to undermine God's people in the past. God's verdict on such a group had been clear and consistent. 'If a prophet, or one who foretells by dreams, appears among you and announces to you a miraculous sign or wonder, and if the sign or wonder of which he has spoken takes place, and he says, "Let us follow other gods" (gods you have not known) "and let us worship them," you must not listen to the words of that prophet or dreamer. The LORD your God is testing you to find out whether you love him with all your heart and with all your soul.'[3] That warning was repeated constantly throughout Israel's history,[4] and was reinforced with the death penalty.[5] That was how important it was to pay attention to what God really had said and not to make it up according to what people wanted to hear.

Alarmingly, *there will be false teachers among* us, because Christians are also *the people* of God. This was a warning that Jesus, Paul, John and Jude all made in their turn.[6] Perhaps Peter calls them by his own invented phrase *false teachers*, rather than false prophets, because their claim played down the supernatural. They were the people who slander (2:10) and scoff (3:3). Nevertheless, teachers occupied a very high place in the early church, bracketed with prophets as possessing one of the esteemed higher gifts.[7] To claim to be a teacher while in reality being a *false teacher*, then, was no minor mistake. It was to occupy someone else's position, and led to misleading people about God, about themselves and about the way of salvation. In the early church there was a clear understanding of the difference between truth and error, and the difference has eternal consequences.

There are always some Christians who find it hard to distinguish between true and false teachers. Perhaps they wonder if they should be more critical than they are, but worry about the danger of being

---

[2] *Cf.* Acts 10:42; 1 Pet. 2:9–10.   [3] Dt. 13:1–3.
[4] *E.g.* Is. 28:7; Je. 23:14; Ezk. 13:1–7; Zc. 13:4.
[5] Dt. 13:5; 18:20.
[6] Mt. 24:11, 24; Acts 20:29–30; Gal. 1:6–9; Phil. 3:2; 2 Thes. 2:1–3; 1 Tim. 1:3–7; 1 Jn. 2:18–19; Rev. 16:13–14; 19:20; 20:10; Jude 3–4.
[7] Acts 13:1; Rom. 12:6–8; 1 Cor. 12:28–29; Eph. 4:11.

too concerned about minor issues. Others become discouraged because the false teachers seem to be more prominent, and they leave churches and denominations to look for purity. Peter warns that this is a futile exercise, because false teaching is an ever-present and inevitable danger in any church or denomination. That is not to advise despair, for truth and error matter. As Calvin saw, 'the Spirit of God has declared once and for all that the Church will never be free from this internal trouble'.[8] Peter will tell us to avoid being either deluded (2:1–22) or despondent (3:1–10). Instead, we need to take radical action to avoid error's consequences.

2. The ever-gullible church (2:1b–3a)

How can we recognize a false teacher? What marks out such people, so that we can avoid their influence? Peter gives five warning signs.

a. Unorthodox teaching

This sign seems obvious, but in reality unorthodox teaching can be hard to spot. These people will not have big signs around their necks, saying, 'I am a false teacher, so please do not listen to me.' They will be highly plausible, and they will *secretly introduce*, or 'smuggle in',[9] their new ideas. The word *heresies* might conjure up something easily recognized, but the Greek word *hairēsis* meant an 'opinion' or 'variant'. Originally, the Sadducees, Pharisees, and even the Christians could be referred to by the word, without any underlying criticism.[10] Within Christianity, however, it began to have the sense of faction or divisiveness,[11] and Peter tightens the meaning even more by adding the word *destructive*. What these men teach is not a permissible variant of the gospel. It is a range of 'damnable heresies' (AV) which lead straight to judgment.

The critical proof lies in the *stories they have made up*. They might be stories about the impressiveness of their ministry or about new truths that God has taught them, but the stinging condemnation is that they have made them up.

Rather than adding to the glory of God, such ideas have only been *denying the sovereign Lord who bought them*. Peter uses an unusually strong word to indicate the right of the Lord God to rule the lives of his people. It is *despotēs*, translated here as *sovereign Lord*. It is the usual word for slave ownership,[12] and stresses an absolute right to possess. There are three possible ways to read what Peter says here.

---

[8] Calvin (*Peter*), p. 345.   [9] Kelly, p. 326.   [10] *E.g.* Acts 5:17; 15:5; 24:5; 26:5.
[11] 1 Cor. 11:18; Gal. 5:20; Tit. 3:10.   [12] 1 Tim. 6:1; Tit. 2:9; 1 Pet. 2:18.

i. The creator God

The word *despotēs* is used in the New Testament of God in his capacity as creator and ruler of his world.[13] It is because of his awe-inspiring greatness that Christians should obey him, can pray to him and may believe in his promises. But since God is the creator and ruler of all people, and not just of believers (those whom he has *bought*), it is difficult to see how the word could be pointing to God's wider rule here. We should therefore look for a more specific meaning.

ii. The saving Christ

In the parallel passage in Jude 4, *sovereign Lord* is clearly intended to mean Jesus Christ, and because of the word *bought* here, he is possibly the reference in this passage. It is one of the great themes of the New Testament that the cross bought us out of slavery to sin and into the new ownership of Jesus Christ. The word 'bought' (*agorazō*) comes straight from the public slave auction. It is used twenty-five times in the New Testament for a simple commercial transaction, but also for the effect of the death of Christ.[14] On this reading, Peter emphasizes the absolute right of Jesus Christ to rule the lives of his people; but the false teachers reject it, and openly *deny the sovereign Lord*.

Yet, if this is the right translation, we must face the issue that while Jesus offers the Christian assured and immovable salvation,[15] according to Peter the false teachers here have lost it. Can a Christian, then, lose his or her salvation? Were the false teachers ever truly converted? Were they among the elect, if Christ had bought them? Can we be sure that, having been bought, we will be saved?

The questions show the problems in this interpretation. Obviously the two situations are different, for Jesus is talking of a group of Christians facing all sorts of pressures and squeezes which, he promises, cannot affect their eternal salvation; while Peter is talking of people who are deliberately flouting the rule of the Master, seeing how far they can go. In Peter's mind these men are not disciples of Christ, even though they may once have professed to be so. One of the key marks of a disciple is a willingness to serve as a slave. Someone who does not do that is very close to not being a Christian, and someone who teaches others not to do that is probably not in the faith. On the other hand, people who suffer agonies of conscience because they are not serving Jesus enough cannot be

---

[13] Lk. 2:29; Acts 4:24; 2 Tim. 2:21; Rev. 6:10.
[14] 1 Cor. 6:20; 7:23; Rev. 5:9; 14:3. For other 'purchasing' verbs see Mk. 10:45; Acts 20:28; Rom. 6:17–18; 1 Tim. 2:6; 1 Pet. 1:18.
[15] Jn. 10:28–29.

placed in that apostate category. Scrupulous Christians can rest assured that they have a powerful sovereign Lord who has done all that is necessary to have bought them. Nevertheless, because of the possible contradiction between Peter and Jesus, we need another way to understand Peter.

iii. The saving God

Wayne Grudem[16] has suggested that Peter is quoting Deuteronomy 32:6. As Moses reminded the people of all that God had done for them, he said,

> Do you thus repay the LORD,
> O foolish and unwise people?
> Is not He your Father who has bought you?
> He has made you and established you.[17]

In this understanding, Peter continues his parallel with the peril of God's people in the Old Testament by pointing back to the work of God in rescuing the people from Egypt, by which they became his possession when he bought them. They needed to respond to that work in faith rather than follow godless leadership. The word 'bought' alerts Peter's readers to an Old Testament theme, and does not make a statement about the cross and whether we may lose our salvation. To quote Grudem, 'The text means not that Christ had redeemed the false prophets, but simply that they were rebellious Jewish people (or church attenders in the same position as rebellious Jews) who were rightly owned by God because they had been brought out of the land of Egypt (or their forefathers had) but were ungrateful to him. Christ's specific work of redemption is not in view in this verse.'[18] Clark[19] puts it very neatly and slightly differently when he says that they refers back to 'the people' in verse 1 ('they even deny the Lord who delivered the Israelites from Egypt').

These words would have an extraordinary poignancy for Peter as he wrote them. He knew the shame of denying Jesus, even though Jesus had foretold it; and he knew the humble wonder of being restored.[20] But where Peter had known a spasm of cowardice, these men were settled in their opposition and showed no inclination to remorse or forgiveness. How did they deny God? It is difficult to be

---

[16] W. Grudem, *Systematic Theology* (Leicester: IVP; Grand Rapids: Zondervan, 1994), p. 615.
[17] This translation is NASB, and Grudem gives his own which matches it. He says that the Hebrew word *qānâ* can mean 'created' (*cf.* 'Creator' in NIV main text), or – more frequently – 'bought' (as NIV footnote). The LXX understood the Hebrew to mean 'bought', although it uses *kataomai* rather than Peter's synonymous word *agorazō*.
[18] Grudem, *op. cit.*, p. 615.   [19] Clark, pp. 38–39.   [20] Mk. 14:30–31.

quite sure. Possibly they denied his ability to save, or denied Christ's return, or just generally denied his claim over them as their Saviour and Lord.

Ironically, the very truth these men deny is creeping up on them. They are dismantling a Christian view of the future, mocking any idea of judgment; but they will very soon find that their *destructive heresies* rebound in *destruction*, as the very teaching they deny comes true. The word *swift* is *tachinos*, used of the abrupt arrival of Peter's impending death (1:14), and here too it means 'unexpected' and 'suddenly' rather than 'imminent'. Peter's warning has not lost its force just because it is two thousand years old.

b. Free morality

Such men lead and encourage others in *shameful ways*. The word *aselgeia* is again a strong one, which Peter repeats in 2:7 ('filthy') and 2:18 ('lustful').[21] Its meaning is sensual, shading off into sexual, and here in the plural means 'either different forms or repeated habitual acts of lasciviousness'.[22] It is an inevitable hallmark of no longer believing in the second coming that ethics becomes a matter of private choice and taste, and the key issues are those of self-expression and fulfilment rather than purity and obedience.

c. Great popularity

Alexander Nisbet wisely said that 'it is not strange to see that the most dangerous heretics have many followers; every error being a friend to some lust'.[23] If there is no longer a master to please, then there will only be ourselves to please; and if someone starts speaking a message that flatters people rather than calling them to repentance and faith, and that encourages them to enjoy their darkest and most secret wishes rather than hard discipleship and learning, it will not be surprising that *many will follow*. Such a message makes no demands other than the ones we want to make on ourselves, and it is the height of enjoyment. This does not, of course, mean that anyone who is popular is automatically a false teacher, or that truth is found only in small and secret sects. It means that one result of having the kind of gospel these men had is a spurious repentance and faith that are really no change and faith at all.

---

[21] *Cf.* 1 Pet. 4:3; Jude 4.   [22] Bigg, p. 273. *Cf.* 2:7, 10, 12, 14, 18, 19, 22; 3:3.
[23] Nisbet, p. 247.

d. Maimed evangelism

The well-meaning non-Christian is no fool, and is repelled by the greedy self-indulgence that is often served up as the gospel. Sadly, that often means running from any kind of Christianity, even the authentic article. Thus Peter observes that the *many* who *follow* these *shameful ways* actually serve to *bring the way of truth into disrepute*. Kelly notes that 'early Christian writers were acutely conscious . . . of the impression, favourable or the reverse, which the pagan world is bound to form from the conduct of its members';[24] and it is certainly a consistent theme throughout the New Testament that the Christians' lives, and especially the Christian leaders' lives, are a shop window for the gospel.[25]

Because of these men *the way of truth*[26] is being brought *into disrepute*. Again Peter's word is strong, *blasphēmeō*. Although 'blaspheme' is probably more than he intends to say here, it is rightly translated 'slander' in 2:10–11, and 'blaspheme' in 2:12, when it refers to what these men themselves are doing. The effect of these men on the church's witness is disastrously evident. It had always been the case; this verse seems to be based on Isaiah 52:5, where God declares, 'All day long my name is constantly blasphemed.'[27] Non-Christians will not take our beliefs seriously unless our behaviour matches them.

e. Suspect motives

In their greed these teachers will exploit you. That is, if the heart of these men's motivation was their *shameful ways*, it is not surprising that the same heart is revealed in the way they propagate their teaching. These are false shepherds who want to fleece the sheep![28] Clark warns us that 'this passage should not be narrowly restricted to money',[29] and he is surely right to say that honour and prestige – even other teachers' wives, he suggests – might be objects of this exploitation. Nevertheless, the word translated *greed* has overtones of extortion, and the word translated *exploit* is a normal commercial word[30] which Paul used in a similar warning about 'men of corrupt mind, who have been robbed of the truth and who think that godliness is a means to financial gain'.[31] Even in honest churches which face deficits and overdrafts, there is always the temptation to

---

[24] Kelly, p. 329.   [25] Rom. 14:16; 1 Tim. 3:7; Tit. 2:5; Jas. 2:6–7.
[26] 'The way' was an early term for Christianity, and one that Peter was fond of; see 2:15, 21. *Cf.* Jn. 14:6; Acts 9:2; 18:25–26; 19:9, 23; 24:14, 22.
[27] Also quoted in Rom. 2:24.
[28] This was not a new problem; see Ezk. 34; 1 Thes. 2:3–9.
[29] Clark, p. 40.   [30] Translated 'carry on business' in Jas. 4:13.   [31] 1 Tim. 6:5.

put fingers in the till, and to ask the preacher to preach in ways that will uplift and make people 'feel good' before the collection is taken up. That is the start of the rot, which lets the bank balance rule the church's priorities. Of course, it may seem a long way from that to the duplicitous extortion of these men, but Peter wrote this as a warning to us too.

The New Testament is unashamed to say that Christian leaders face temptations over money, which is why they were to be chosen partly for their financial honesty. Peter instructed that a new teacher should be 'not greedy for money, but eager to serve'.[32] Paul took especial care to be seen to go beyond the minimum that honesty required: 'we are taking pains to do what is right, not only in the eyes of the Lord but also in the eyes of men'.[33] The counter-balance to the pastor's honesty must be the church's generosity, for 'the Lord has commanded that those who preach the gospel should receive their living from the gospel'.[34] Handling money is a dangerous occupation for Christian leaders, and requires that we hold the two safety rails of choosing honest pastors and then paying them enough to keep them honest!

3. The ever-wakeful God (2:3b)

If these people deny that there is a condemnatory judgment from God on their actions, and if the absence of the second coming gives them freedom to carry on, are they not vindicated? Are Christians who do obey what the apostles said not foolish rather than wise? These questions take us to the heart of the letter, and the last half of verse 3 acts as a bridge between Peter's raising the issue of *their condemnation*, and the way he answers it. Notice how verse 4 begins with the word 'For'. This sentence, then, makes assertions which the rest of the chapter will prove. It is a finely balanced sentence which gives 'a solemn rhythm to the threat',[35] and more literally translates as 'their condemnation from long ago has not been idle, and their destruction has not been sleeping'.

These men were accusing God of dozing off, rather as Elijah had taunted the prophets of Baal. 'Perhaps he is deep in thought, or busy, or travelling. Maybe he is sleeping and must be awakened.'[36] But while Elijah pokes fun at a non-existent deity, Peter sees people poking fun at the living God, and 'he who watches over Israel will neither slumber nor sleep'.[37] God watches to bring judgment and salvation. Isaiah says that God used pagan nations to punish Israel,

---

[32] 1 Pet. 5:2; cf. 1 Tim. 3:3; 6:3–10; Tit. 1:7.   [33] 2 Cor. 8:21.   [34] 1 Cor. 9:14.
[35] Kelly, p. 329.   [36] 1 Ki. 18:27.
[37] Ps. 121:4. In LXX this verse seems to have influenced Peter's vocabulary.

and 'not one of them grows tired or stumbles, not one slumbers or sleeps'.[38] Peter reminds us that God has decided on the verdict already – *condemnation* – and on the sentence, *destruction*. As Moffatt says, 'they may pooh-pooh the idea of a final retribution, but they are doomed men, on the edge of punishment'.[39] God's verdict on sin has been crystal clear from the very first warning about the tree of the knowledge of good and evil in the garden: 'when you eat of it you will surely die'.[40] The miracle was that when the man and the woman were banished from the garden, they were banished with a promise that judgment would not fall until a sin-bearer had been found.[41] In order to explain why we would be very foolish to presume on God's patience, Peter uses the important principle that God delays judgment so as to exercise mercy.

[38] Is. 5:27.   [39] Moffatt (*Peter*), p. 192.   [40] Gn. 2:17.   [41] Gn. 3:15.

2 Peter 2:4–9
7. Putting the world on hold

If God's judgment is real but future, how are Christians to live in the meantime? Peter now gives three examples from the Old Testament to prove that God has judged in the past and will judge again in the future, and to show how he therefore expects us to live in the present.

For if God did not spare angels when they sinned, but sent them to hell, putting them into gloomy dungeons to be held for judgment; ⁵if he did not spare the ancient world when he brought the flood on its ungodly people, but protected Noah, a preacher of righteousness, and seven others; ⁶if he condemned the cities of Sodom and Gomorrah by burning them to ashes, and made them an example of what is going to happen to the ungodly; ⁷and if he rescued Lot, a righteous man, who was distressed by the filthy lives of lawless men ⁸(for that righteous man, living among them day after day, was tormented in his righteous soul by the lawless deeds he saw and heard) – ⁹if this is so, then the Lord knows how to rescue godly men from trials and to hold the unrighteous for the day of judgment, while continuing their punishment.

Structurally, this section is one sentence, with the *if* of verse 4 being answered by the concluding *then* of verse 9, but the NIV has rightly smoothed it by adding *if* in verses 5, 6, 7 and 9. It is a section which, for its vocabulary and structure, is very similar to Jude; and debate hovers over which letter came first. The best solution seems to be that Peter came second, adapting Jude to a wider audience not used to Jude's background material;[1] but the argument is largely redundant, because both writers have clear and independent lines of

---

[1] See Appendix. The main background material to Jude is *1 Enoch*; see comments there. Green (1987) says that 'if Peter alludes to it at all he does so with the utmost discretion' (p. 110). Bauckham (1983) thinks Peter is 'probably not familiar' with it (p. 247).

thought. Peter shares with Jude the examples of the angels and Sodom and Gomorrah, but replaces the wandering Israelites with the flood and introduces his important theme of living in an impure world. He shapes his three[2] examples carefully.

Chronology. Peter's examples follow the order in Genesis: 6:1–4 (the angels); 6:5 – 9:17 (the flood); 18:16 – 19:29 (Sodom and Gomorrah).

Locality. The examples of judgment gradually reduce in scale, from the cosmic (angels) through the widespread (flood) to the local (cities of the plain). This helps Peter explain why we are still waiting for a final, cosmic judgment.

Theology. Peter carefully accumulated his key words. The angels have *sinned* and are being *held for judgment* without exception. Noah's world may be *ungodly*, but he stands for *righteousness*, and so he and those who believe him are *protected*. Sodom and Gomorrah are not only *ungodly* but also *lawless* (twice), but Lot is *righteous* (three times), and so is *rescued*. Peter concludes in verse 9 that God *knows how to rescue godly men and to hold the unrighteous for the day of judgment.*

1. Three biblical examples of God's wise judgment (2:4–8)

a. The fallen angels (2:4)

The first example gives an intriguing but partial glimpse into a world beyond human experience, of wonderful beings who served God face to face, yet still rebelled against him. Jesus 'saw Satan fall like lightning'[3] during his ministry, and John saw a vision of Satan and his hordes as 'they lost their place in heaven'.[4] But Peter is probably taking us back to the dawn of human history and a mysterious moment from Genesis 6:1–4a.

> When men began to increase in number on the earth and daughters were born to them, the sons of God saw that the daughters of men were beautiful, and they married any of them they chose. Then the LORD said, 'My Spirit will not contend with man for ever, for he is mortal; his days will be a hundred and twenty years.'
> The Nephilim were on the earth in those days – and also afterwards – when the sons of God went to the daughters of men and had children by them.

---

[2] Elliott (pp. 147–149) suggests two pairs of examples: the angels and Noah's world contrasted with Noah; the angels and the cities contrasted with Lot. But this is unnecessarily complicated.
[3] Lk. 10:18.   [4] Rev. 12:7–9.

That strange tale of the angels (as the phrase 'the sons of God' was understood)[5] mating with human beings was frequently used as an example of sin, sometimes specified, sometimes not. Here, although we might guess at pride or lust, Peter has simply said that they *sinned*, which is open enough to include the excesses of the next two examples as well. Peter uses this illustration to make two points.

First, no-one is exempt from judgment, not even the angels; *God did not spare angels*. Peter omits the definite article before *angels*, and Bigg says that 'the absence ... gives the sense of "even angels".'[6] The proud false teachers claimed that they, at least, were beyond God's judgment, and they mock Peter's naïve and primitive faith in a day of judgment. But Peter says that no-one, not even the most glorious and powerful of those who stand against God, can avoid him.

Secondly, judgment, although delayed, is still real. The angels sinned in the past, but they are only being *held* in the present *for judgment* in the future. These majestic but flawed beings still await their final, inevitable punishment. Built into the way God runs the universe is the principle that punishment does not immediately follow rebellion. There will be no exceptions to the adverse verdict on the rebellious angels, but at the heart of Peter's second and third examples is the possibility of salvation for rebellious mankind.

Peter draws a discreet veil over what has happened to these angels in the meantime, and this is made more opaque by a manuscript problem. The veil is that God *sent them to hell*, one word which, as the NIV footnote suggests, could be translated 'sent them to Tartarus'. Tartarus was a standard term in non-biblical Greek mythology for a part of hell to which rebellious gods were sent, and this is its only biblical appearance. Peter does not seem to allude to this myth for any particular reason.[7] Probably it is just a synonym for hell which had lost its pagan overtones, and had 'become fully acclimatised in Hellenistic Judaism'.[8]

The manuscript problem is whether God has held them in dark *dungeons* (*sirois*, from which our word 'silo' is derived) or, as in NIV footnote, 'chains' (*seirais*). In the parallel passage Jude uses a different word altogether, *desmois*, clearly meaning 'chains', and the

---

[5] Jb. 1:6; 2:1; 38:7. See Bauckham (1983), pp. 246–247, for similar contemporary non-biblical references.

[6] Bigg, p. 274.

[7] Green (1987) says, 'Just as Paul could quote an apt verse from the pagan poet Aratus (Acts 17:28) so Peter could make use of this Homeric imagery' (p. 110). That is true, and is certainly why many NT writers quote non-biblical works (see comments on Jude 9–10, 14–16), but Peter has no similar reason here; he seems to use the word without thinking of its pagan overtones.

[8] Kelly, p. 331; see LXX of Jb. 40:15; 41:23.

argument here is very finely balanced.[9] In reality it matters little, because the creatures are out of harm's way under God's lock and key. 'It would be hazardous to dogmatize with undue definiteness, on the strength of this passing allusion, as to the condition of these inhabitants of the unseen world,' is Plumptre's wise comment.[10]

We might expect the conclusion to be: 'Just as God did not spare the rebellious angels, so he will not spare the false teachers.' But Peter employs much greater subtlety than that, as his second example shows.

b. The flooded world (2:5)

Just as God 'did not spare angels', *so he did not spare the ancient world when he brought the flood.* In the story that follows that of the fallen angels in Genesis, humankind's rebellion also provoked God's anger, and he was 'grieved that he had made man on the earth, and his heart was filled with pain'. There is one crucial difference between men and angels, however. Although God determines to 'wipe mankind, whom I have created, from the face of the earth', a complete removal was unthinkable because 'Noah found favour in the eyes of the LORD'.[11]

Noah 'found favour' because he stood out in contrast to his setting, the *ungodly people. Ungodly* translates *asebēs*, a word Peter has probably chosen because of its similarity to his word *eusebeia*, *godliness* (1:3, 6–7; 2:9; 3:11). Genesis says that society 'was corrupt ... and full of violence',[12] but that by contrast 'Noah was a righteous man, blameless among the people of his time'.[13] Noah was no passive believer. He is commended in Genesis because he expected God's promised judgment and made provision to escape it. Hebrews' verdict on him is that 'by faith ... when warned about things not yet seen, in holy fear [he] built an ark to save his family. By his faith he condemned the world and became heir of the righteousness that comes by faith.'[14]

Noah not only built; he was a *preacher of righteousness*, which is a strange description because in Genesis he is famous only for making the ark. Michael Green asks, 'How could a good man keep quiet when he saw others going to ruin?'[15] – a fair comment, because the odd structure would undoubtedly have led to questions and answers. Blum also thinks that 'this could refer to his preaching activity not recorded in the OT, or to the fact that his lifestyle

---

[9] Green (1987), p. 110, prefers the translation 'dungeons'; Bauckham (1983) prefers 'fetters', but says 'it is almost impossible to decide' (p. 244).
[10] Plumptre, p. 179. [11] Gn. 6:6–8. [12] Gn. 6:11. [13] Gn. 6:9.
[14] Heb. 11:7. [15] Green (1987), p. 111.

condemned sin and proclaimed righteousness to his contemporaries',[16] which is possible. There were certainly teachings in Jewish circles that referred to Noah as a prophet.[17] But simply by being a boat-builder in a desert, Noah would have displayed his faith in the judgment and mercy of God. He displayed it to the mocking incomprehension of his contemporaries, but also to the saving faith of the *seven others* who believed and joined him (his wife, three sons and their wives).[18]

Peter makes two further points by this illustration. First, although God's judgment on a sinful creation is inevitable, it is not inescapable. God *protected* Noah and those who believed his message. Peter's message of inevitable judgment on a sinful world is not one of unrelieved gloom and pessimism, for he offers the way of escape through faith in Jesus Christ. He will protect us on the day of universal judgment. *Seven* may indicate the relatively small number who believed Noah, and the small number who will believe Peter. By contrast, the 'false teachers, notwithstanding their multitude of followers, and long success in propagating their errors, have no reason to imagine to themselves an escape from the wrath of God'.[19]

Secondly, Noah spent many weary years building his ark, holding out *righteousness* to an *ungodly people*. They would have laughed at the idiot building a boat in the desert. We too live among ungodly people who will perhaps mock our faith in a judging, saving God. We will find it hard or even foolish, and be beguiled into giving up, but we are to persevere in copying Noah. We must, unlike the false teachers, hold out and hold on to *righteousness*. We must actively believe it, as Noah's family did; and we must live it and speak it, as Noah himself did. And, as Peter's third illustration will show, doing that can be very tough indeed.

c. The filthy cities (2:6–8)

Sodom and Gomorrah were a common pairing that represented sin and rebellion throughout the Old Testament, sometimes along with the other 'cities of the plain'[20] that were destroyed at the

---

[16] Blum, p. 278.
[17] That is the way Peter treats the story in 1 Pet. 3:20, where he compares Noah's saving activity to Christ's. The most frequently quoted Jewish reference is to Josephus, *Antiquities*, 1.3.1.
[18] Peter sees this picture in his first letter too (1 Pet. 3:20), where Noah's saving activity is compared to Christ's.
[19] Nisbet, p. 250.
[20] Dt. 29:23; 32:32; Ps. 107:34; Is. 1:9–10; 3:9; 13:19; Je. 23:14; 49:18; 50:40; La. 4:6; Ezk. 16:46–55; Ho. 11:8; Am. 4:11; Zp. 2:9.

same time.[21] The particular sin of the towns was some form of sexual sin – probably homosexual practice – and that should be at the forefront of our thinking about them. But Ezekiel added that they were also 'arrogant, overfed and unconcerned; they did not help the poor and needy'.[22] Peter seems to want to keep a broad focus on sin rather than being too detailed in his comparison.[23] It is not enough to say that these cities were, as those of Noah's day, *ungodly*; he now says that the inhabitants were *lawless* (7, 8) and their *lives* were *filthy* (7). *Lawless* is a word Peter uses only in this letter, but *filthy* (*aselgeia*) is part of his description of paganism in his first letter, saying that Christians 'have spent enough time in the past doing what pagans choose to do – living in debauchery (*aselgeia*), lust, drunkenness, orgies, carousing and detestable idolatry'.[24] This is a very generalized view of sin, and shows both the disgust that a right-thinking Christian shares at the results of rebellion, and the rightness of God's holy judgment.

God judges all such practices as he did the behaviour in the cities, *burning them to ashes*. Genesis mentions 'burning sulphur' and 'dense smoke ... like smoke from a furnace',[25] and Peter elaborates the picture with a word that one writer would use to describe the horrific devastation caused by the eruption of Vesuvius in AD 79.[26] Just like the flood, this annihilation is meant as a warning to us, because God *made them an example of what is going to happen to the ungodly*.

Just as with the flood, though, there is grace as well as mercy, for Peter stands *Lot, a righteous man*, alongside 'Noah, a preacher of righteousness'. That Lot was righteous might come as a surprise if we are only superficially familiar with the Genesis account, for he comes across as greedy, cowardly and weak, perpetually attracted towards the sinful cities which he finds so hard to leave. Yet Peter insists that Lot was *distressed by the filthy lives of lawless men* and *tormented ... by the lawless deeds*, so perhaps there is more to Lot's character. Peter certainly tells us of his pain; *distressed* translates *kataponoumenos*, which occurs in Acts 7:24 for the way an Egyptian 'ill-treated' an Israelite in Moses' presence; and *tormented* translates *basanizō*, which Mark used for 'torture' and 'straining at the oars'.[27]

---

[21] Gn. 19:1–29.   [22] Ezk. 16:49.
[23] Jude 7, by contrast, highlights the specifically sexual side of their sin. See the comments there for an analysis of the idea that Sodom's sin may not have been homosexual practice.
[24] 1 Pet. 4:3. See also above on 2:2.   [25] Gn. 19:24, 28.
[26] *Tephroō*; MM, p. 632.   [27] Mk. 5:7; 6:48.

There is certainly evidence for Lot's tortured righteousness in Genesis. When Abraham was interceding with God for the cities, he did so because God would not have wanted to destroy anyone who was righteous. The person Abraham had in mind was the one whom God eventually rescued: Lot (like Noah, with his family).[28] Here in verse 8 he is called, literally, 'the righteous one' (*ho dikaios*), which Plumptre calls 'half-generic, half-individual',[29] and that would fit the external verdict of Abraham. There is also the internal evidence of Lot's repulsion at the city where he lived, for when God's messengers arrived to confirm the reports of the cities' wickedness, he would not let the men of Sodom do what they wanted. 'Don't do this wicked thing,' he pleaded, and the men complained that this outsider 'wants to play the judge'.[30] Whatever the precise intentions of the men, and however we explain the difficulties of the way Lot handled it by offering his unmarried daughters as substitutes, the stubborn truth remains that he was *distressed* and *tormented* by what he *saw and heard*, and so Peter is right to call him a *righteous man*.[31] Clark notes sharply that 'However strange this may seem, there are many Christians today who are in no position to criticise. They should listen to the rumblings of the volcano beneath them.'[32]

Peter makes two further points with his third illustration. First, not only is judgment promised, but its pattern has been revealed; for Sodom and Gomorrah are an *example*, a warning. When Peter finally builds his picture of the destruction of our world he combines the images of the flood and the ashes by talking of 'waters' and 'fire' (3:6–7).

Secondly, living the kind of life God approves in a world under judgment will be tough. Like Lot, we should be distressed and tormented by what we see and hear. Like the Israelites whom God approves of in Ezekiel's vision, we should 'grieve and lament over all the detestable things that are done'.[33] Although we share Lot's vision of a future judgment and salvation, the stress in this third example is even more on the present ungodliness that Peter mentions twice, and the lawlessness he also mentions twice. We may know nothing of angels and their rebellion, and the loneliness of Noah's faithful witness may be alien to us, but Lot lived in our world, facing the pressures to conform and compromise that are so familiar to us.

---

[28] Gn. 18:22–33; 19:29–30.   [29] Plumptre, p. 180.
[30] Gn. 19:6, 9.
[31] In non-biblical Jewish writings, he was 'the wise one'; Wisdom 10:6; 19:7.
[32] Clark, p. 44. See T. D. Alexander's helpful article, 'Lot's Hospitality; A Clue to his Righteousness', *JBL* 104/2 (1985), pp. 289–300.
[33] Ezk. 9:4.

The three illustrations: a summary

Each of the three illustrations has made two points which Peter is using to build a cumulative case. To sum them up, the six are as follows.

From the fallen angels
1. No-one is exempt from judgment.
2. Judgment, though delayed, is real.

From the flooded world
3. God's inevitable judgment can be escaped.
4. We are to hold that offer out to others, even if they mock.

From the filthy cities
5. The pattern of that judgment has been revealed.
6. Living a godly life in an ungodly world will be hard.

2. God is in control (2:9)

Peter reaches two conclusions, as the 'For it' clause from verse 4 reaches its pairing, *then*. Having said that Noah and Lot were marked out by being righteous (2:5, 7–8), and that the people of their day were marked out by being ungodly (2:5, 6), he reverses the terms and says that God is in control of both the godly and the unrighteous. He is now equipped to address the hard topic of why, if God is so firmly in control, the godly and righteous suffer while the unrighteous and ungodly go free.

a. God is in control of the godly

The lesson so far could be that the way out of *trials* is through what God will effect on the last day, just as he 'protected' Noah during the flood (verse 5). Ultimately, that will be the case. But the emphasis in the three examples has been much more on what happened before judgment. Even the angels are still waiting for their judgment. Peter says that *the Lord knows how to rescue godly men*, shown in the way he 'rescued Lot' (verse 7). The difference between Noah and Lot was that the flood was a widespread and effective judgment enabling God to start again, but the destruction of Sodom and Gomorrah was local and exemplary. It changed nothing, but set the alarm bells ringing. So we must copy those two heroes and stand out against the prevailing immorality of our world, especially (as Peter is about to show) when that same immorality has infected the church. It could be that the answer in our lifetimes is the final judgment, but it may be that we have to endure trials. These are the tough times all Christians have gone through, where the only way of safety is adherence to God and his faithfulness. The temptation is to think that because the unrighteous seem to run the world, and sometimes the churches too, God has ceased to rule. He has not, but the alert Christian will find it a painful business to be faithful surrounded by filth. If we do not find it painful, then Peter's letter should alert us to the likelihood that we have become more compromised in our world than Lot was in Sodom. Ruth Graham has said, 'If God does not one day judge America' – and, we might add, whichever country we live in – 'he will have to apologise to Sodom and Gomorrah!'[34]

b. God is in control of the unrighteous

The rebellious angels are being 'held for judgment' (4), and the same is true of the rebellious humans, for God *knows how to hold the unrighteous for the day of judgment, while continuing their punishment*.[35] God is in control, and the men and women who run the world and the church their own way will one day find that out to their cost. That was the lesson Jesus himself taught from the stories of the flood and the cities of the plain.[36] In the meantime, those who hold on to their belief in God must not lose heart because he has not yet vindicated himself. He will.

[34] Quoted in L. Dixon, *The Other Side of the Good News* (Wheaton: Victor Books, 1992), p. 23.

[35] Once again there is a critical watershed, over the word *kolazomenous*, translated here 'while continuing their punishment' (*cf.* Acts 4:21). The problem is whether the word should be translated in its normal sense, in the present tense as the NIV does, or with a future sense, as the NIV footnote. The latter gives the meaning 'for punishment until the day of judgment'. Most translators go for the literal present tense; most commentators (who have to explain it!) go for the future. The question boils down to whether, as God holds rebellious men and women for the day of judgment, they are already being in some measure punished, or whether all the punishment lies in the future. It is finely balanced, but the evidence probably favours the future sense.

[36] Lk. 17:26–30.

2 Peter 2:10–22, Part I (2:10–16)
8. Profile of a deadly minister

So far the group known as the 'false teachers' (2:1) has been sketch-ily drawn because Peter has wanted to alert us to the inevitability of their existence, popularity, fraudulence and eventual judgment. He has said that such people are regular features of the living church of God. As he now applies this fact to the ministers (2:10–16) and ministries (2:17–22)[1] that we are to flee, it becomes clear that he can name the false teachers he has in mind. The exact details of their errors will not always be clear to us two thousand years later, for the New Testament often seems opaque on the precise details of error, in order to make its antidotes of the widest possible relevance. But the profiles of the kinds of people who will try to lead us astray and the kinds of error they will try to introduce are strikingly contemporary. Peter's abhorrence of the errorists produces some of the most colourful and shocking language in the New Testament, and Kelly reflects much modern sentiment when he talks of Peter's 'violent and colourfully expressed tirade' and his 'repertory of abuse'.[2] But before we become too embarrassed, we should remem-ber our twentieth-century tendency to assume that all positions are right, rather than some being 'damnable heresies' (as AV translates 2:1). Clark says wisely, 'What twentieth-century Christians might well notice is the sharp difference between the respect paid to false teachers today and the treatment they received from the apostles.'[3]

This is the section where Peter's letter is most obviously similar to Jude's (Jude 8–12). Peter's letter is simpler (for instance, he omits Cain and Korah, in order to deal with the highly appropriate

---

[1] Structurally, verses 4–9 are one long sentence in the Greek, and most com-mentators take the first half of verse 10 as a conclusion to verses 1–9. While it is that, it is also a bridge section, and the outline suggested here is that both verse 10a and verse 17 stand as introductions to their respective sub-sections. The following verses have been subdivided accordingly. A similar structure emerges from chapter 3, and this argues strongly for this letter being a unit. See Appendix.

[2] Kelly, p. 337.   [3] Clark, pp. 50–51.

Balaam at greater length); he strains out the material his readers would not have been familiar with (such as the debate in Jude 9); and he alters the material that is not applicable (for example, the 'love feasts', *agapais*, of Jude 12 have become 'pleasures', *apatais*, in 2:13).[4] The simplest option is that Peter probably adapted Jude,[5] but the decision should not affect how either letter is read. Occasionally, if the two letters are put side by side, then the differences will clarify the meaning and emphases of each.

1. What happened then still happens today (2:10a)

This is especially true of those who follow the corrupt desire of the sinful nature and despise authority.

Peter's gaze turns to the living church of his day. He says that *this* (*i.e.* the fact that 'the Lord knows how to rescue godly men from trials and to hold the unrighteous for the day of judgment, while continuing their punishment', 2:9) is how Christians are to understand their own difficulties with *those* false teachers in their groups. Peter argues carefully, and we must follow him closely as he leads into this important section.

He has already warned that the false teachers 'deny the sovereign Lord who bought them' (2:1). His Old Testament examples have illustrated that principle at work: the angels 'sinned' against God's authority (2:4), the ancient world ignored a 'preacher of righteousness' (2:5), and the inhabitants of Sodom and Gomorrah were 'lawless' (2:7). They were mutinous. Peter warned secondly that they 'follow ... shameful ways' (2:2), and again his examples pointed to this in the wickedness of the angels, the 'ungodly people' of Noah's day (2:5) and the 'filthy lives' of Lot's contemporaries (2:7). Those who are free from what God commands are free to do as they like. Now Peter lifts his eyes from the Old Testament and sees the same two phenomena in the churches he loves, for the false teachers *despise authority*, and they *follow* their *corrupt desire*. Since he has used such vivid Old Testament examples, he is in a strong position to show that the false teachers are as wrong to attempt to justify their greed as they always have been (2:1a).

What was the *authority* that these men *despised*? There are broadly five options, which are tied in with the way the rest of this section is interpreted. Peter may mean the civil authorities (so

---

[4] In Greek capitals (as Jude would have written) the two words are almost identical.
[5] See Appendix. The danger to avoid is trying so hard to reach the original document(s) to see what 2 Peter and Jude have in common that each letter loses its distinctive teaching.

Luther, Calvin, and most recently, Reicke), but this is unlikely simply on the ground that this theme does not surface in the rest of the letter as part of the problem.[6] Secondly, they could be angelic authorities; the word translated *authority* (*kyriotēs*) appears in such contexts as Ephesians 1:21 and Colossians 1:16 in reference to 'principalities and powers'. This possible interpretation would fit in well with the 'angelic' flow of the rest of the passage, and is certainly what Jude means in his corresponding section.[7] Thirdly, 'authority' may refer to local church leaders, an idea which fits well here but is awkward in the context of the difficult next verse.[8] Fourthly, it may be the authority of the apostles themselves, who, although not elsewhere called 'glories' (*doxai*, translated 'celestial beings' in verse 10b), are certainly highly honoured.[9] The fact that Peter has had to defend himself against charges of telling fairy stories, and will have to defend himself from patronizing scorn, would match this theory. Fifthly, it may be God's own authority which is being flouted, and Peter has talked of 'the Lord' (*kyrios*) repeatedly in this letter.[10] It is not at all easy to decide which is right, although the second option (angelic authority) is perhaps the most broad-ranging and appropriate, with the fifth (God's authority behind the angelic authorities) close behind. Yet although the exotic details of these men's error are hidden, the root of it is clear in the way they take it on themselves to *despise authority*. Whether that authority is Christ's own or delegated by him to others is in large measure a side-issue, for their self-willed arrogance is clear.

2. False teachers despise legitimate spiritual authority (2:10b–13a)

Fools, it is said, rush in where angels fear to tread, and certainly this principle applies to the arrogant stupidity of the false teachers.

> *Bold and arrogant, these men are not afraid to slander celestial beings;* [11]*yet even angels, although they are stronger and more powerful, do not bring slanderous accusations against such beings in the presence of the Lord.* [12]*But these men blaspheme in matters they do not understand. They are like brute beasts,*

---

[6] Calvin (*Peter*), p. 352; Luther, p. 272; Reicke, p. 167. Reicke sees a political background to the whole letter, but has not convinced others.

[7] Bauckham (1983), p. 260.

[8] Bigg, p. 280, partially supported by Green (1987), pp. 116–117.

[9] 2 Cor. 8:23 is not about the twelve apostles, neither does it use the word 'glory' in the technical way Jude does here.

[10] 2 Pet. 1:1, 8, 11, 14, 16; 2:9, 11, 20; 3:2, 8, 10, 14, 18.

creatures of instinct, born only to be caught and destroyed, and like beasts they too will perish.
[13]They will be paid back with harm for the harm they have done.

a. The crime (2:10b–11)

The broad outline of these men's crime is fast becoming apparent. They are *bold and arrogant*, a punchy two-word description: 'impudent egoists', 'undisciplined dare-devils'.[11] Their audacity takes Peter's breath away as they remove the inconvenient parts of Christian doctrine that limit their self-indulgence.

The precise details of their crime are less obvious. They *slander celestial beings*. Which celestial beings is Peter talking about? Those who understood 'authority' in verse 10a to mean 'church leaders' tend to want to do the same here, but the term is far too spectacular for that. No doubt these men were saying some colourful and slanderous things about their church leaders if those leaders were trying to curb their excesses, but Peter's defence is on a different plane from church discipline. The word behind the phrase (*doxai*, 'glories') clearly means 'angels' in Jude 8.[12] Although Jude's meaning must not automatically serve as Peter's, it is a useful cross-reference, especially when some non-biblical material may have been quoted. This will be true whichever writer wrote first. Here Jude's meaning, 'angels', does seem to fit. It is not clear whether they are the fallen angels of 2:4 or the perfect angels of 2:11, but that is not too important. In the latter case Peter would be thinking of the prime role of angels in the Old Testament: they were God's law-bringers.[13] As Kelly says, 'angels of any sort belong to a higher order than men'.[14]

The next verse (11) is much more complicated, and there is no way to avoid some hard thinking. In Jude 9, and so partially in the background here, lies a legend of the archangel Michael who refused to support Satan in bringing a legal judgment against Moses, but instead trusted God to uphold his gracious law (see comments on Jude 9–10). If it is likely that this does lie behind Peter's words here, has he so adapted his material for his readership that he has muddled the story? Certainly, on the surface, Peter seems to say that since

---

[11] Reicke, p. 166; Wand, p. 167. The word translated 'arrogant', *authadēs*, occurs in a similar setting in Tit. 1:7, where the NIV translates it 'overbearing'.

[12] Lenski's suggestion that 'glories' refers to the results of the cross, as in 1 Pet. 1:11, is well meant but does not really fit the context of 2 Peter. The false teachers are denying the second coming, and it will indeed be glorious; but Peter does not make that second point.

[13] Dt. 33:2; Gal. 3:19; Heb. 2:2; *cf.* Green (1987), p. 118.   [14] Kelly, p. 337.

even angels refuse to slander other angels, Christians should refuse to slander evil angels, which is what the excesses of the false teachers were leading them into. If that is the case, at the very least Peter has altered Jude completely to mean something he did not intend; or possibly he has not grasped Jude's meaning. Bauckham thinks this, and says that 'probably the author of 2 Peter did not know the story, and therefore he misunderstood the point of Jude'.[15] But it is unnecessary to take such an extreme view as to make one part of the New Testament misunderstand another.

Peter certainly makes the same legal point as Jude:[16] *These men are not afraid to slander (blasphēmountes) celestial beings; yet even angels … do not bring slanderous accusations (blasphēmon krisin) against such beings in the presence of the Lord … these men blaspheme (blasphēmountes) in matters they do not understand.* The NIV is helpful here, for although the Greek phrases are similar, the middle one ('bring slanderous accusations') is a legal one meaning 'pass a judgment on the question of slander or blasphemy'. These men may blaspheme, but the angels refrain from making a slanderous accusation. Putting Peter's story alongside Jude's, we see that Peter is making the same points, although he is using other characters more familiar to his readership.

Who are the accused? In Jude it is Moses; in Peter it seems to be the fallen angels being 'held for judgment' (2:4). In both cases the accused are clearly guilty.[17]

Who are the witnesses? In Jude it is Michael, in Peter it seems to be the perfect angels. They are being invited to support a charge against the accused, but they express reluctance to do so.

What are the charges? In both Jude and Peter the accusation is slander. It is easy to imagine the fallen angels slandering God as they plotted their revolt, executed it, and now sit awaiting their final judgment.

What is the lesson? The archangel (Jude) or the perfect angels (Peter) show a marked reluctance to come into *the presence of the Lord* and enforce the demands of the law, even though they (and by implication, their cases) are much *stronger than* the accused. We find out the reason for this only from Jude 9 and his Old Testament control (Zc. 3:2), where Michael realizes that God wants not only to uphold the law but also to extend forgiving grace. Archangels do not have the authority to do away with the law, but Michael knows

---

[15] Bauckham (1983), p. 261.   [16] See comments on Jude 9–10.

[17] Hillyer says, helpfully, that if 'glories' seems too strong a word for fallen angels, 'this is to attach too positive and unsullied a character to "glories", which in today's colloquial terms might be called "leading lights" without any necessary implication of their moral standing' (p. 197).

that God has a higher work than judgment, and so he stands aside. We do not need that final reason to follow Peter's argument here, which is that ultimate judgments in matters of the law can be made only by God.

What is the application? In both letters, Jude and Peter change their words to show that what the false teachers are doing is not precisely the same as what is going on in the heavenly courtroom. Bare-faced *slander* is not the same as legal *slanderous accusations.* Peter is not saying that the false teachers are daring to do what the angels dare not do (*i.e.* slander another angel), and that we should take care to speak respectfully of even fallen angels. Rather, the lesson is that just as the angels know that decisions of the law are not to be made by them but to be handed over to God, even when the case is obvious, so Christians are not to treat God's Old Testament law lightly but to recognize that only God has the power to enforce or alter it. The writer to the Hebrews faced the same problem, for, having taught Christians that Jesus Christ is 'as much superior to the angels as the name he has inherited is superior to theirs', he does not want them to treat the law as less than holy. So he reminds them that 'the message spoken by angels was binding, and every violation and disobedience received its just punishment'.[18]

Although it is difficult to decide on these details, the basic weakness in the false teachers' position is clear. Peter is comparing their brazen egoism with the respect for God's word that the angels demonstrate. Angels are obedient messengers, who do not take it on themselves to alter the message they deliver. Whoever it is whom the angels exceed in strength and power, they refuse to take advantage of that strength to bring slanderous accusations against them. The false teachers, on the other hand, find such humility offensive and inappropriate, and quite possibly they find the very talk of angels a quaint and irrelevant myth in their secular eyes. So they slander such beings. Are they laughingly copying the rebellious angels in their daring defiance, mocking the lack of freedom of the angels who remained obedient? Are they sniggering over the idea that angels brought God's law from heaven to earth? Do they deny that there is a real power of evil who has an authority over those who rebel against God?

Once again, Peter's precise meaning is difficult to grasp, but the two-thousand-year-old prototype is still awesomely relevant. There are still those today who will all too easily discard inconvenient Christian doctrine and ethics in order to make life seemingly more pleasurable and the gospel more attractive (2:2). What could do that

[18] Heb. 1:4; 2:2.

better than dismantling any idea of ultimate personal judgment according to a revealed and fixed set of morals? But in that case Christ no longer rules his world; we do. He no longer rules his church; we do. He no longer even rules our lives; we rule there as well. 'The sensual man is always [self-willed], for in the last analysis self is all that matters to him. His hell is this, that his world contracts until the only thing he has left is the self he has corrupted.'[19]

b. The verdict (2:12a)

Although these people taught impressive, new ideas that held ordinary Christians spellbound by their daring, Peter says that they do not know what they are talking about, for they *blaspheme in matters they do not understand* (*agnoeō*). They are probably claiming some insightful knowledge (*gnōsis*), but they are actually ignorant. What is worse, their empty-headedness is leading them to *blaspheme* (*blasphēmeō*), which is the verb translated 'slander' in 2:10. It is a sobering thought that not only are we not free to make up our own forms of doctrine and ethics, but if we do presume to do so our apparent free thought is actually blasphemy.

Such teaching leads us to be *creatures of instinct*, who are 'primitive'.[20] Although it promises that we will be better, fuller human beings, it actually offers lower, not higher, possibilities, even if they are dressed up in impressive language and ideas. Well-explained rationalism and modern reinterpretations of Christian ethics are an excuse for people to get away with what they want, by following their instinct to sin.

c. The sentence (2:12b–13a)

The NIV has smoothed the Greek here, and made the main two ideas clear. First, these people *are like brute beasts . . . born only to be caught and destroyed*. This figure of speech plays on the idea of what is natural to animals. Like farm animals reared for slaughter, these teachers have ahead of them only judgment and condemnation. Once again, Peter has raised the certainty of future judgment, although his emphasis is still on living beforehand. Is he saying that these people are unwittingly locked into a judgment from which, even if they repented, there would be no redemption? Peter's three examples from the Old Testament would have had little force were it not for the fact that in each case there was open-eyed rebellion against God, and that despite full knowledge

[19] Green (1987), p. 117.   [20] Reicke, p. 167

of the consequences there was no desire to repent at all. As he will go on to say, these people 'have escaped the corruption of the world by knowing our Lord and Saviour Jesus Christ and are again entangled in it and overcome' (2:20). The position Peter is attacking is that adopted by people who know the gospel to be true but have decided that it is preferable to adapt it in order to permit greater freedom.

This leads to Peter's second point: *like beasts they too will perish. They will be paid back with harm for the harm they have done*. The animal inevitably ends up in the abattoir; the trickster inescapably ends up being tricked. Peter indulges in one of his acid puns here; literally, he says something like 'they will be done out of the profits of their wrong-doing' (Moffatt). But it is difficult to reproduce the word *adikoumenoi* ('having been wronged') in English without giving the impression that they suffer an injustice at God's hands, which is not in Peter's mind at all.[21] There is a sickening inevitability about the destiny of the false teachers. In the long run, if they behave like animals they are treated like animals, and if they cheat they will find they have been out-witted.[22]

3. False teachers follow the corrupt desire of the sinful nature (2:13b–16)

> *Their idea of pleasure is to carouse in broad daylight. They are blots and blemishes, revelling in their pleasures while they feast with you. *[14]*With eyes full of adultery, they never stop sinning; they seduce the unstable; they are experts in greed – an accursed brood! *[15]*They have left the straight way and wandered off to follow the way of Balaam son of Beor, who loved the wages of wickedness. *[16]*But he was rebuked for his wrongdoing by a donkey – a beast without speech – who spoke with a man's voice and restrained the prophet's madness.*

Having shown that the errorists 'despise authority', Peter now shows how they 'follow the corrupt desire of the sinful nature' (2:10). He has already begun to do so by warning of their animal instinct, but the time has come for a full-blown denunciation. He first of all indicates what is wrong in the way they are behaving among the Christians, and then gives a further Old Testament example to warn and encourage.

---

[21] Some Greek copyists thought so too, and substituted *komioumenoi*, 'having received'. To see this as a pun means that one does not have to defend an apparent unfairness on God's part, which some more straight-faced commentators try to do.

[22] 2 Sa. 22:26–27.

a. Behaviour (2:13b–14)

Drunkenness in the daytime was a sign of dissipation that brought down the condemnation of all decent people in the ancient world, whether they were Jews, Christians or pagans.[23] Presumably that was why Peter had to work so quickly on the day of Pentecost to stop the rumour that the Christians were drunk.[24] But Peter here seems to have a more serious point in mind. The word translated *pleasure* is *hēdonē*, from which we derive 'hedonism', and it has overtones of self-indulgence and vice. Peter has called the combined message of the apostles and prophets 'a light shining in a dark place, until the day dawns and the morning star rises in your hearts' (1:19), 'day' and 'light' being common biblical metaphors for the gospel and its implications.[25] By contrast, the rebellious angels are held in 'gloomy dungeons' (2:4), and Peter will conclude that 'blackest darkness is reserved' for the false teachers (2:17). He is saying that in the light of the full knowledge of the gospel, these men still engage in deeds that are appropriate to the dark, non-Christian world.[26] Among Christians, with enticing words for new or *unstable* believers, these people revel *in their pleasures while they feast with you.* In the parallel passage in Jude, these people indulge themselves in the *agapē* meal, the Lord's supper. Here in 2 Peter the word is *apatais, pleasures.* It is possible that the problem does not focus on Christian meetings, but it is unlikely that Peter would have deliberately chosen a word so similar to Jude's. It is probably better to see this as another grim pun, for the Lord's supper is turning into a time of sensual indulgence and sexual excess.[27]

God's people are to be 'spotless' (*aspiloi*) and 'blameless' (*amōmētoi*) (3:14),[28] but these people *are blots* (*spiloi*) *and blemishes* (*mōmoi*),[29] 'like the blemishes on an animal not fit for sacrifice (Lev. 1:3) or on a man not fit for priestly service (Lev. 21:21)'.[30] They are tainting and making unsavoury the entire Christian community by their continuing bad behaviour. Now they are not only bringing 'the way of truth into disrepute' (2:2)

---

[23] Is. 5:11; 1 Thes. 5:7. The commentaries offer lists of pagan disapproval of drunkenness.

[24] Acts 2:13–15.

[25] 'Day', *e.g.* 1 Cor. 5:5; 1 Thes. 5:2–4. 'Light', *e.g.* Jn. 1:5–9; Rom. 13:12.

[26] *Cf.* Rom. 13:11–13.

[27] *Cf.* 1 Cor. 11:17–22. These occasions were real meals with proper food and wine, so it would have been possible to be gluttonous and drunk at them.

[28] *Cf.* 1 Pet. 1:19.

[29] The Greek prefix *a-* means the same as our English suffix '-less'.

[30] Bauckham (1983), pp. 265–266.

with non-Christians, they are making the church unsavoury to its Master, and unready for his return (3:14).

What they do is quite out of their control, for they *never stop sinning*. Peter has already told us to make a decisive break with our past and to remember that a Christian 'has been cleansed from his past sins' (1:9). He held up as a frightful example the angels 'when they sinned' (2:4). It is hardly a surprise that sin is out of control in these people's lives. Even so, Peter's language is graphic. He says that they have *eyes full of adultery* (literally, 'full of an adulteress'),[31] as though there is nothing they can see that does not suggest and encourage sin. They carry the problem around with them.

Yet they are culpable for their active recruitment, because they *entice the unstable*. *Entice* translates *deleazō*, a fishing word[32] which describes their careful luring of unwary Christians. If the Christians are unstable, of course, they are asking for trouble, and Peter is again using a word-play to drive the point home to those who first heard the letter read aloud. *Unstable* translates *astēriktous* (here and in 3:16), which is very similar to the words translated 'firmly established' (*estērigmenous*, 1:12) and 'secure position' (*stērigmou*, 3:17).

Peter moves from one sport to another, for these men exercise at their local gym: they are *experts in greed*, and the word behind *expert*, *gymnazō*, produced the modern 'gymnasium'. They have tried a variety of sins and discovered which ones are to their taste and which are not. They have practised how to enjoy their lusts to the limit, and they never know when to stop. This sickening picture is summed up in two words: *accursed brood*, a Hebrew-style phrase which is literally 'children of a curse'.[33] It is the hardest denunciation Peter has used so far, and it paves the way for his final Old Testament character study, Balaam, who was hired to curse Israel.

b. Balaam (2:15–16)

Balaam, the prophet who worked for profit, would have been familiar to Peter's readers. Not only does the Old Testament tell his story at some length,[34] but it repeatedly holds him up as a warning.[35] He also appears here, in Jude, and (much more briefly)

---

[31] *Cf.* Jesus' vivid teaching in Mt. 5:28, and Job's pure decision, 'I have made a covenant with my eyes, not to look lustfully at a girl' (Jb. 31:1).
[32] Also in 2:18 and Jas. 1:14.
[33] For a similar construction see 1 Pet. 1:14; Eph. 2:2, 3; 5:6, 8.
[34] Nu. 22:2 – 24:5; 31:16.
[35] Dt. 23:4; Jos. 13:22; 24:9; Ne. 13:2, 27; Mi. 6:5.

in Revelation as the patron saint of the mysterious Nicolaitan sect.[36] The most famous episode in Balaam's story is the one Peter quotes, where his journey is halted by his more perceptive donkey. That might have inspired Peter's continuing use of the metaphor of the *way* (2:2, 21). They have *left the straight way and wandered off to follow the way of Balaam son of Beor*,[37] *who loved the wages of wickedness*. So what exactly did Balaam do?

i. Balaam loved the wages of wickedness

Peter has already mentioned this motivation, because the phrase 'paid back with harm' (2:13) is the same Greek phrase as *the wages of wickedness* here (*misthos adikias*). The NIV is right to translate it in two quite different ways (as was explained above), but the repetition underlines the facts that Balaam was a man who did what the false teachers are doing, and that they are following him to his (and their) destruction.

Balaam was willing to take money in order to entice God to curse the Israelites.[38] Balak, the king of Moab, at the request of the Midianites, tried to use Balaam's prophetic gift to rain curses on the Israelites, but Balaam could not use his God-given talent to achieve that. Instead, he tells Balak that the Israelites are God's blessed people. Peter is not doing detailed exegesis here, and so the question of Balaam's prophetic gift is not explored. Instead, we are just to notice that Balaam was willing to put his greed above his concern for the Israelites, but that the plan failed because God's purposes are never thwarted. Balaam explained that 'even if Balak gave me his palace filled with silver and gold, I could not ... go beyond the command of the LORD my God.'[39] Yet he still tried. In the same way, Peter's false teachers are putting their greed for the wages of wickedness above their concern for the Christians, for 'in their greed' they 'will exploit you with stories they have made up' (2:3). But they will not always have their way in the church of God.

Balaam also led Israel into idolatry and adultery.[40] Having failed by direct means, he tried indirect ones; and since he could not alter God's view of Israel, he tried to change Israel's view of God. He tempted many of the people down a path of moral and theological

---

[36] 'You have people there who hold to the teaching of Balaam, who taught Balak to entice the Israelites to sin by eating food sacrificed to idols and by committing sexual immorality' (Rev. 2:14). The application is along lines parallel to Peter's.

[37] According to many manuscripts, Peter actually wrote 'son of Bosor'. Although suggestions have been made that 'Bosor' reproduced the guttural Hebrew pronunciation of 'Beor', or that it drew attention to the similarity to the Hebrew word for 'flesh', *bāśār*, the honest answer to the question 'Why Bosor?' is Lenski's: 'Nobody knows.' Lenski, p. 325.

[38] Nu. 22:2–20, 36 – 24:25

[39] Nu. 22:18.   [40] Nu. 31:16.

compromise, and that did indeed incur God's curse on them. Again the parallels are clear. Peter's false teachers are also enticing God's people, the church, down a path of moral and theological compromise, for *with eyes full of adultery, they never stop sinning; they seduce the unstable.*

ii. Balaam was rebuked for his wrongdoing by a donkey
The heart of the Balaam story and the crux of his dilemma was that he knew what God wanted him to do, and yet for reasons of personal profit he was willing to do the opposite. His moment of decision came when an angel blocked his path with a message from God.[41] Balaam was so self-absorbed and unspiritual that he could not see the angel, and spurred the donkey on. But the animal spoke, rebuking his cruelty and spiritual blindness. The Lord then enabled Balaam to see the angel and hear his message. It is a strange story,[42] but we must not cut it out of our Bibles because we find it embarrassing. It is no more 'nonsensical' than any other miraculous occurrence in the Bible might appear to be to a sceptic, even if it does have deliberate overtones of the humorous. Peter uses this story because he has already drawn the parallel between the greed of Balaam and that of his errorists, and now he wants to draw another – they may be stopped in their tracks by someone who (no matter how foolish he or she may feel) points out that they are flying right in the face of God.

In other words, the *donkey* is the ordinary Christian today who tries to restrain the *madness* of the errorists' *wrongdoing.*[43] It is even possible that Peter is making a mildly self-deprecating remark. In order to uncouple themselves from the apostles' teaching, the false teachers say that it was made up. So Peter says, in effect, 'Let me answer you as a man to a man – no, let me answer you as *a donkey ... with a man's voice* – you are wrong.' If Peter is right, the people he is describing will be present in churches all the time, often in positions of leadership. We must not be afraid to confront them, even if at times we feel a bit foolish because they are unable to see what clearly lies ahead of them – the very word of God, carried by one of the 'celestial beings' they affect to despise.

---

[41] Nu. 22:21–35.
[42] It was equally strange to the ancient world which worked with donkeys every day. We must not assume that the original readers were gullible and that we are the first generation with questions. They knew that donkeys do not speak, even better than we do.
[43] It is just possible that these people claimed to be prophets (see above on 2:1), but their trenchant anti-supernaturalism makes it unlikely.

2 Peter 2:10–22, Part II (2:17–22)
9. Profile of a deadly ministry

It is clear by now that Peter is a concerned and angry pastor. He sees young Christians being deliberately muddled on basic issues and so set on a course to lead them away from Christ. While this section is about the false teachers, his target audience is the mature Christians whom he wants to wake up to the danger he sees coming.

1. How to spot the problem (2:17)

Peter's mind has moved on from the deadly ministers to their deadly ministries, and in particular to those whom they aim to influence and how they proceed.

These men are springs without water and mists driven by a storm. Blackest darkness is reserved for them.

Commentators often complain that Peter's 'metaphors are mixed: "the nether gloom of darkness" has not been reserved for "waterless springs and mists".'[1] But a closer reading shows that Peter knows exactly what he is doing in adapting Jude's material for his own train of thought. Jude has a chain of three vivid metaphors, of which the first is: 'They are clouds without rain, blown along by the wind' (Jude 12). Peter, while familiar with Jude, has expanded this one image into two separate metaphors: the first speaks of dryness (*springs without water*) and the second of impotence (*mists driven by a storm*).[2] The third statement, *Blackest darkness is reserved for them*, is a different kind of word picture: blackest darkness is indeed not reserved for dry springs or driven mists (which would make Peter's language very muddled),

---

[1] Sidebottom, p. 116.
[2] Most commentators assume that this is a second example of being waterless, but Peter does not say that.

but for 'these men' (17a) who are causing the havoc.[3] Peter uses his key words, *darkness* and *reserved* (2:4),[4] to make sure that his theory is applied. Structurally, this verse introduces the themes of the next few verses.

2. Dry springs: they have nothing of value to say (2:18)

For they mouth empty, boastful words and, by appealing to the lustful desires of sinful human nature, they entice people who are just escaping from those who live in error.

'Wells without water are a most tragic disappointment to the Eastern traveller',[5] and so are teachers without truth. In the Old Testament, teachers were often compared to thirst-quenching wells.[6] God explained the tragedy of Jeremiah's time thus: 'My people ... have forsaken me, the spring of living water, and have dug their own cisterns, broken cisterns that cannot hold water.'[7] Jesus himself promised that he would quench our spiritual thirst, and then use us to quench that of others.[8]

What, though, if the people who teach us are not full, bubbling fountains of life-giving water? What if they are 'without water' and *empty*? That was the tragedy in Peter's churches. People claiming the right to lead produced *empty, boastful words*. Their experiences and teaching were 'swollen beyond [their] natural size'.[9] Overblown, with exaggerated claims dressed in fancy words, these people were like spiritual puffer fish, inflating themselves to impress and intimidate. When these people operate today, then, we would expect great claims for what God has done and will do through them, and for the remarkable spiritual benefits and freedom that have come from following their simple programme. But, of course, we are disappointed.

We would also expect young Christians to be especially easy prey, and indeed Peter says that *they entice people who are just escaping from those who live in error*.[10] A recent convert from

---

[3] See Bauckham (1983), pp. 271ff. His conclusion that 'it leaves the last clause ... without the special appropriateness it had in Jude' (p. 272) is unnecessary. See below for Peter's link, which is admittedly different from Jude's, but more appropriate for his own readers.

[4] There translated 'gloomy' and 'held'.   [5] Wand, p. 170.

[6] *E.g.* Pr. 10:11; 14:27.   [7] Je. 2:13.   [8] Jn. 4:13–14; 7:37–38.

[9] Bigg, p. 285, translating *hyperonka*, 'empty'.

[10] This sentence is a minefield which the NIV crosses well. Most scholars agree that the verb is in the present ('are fleeing'), rather than the aorist ('have fled') which has occurred in some manuscripts by assimilation to the aorist in 2:20 (and 1:4). This meaning would be appropriate to young Christians. Again, most scholars agree that

idolatrous paganism,[11] then, would find these people waiting to teach them their version of truth. Once again, Peter has used the same fishing imagery as in 2:14b (*deleazō*, there translated 'seduce'), for they are angling for the young Christians. 'Like carnivorous animals that prey on the weakest members of a herd, so the false teachers focus their attention on the weakest converts.'[12]

Their means of trapping the young Christians is enticing, for they speak on those areas of life which the new disciple will find hardest to change. They say that if their way is followed, new Christians need not change at all, and can have the best of both worlds. They appeal *to the lustful desires of the sinful human nature*. Peter has already warned of the attractiveness of this recruiting method; the phrase *lustful desires* translates the same Greek word[13] as the errorists' 'shameful ways' (2:2) and the 'filthy lives' of the people of Sodom (2:7). He has also promised that Christians will 'escape the corruption in the world caused by evil desires' (1:4). The false teachers, on the other hand, tell those who *are just escaping* that they need not leave their *lustful desires*[14] behind them.

Of course, this will not satisfy the deep thirst that only Jesus can quench, but in the meantime it fulfils a basic quest for religion without having to make any serious effort. In fact, if the false teachers are right, Christians can indulge themselves in any way they like.

3. **Driven mists: they are powerless in the face of sin (2:19)**

They promise them freedom, while they themselves are slaves of depravity – for a man is a slave to whatever has mastered him.

Freedom! That was the great catchword. Jesus had promised true freedom,[15] and Paul had taught it,[16] but it was an easily misunderstood position . If I am truly free, does that mean I am free to do as I like? No. 'To be free as a Christian is to be a *slave* like Peter (1:1), not of *corruption* (v. 20, cf. v. 12) but of the *Master* who paid the price of his own life in order to free humans to be holy.'[17] The ultimate destiny of Christians is no longer controlled by sin, because they face Christ as Saviour as well as Judge; but that does

---

we should read the rare word *ologōs*, 'just', rather than the more common *ontōs*, 'really' (as AV). The discrepancy probably occurred because in Greek capitals the two words are almost identical and a scribe would guess that the more common word was right. But the 'just' reading again fits the context of young Christians.

[11] *Planē* ('error') has this overtone in Rom. 1:27; Tit. 3:3.

[12] Kistemaker, p. 308, changing the imagery.   [13] *Aselgeia*.

[14] 'Evil desires' (1:4) and 'lustful desires' here translate the same Greek word, *epithymia*.

[15] Jn. 8:32.   [16] Gal. 5:1-7.

[17] Elliott, p. 151. See Rom. 6:16; 1 Cor. 6:12.

not mean they are free from the rule of God's law. As Peter wrote in his first letter, 'Live as free men, but do not use your freedom as a cover-up for evil.'[18]

The false teachers have abandoned this, of course, because they have turned their backs on God's 'promise' to come as Saviour and Judge (3:4, 9). So they are free to set up their own stall, and *promise them* (the new Christians) *freedom* – their own brand, naturally. They promise freedom in the future and freedom in the present, because 'freedom from moral constraint is a consequence of freedom from fear of judgment'.[19] It would sound very attractive, and there are sufficient verbal echoes of 1:3–4 here to make it possible that they are deliberately echoing the true promises of the gospel[20] by hijacking the current Christian evangelistic jargon and turning it on its head. Alexander Nisbet, obviously a wise old pastor who had encountered this problem many times, says, 'They that do most hurt to the souls of the Lord's people by venting most dangerous errors among them make often times the fairest promises of doing most good to them.'[21] We must beware of people whose promises differ from God's.

Their message is worse than useless. They themselves are 'mists' (17), an unusual word that means 'the haze which is left after the condensation of clouds into rain'.[22] Peter moves on from his point about the false teachers' dryness, and describes them as 'driven by a storm'. Peter encountered storms on the sea of Galilee,[23] and knew the powerlessness the crew of a small boat feel in the face of such strong gales. The false teachers are equally out of control; ironically, although they *promise ... freedom*, they are themselves *slaves of depravity*. The word translated *depravity* (*phthora*) is the word Peter has used in 1:4 ('corruption') and 2:12 ('destroyed'), and here too we should sense the overtones of both corruption and destruction. The irony is that while they claim to be cut free from a future judgment, and teach new Christians to follow them, they are shackled to the destructiveness of sin both now and in the destiny to which sin leads. Peter, like Paul, holds out the possibility of incorruption[24] and salvation, but that means submitting to our Master.

Peter's lucid and penetrating analysis of these people concludes with a common pithy proverb that Jesus knew[25] and Paul used.[26] No-one is without a master, and if the false teachers do not serve

---

18 1Pet. 2:16.   19 Bauckham (1983), p. 275.
20 Bauckham (1983) has a full and very perceptive list, pp. 276–277.
21 Nisbet, p. 267.   22 Kelly, p. 345.
23 Mk. 4:27 and Lk. 8:23 use the same word for 'storm', *lailapos*.
24 1 Pet. 1:4, 23; 1 Cor. 15:42, 50; Eph. 6:24; 2 Tim. 1:10.   25 Jn. 8:34.
26 Rom. 6:16.

Christ as his slaves, then, by definition, they serve sin and its master. Peter's words, *a man is a slave to whatever has mastered him*, refer to the military custom of taking the defeated enemy in chains as slaves of the victorious army. These *boastful, lustful* popular teachers are the captured cat's-paws of the rebels who are themselves, in time, bound to submit to Christ.

Pause for thought

Unpleasant though it may be, we ought at this stage to pause and review the poisonous strategy that will be eating away at churches even now, if Peter is right. The target group will be gullible Christians, who are either so new or so untaught as to be 'unstable' (2:14). The offer will be of true freedom, perhaps carrying the implication that the New Testament message that converted them did not truly liberate them. That freedom will operate in two areas: freedom to think their own thoughts, so they need not submit to the authority of the apostles and their promise of the return of Christ; and freedom for self-expression, because everything – including *the lustful desires of sinful human nature* – is to be affirmed. The whole package will be wrapped in *empty, boastful words*. This probably means that although it will sound attractive, closer examination will reveal a gap between (on the one hand) what these people claim publicly for their relationship with God, and (on the other) their private self-indulgence. A non-judgmental ethic and an open-ended theology will be on offer to immature Christians, who do not know enough to refuse it and cannot see the selfishness masquerading as spirituality. It is sharply contemporary.

4. Darkness is reserved: they are destined for judgment (2:20-22)

We saw that Peter's three Old Testament examples (the fallen angels, the flooded world, and the filthy cities of Sodom and Gomorrah) share two main characteristics – lawlessness and licentiousness. These characteristics are shared too by the false teachers. It is inevitable, therefore, that they share the same destiny. Until that day of judgment, though, Peter wants the Christians to know that however strong and persuasive these people may be, they share the fate of the fallen angels (2:4), for 'blackest darkness is reserved for them' (2:17). His concern is not yet with their final judgment,[27] which is why what is reserved for them is the rebellious

---

[27] Failure to notice this leads many commentators to miss the connection between the end of verse 17 and verses 20–22; these verses describe the errorists' *present* status, not their *future* one.

angels' temporary cell. Although the verdict has been announced, the sentence (described in chapter 3) is not yet operative.

If they have escaped the corruption of the world by knowing our Lord and Saviour Jesus Christ and are again entangled in it and overcome, they are worse off at the end than they were at the beginning. ²¹*It would have been better for them not to have known the way of righteousness, than to have known it and then to turn their backs on the sacred command that was passed on to them.* ²²*Of them the proverbs are true: 'A dog returns to its vomit,' and, 'A sow that is washed goes back to her wallowing in the mud.'*

The false teachers are at the moment *entangled* in the nets of *the corruption of the world* ('slaves of depravity', 19) and *overcome* ('mastered', 19) by it. The word-picture is of a gladiator caught in the thrown net of his opponent, or, more appropriately, of a hunted animal caught in the trap of the hunter. This had not always been the case, for those in such present peril had given good evidence in the past of having been fully committed followers of Christ. Peter says that *they*²⁸ *have escaped the corruption of the world by knowing our Lord and Saviour Jesus Christ* and *have known the way of righteousness.* These verses have caused great anxiety and discussion over whether it is possible to be saved but then to lose salvation. Worried Christians wonder whether they are Christians at all. Confident Christians count raised hands at evangelistic meetings as denoting new believers, and then wonder why so many fall away. Because it would be unwise to take Peter's few words as representing the whole of New Testament thought, we need to take a broader view.

First, *the salvation Christ has won is full, final and free.* The cross is God's ultimate solution which has paid the price of sin once and for all, and its benefits are available to all who believe.²⁹ We must rest on Jesus' foundation promise that 'I give them eternal life, and they shall never perish; no-one can snatch them out of my hand'.³⁰ The false teachers Peter describes would find the terms and exclusivity of Jesus a major stumbling-block.

Secondly, *there will always be non-Christians in the church.* Jesus warned us of that in the parable of the wheat and the weeds, and warned us not to take upon ourselves the task of judging who are rightly his.³¹ The experience of the New Testament churches

²⁸ Kelly (pp. 347–348) is almost alone among modern commentators in arguing that 'they' are the new Christians in peril. Although the Greek is ambiguous, understanding 'they' as the false teachers makes much better sense. Blum (p. 282) gives a succinct analysis.
²⁹ Rom. 3:21–26.
³⁰ Jn. 10:28.　³¹ Mt. 13:24–30, 36–43.

confirmed that: they were always a mixed bag.[32]

Thirdly, *from the outside it is extraordinarily difficult to tell a real from a fake Christian.* Who would have thought that Judas, one of the twelve and presumably a member of the teaching and healing expeditions, was 'a devil'?[33] Jesus had taught them: 'Many will say to me on that day, "Lord, Lord, did we not prophesy in your name, and in your name drive out demons and perform many miracles?" Then I will tell them plainly, "I never knew you. Away from me, you evildoers!"'[34] Only Jesus will be able to judge our hearts.

Fourthly, *in cases where there is blatant disobedience, the church leadership has the responsibility to discipline.* While it is often beyond us to decide whether someone who professes faith is genuinely a Christian, there will be notorious cases where either words or actions are at such a distance from the Bible's requirements that the local church leadership has to act for the good of that person and the good of the church.[35] The aim is a restored Christian fellowship, not an illusory 'pure' church, which will come only when Jesus transforms us to be like him.[36]

Fifthly, *the acid test is whether we are merely hearers of God's words or doers as well.* Of course, we all sin and so there will frequently be times when God's Word rebukes us (that is partly what it is there for).[37] But that attitude is a long way from the one that refuses to acknowledge that Jesus has any rights over us as our Lord and Master, and sees his words as merely an opinion. 'Why do you call me, "Lord, Lord," and do not do what I say?'[38] asked Jesus. These are those who profess faith in and obedience to Christ, but have no performance to back it up. If those two elements are separated, we have the condition known as 'apostasy', in which people heard the gospel and seemingly accepted it, but made no growth, and then turned their backs on it. Hebrews[39] tells us that there is no 'second gospel' for such people, who have rejected the first.

Finally, *some measure of self-examination in spiritual growth is always healthy.* If we are concerned about our sin and ask Jesus Christ to forgive us and equip us to serve him again, then all is well. Jesus' promise of eternal life and eternal protection stands for us. If, however, we notice a dullness to sin, a reluctance to confess, and a stubborn refusal to bow the knee to Christ, then we should be alarmed, because that is the classic diagnosis of unbelief. We should

---

[32] *E.g.* 2 Cor. 13:5; 2 Tim. 2:17–19; 1 Jn. 2:19.
[33] Jn. 6:70. [34] Mt. 7:22–23.
[35] Mt. 18:15–17; Lk. 17:3; 1 Cor. 5:1–5; Gal. 6:1–2; 2 Thes. 3:6–15.
[36] Rev. 21:1–27. [37] 2 Tim. 3:16. [38] Lk. 6:46. [39] Heb. 6:4–6; 10:26.

stir ourselves to turn to Christ, expose our sin to his penetrating but forgiving eyes, and be welcomed home. If the thought of that does not make us run to him, and that is our considered and consistent will over a period of time and a number of areas, then the result of our self-examination will be that we are not believers at all, and we probably find the gospel a dull irrelevance and constriction. That is why wilful refusal to accept what is known to be true is so serious a sin, and in its most vivid encounter with Jesus he says that such a person 'blasphemes against the Holy Spirit'.[40] That person cannot be forgiven, because he or she refuses to recognize the one who can forgive.

We are now in a stronger position to look at the false teachers and learn from their error. Peter does not shrink from describing them as publicly confessing Christ. They knew[41] our Lord and Saviour Jesus Christ – but did they know him as Lord and Saviour in the way a Christian does? It seems unlikely. To know Christ as Lord means *to have known the way of righteousness*.[42] That is the standard he requires – but that is precisely the standard they reject. And to know Christ as Saviour means to 'look forward to the day of God and speed its coming' (3:12), but that is the very day they refuse to believe in, 'scoffing and following their own evil desires' (3:3).

Whatever their public confession had been, currently they demonstrate a public rejection of Christ as they *turn their backs on the sacred command that was passed on to them*. Their condition is grave, for what they reject is the *command*. This word, in the singular, was standard Christian shorthand for the entire message, Old Testament, New, or both (3:2).[43] The command was from God, which is why it is *sacred*, and it was *passed on to them* with the unique authority of the apostles.[44] Yet although they have known God's gospel, they now spurn it as a pathetic joke.

Peter's final words on these men are two proverbs,[45] which, in a rough-hewn way, describe the choice they have made. A *sow* was a ritually unclean animal in the Old Testament, and a *dog* was a

[40] Mk. 3:29.
[41] *Epignōsis*, the word for 'knowledge' in 1:1; see the discussion there. It would be a linguistic error to assume that what it means in 1:1 it necessarily means here, because every word has a field of meanings, and precise meaning is determined by context. Whatever it means in 1:1 it *cannot* mean 'saving knowledge' here.
[42] *Cf.* Mt. 21:32.   [43] *Cf.* Rom. 7:12; 1 Tim. 6:14; Heb. 7:18; 1 Jn. 2:7.
[44] *Paradidōmi* has a technical force; see Lk. 1:2; 1 Cor. 11:2, 23; 15:1–3; 2 Thes. 3:6; Jude 3.
[45] The first is biblical (Pr. 26:11), the second a common one of the time. See Bauckham (1983), p. 279.

repulsive scavenger.[46] Coupled together by Jesus, they came to describe those who reject the gospel.[47] The scavenging dog eating its own *vomit* and the sow *wallowing in* its own *mud* are both revolting pictures of 'brute beasts, creatures of instinct' (2:12), and they vividly describe the false teachers. After an initial display of repentance and reformation, they show that nothing in their nature has changed at all, which is the last proof that these people never were Christians.[48] Whatever they vomited up from the inside or washed off from the outside, nothing has fundamentally changed.[49]

This whole section from 2:10 has been full of strong language, and talk of vomit and mud[50] is merely the last and strongest. In our sanitized society, we might view such terms as bad taste. But we must not be too fastidious about describing the utter corruption of sin as it really is. 'Sin ought to be represented by the Lord's ministers in its abominable vileness, especially when men labour to palliate its filthy practices with fair pretences.'[51] If such ideas still strike us as strong, then it indicates how lightly we take the most important and ghastly division in eternity. The horrific picture that these people are *worse off at the end than they were at the beginning* echoes Jesus' tale of the fate of the demon-possessed man who was exorcised of one demon but ended up with seven, and so 'the final condition of that man is worse than the first'.[52] Peter does not spell out how they are worse off. Perhaps he means that their sin is more serious, their hearts more hardened, their minds more cynical or their slavery to self more intense. But that is the condition of those who are put in 'gloomy dungeons' (2:3) awaiting judgment. Now we have to await the Judge.

[46] Pigs: Lv. 11:7, *etc.* Dogs: *e.g.* 1 Ki. 21:19.   [47] Mt. 7:6; Phil. 3:2; Rev. 22:15.

[48] Plumptre's statement (p. 189), 'the old nature has returned in both cases', has missed the point; the old nature never went away.

[49] Any link with baptism here is a 'happy coincidence'; Bauckham (1983), p. 280. Nothing corresponds in Christian liturgy to the canine emetic!

[50] The word used for the filth at the bottom of Jeremiah's cistern-cum-cell in Je. 38:6, LXX.

[51] Nisbet, p. 272.

[52] Mt. 12:45. In its original setting it warns the Jewish leadership that if they reject the wrath of Jesus they will end up with someone far worse: the Romans.

2 Peter 3:1–2
10. Have you forgotten anything?

Dear friends, this is now my second letter to you. I have written both of them as reminders to stimulate you to wholesome thinking. [2]I want you to recall the words spoken in the past by the holy prophets and the command given by our Lord and Saviour through your apostles.

A good teacher repeats the lesson until the class has learned it, and Peter again goes over ground that he has covered in 1:16–21. This indicates a new direction in the letter, and we are meant to recall what he has said earlier in order to prepare ourselves for the next topic.

This section starts with a sudden jolt as Peter turns from the false teachers to the Christians. The phrase *Dear friends* marks a clear transition point in the argument.[1] But the break between the two chapters is a deep one, and causes many readers difficulties with Peter's logic. For some, 2:4–22 is a digression where Peter quotes and adapts Jude, and now he returns to his main thesis.[2] For others, this is the start of a whole new letter which later editors attached to the first part.[3] Others again see the break as a reminder to the readers that the letter is not really by Peter.[4] But these solutions are too savage.

---

[1] As it does in 1 Pet. 2:11; 4:12.

[2] *E.g.* Kelly, for whom most of chapter 2 is a 'long tirade' (p. 352). But would a writer have wasted valuable parchment on what was not his 'principal theme'? See Appendix.

[3] M. McNamara, 'The Unity of Second Peter: A Reconsideration', *Scripture* 12 (1960), pp. 13–19.

[4] *E.g.* Bauckham (1983): 'These verses . . . are doubtless intended to reestablish in the readers' minds the fact that it is Peter's testament they are reading, after a long section in which this has not been evident' (p. 282). But if the testamentary style was as well known and recognizable as Bauckham claims, would his readers really have forgotten it in half a chapter?

1. The connection with 2 Peter 2

The obvious connection with the end of chapter 2 is the word *command*. The contrast is between the false teachers, who 'turn their backs on the sacred command that was passed on to them' (2:21), and the Christians, who should *recall . . . the command given by our Lord and Saviour through your apostles* (3:2). The phrase *Lord and Saviour* has occurred only a few verses before too, in 2:20. Is Peter hinting that the false teachers have separated these two, and he wants the Christians to keep them together?

The contrast takes further shape as Peter turns from the 'dog' and 'sow' of 2:22 to the *dear friends* of 3:1. This is the first of four times Peter uses the word *agapētoi* in this chapter (the others are in 3:8, 14, 17). The word comes from *agapē*, love. While Peter is repelled by the false teachers, he sees a deep tie between himself and those to whom he is writing; perhaps they needed that assurance after the colourful language of chapter 2! Each time he uses the phrase *dear friends* in this chapter, he is increasingly wooing his readers away from friendship with the false teachers into a deeper love for God and his gospel.

2. The connection with 2 Peter 1

The links with chapter 2 are merely stylistic compared to the obvious break in thought. Much more impressive are the links back to the end of chapter 1. First, there is the now familiar coupling of the *apostles* and the *prophets*, echoing their authority in 1:16–21. Secondly, there is his writing *reminders to stimulate you*, the same Greek phrase which is translated *refresh your memory* in 1:13. So his aim is still the same. He is worried that the Christians are going to wander from what the prophets and apostles have taught them, and he is going to remind them this time by attacking the false teachers' doctrine directly.[5]

3. The connection with the past

This is evidently something he has had to do before, since this is his *second letter* to them on the subject. The obvious candidate for the first letter is 1 Peter, but various objections to that have been raised. The readership is said to be different, for 1 Peter had a wide readership in Asia Minor (1 Pet. 1:1–2), but 2 Peter a narrower one tied to the areas where Peter had actually ministered (1:12–15).

---

[5] Plumptre (p. 189) wants to make the false teachers and the mockers two groups, but this is unnecessary.

1 Peter has a different theological content from 2 Peter, and so it is difficult to see how the latter can be a *reminder* of the former. Those who claim that 2 Peter is not by Peter at all say, therefore, that this phrase is a deliberate literary device to tie the two letters together.[6] All these arguments have opponents,[7] but the likelihood is that here Peter is referring to an earlier letter which was subsequently disregarded because of this letter's fuller statement on the subject. Lost letters by apostles are not unknown.[8] It might seem unnecessary to posit one more letter, and Kelly calls it a 'desperate expedient'.[9] But there is the tantalizing possibility that if Peter is a redrafting of Jude for a more Gentile readership, then the earlier letter might have been a copy of Jude with a brief covering note from Peter.

4. The connections

What these verses confirm is that Peter is still concerned with the issue of right belief leading to right behaviour. The end result of his reminders, he hopes, will be *wholesome thinking*[10] among his readership, so that they will be fruitful and productive in their 'knowledge of our Lord Jesus Christ' (1:8). That contrasts with the 'dry springs' and 'driven mists' who are currently challenging Peter for the right to teach (*cf.* 2:17). The word translated *wholesome* (*eilikrinēs*) means 'that which will bear the full test of being examined by sunlight, and so it carries with it the sense of *transparent* sincerity'.[11] This certainly contrasts with the repulsive behaviour of the false teachers at the end of chapter 2.

These verses also confirm the continuing authority of Peter's witnesses. Not content with saying that the prophets were 'carried along by the Holy Spirit' (1:21), he now says that they are *holy prophets*, a standard phrase to show his reverence for them – reverence that the Christians should share.[12] Partnering them are *your apostles*, which to many sounds an odd phrase if Peter is the writer. Kelly says that it 'inadvertently betrays that the writer belongs to an age when the apostles have been elevated to a venerated group who mediate Christ's teaching to the whole church'.[13] But as Blum says, it is difficult to imagine what Peter could have said here that would

---

[6] Watson, p. 124.
[7] Most notably Boobyer, for whom 2 Peter is pseudepigraphic but deeply influenced by 1 Peter. Kelly (p. 353) sees broad layers of overlap.
[8] *E.g.* 1 Cor. 5:9; Col. 4:16. [9] Kelly, p. 352.
[10] Peter uses the same word in 1 Pet. 1:13, 'prepare your minds for action'.
[11] Plumptre, p. 189.
[12] Peter calls them 'holy prophets' in a speech in Acts 3:21. *Cf.* Lk. 1:70.
[13] Kelly, p. 354.

not be open to that criticism, for 'if Peter had written "my command" or "from us", the same objection would be raised'.[14] That the apostles often had to battle to be recognized is evident not just from this letter but from the very earliest one which the New Testament preserves – Galatians. In both letters there is a call to recognize apostolic authority over the church. Perhaps the word *your* here is a simple call to loyalty away from the interloping false teachers who have no similar right to be heard.

In particular, Peter is reminding his readers of the *words* and *command* which come from these two groups. Just as the prophets 'spoke from God as they were carried along by the Holy Spirit' (1:21), so now there is a *command given by our Lord and Saviour through your apostles.* The urgency comes from Peter's concern at the cavalier attitude the false teachers are adopting to basic Christian doctrines. Throughout this chapter, the false teachers are questioning the *words spoken in the past*, so Peter talks about creation, flood and future judgment all being dependent on 'the same word' (3:5–7). The future promises of God emerge in verses 8–13, where Peter says that God 'is not slow in keeping his promise', and 'in keeping with his promise we are looking for a new ... home of righteousness' (3:9, 13). Verses 14–16 put the writings of an apostle in the same bracket as Old Testament 'Scriptures' (3:16), and verses 17–18 conclude, again, with the balance between what we believe and how we behave. If the theme of chapter 2 was 'the power of God to judge and save (despite appearances to the contrary)', the theme of chapter 3 will be 'the promise of God to come (despite appearances to the contrary)'. The connections between the two chapters form an overall structure for the letter.

[14] Blum, p. 284.

2 Peter 3:3–7
11. God's powerful Word

Peter now has to face the key question of his letter. Was Jesus wrong to promise that he would return in power? May not the false teachers have a point when they argue that the long delay they have experienced effectively invalidates the promise? The issue is all the sharper after two thousand years. Questions about whether Jesus will return, the manner of his return and why he has not returned have grown in relevance. If he is not going to return physically, then 'it would be stupid to wait – the promises are false',[1] and we can give ourselves over to the enjoyable self-centredness of the people Peter is attacking. How can Peter argue that they are wrong and he is right? How can he justify the continuing embarrassing wait for Jesus?

1. Scoffers will come (3:3)

First of all, you must understand that in the last days scoffers will come, scoffing and following their own evil desires.

When Peter says *First of all*, our tidy minds assume that further on he will have a second item for us to understand. But that would be to misunderstand him. It is helpful to look at 1:20, where he uses the same phrase, there translated 'Above all'. He means he is about to say something of overwheming importance.[2] Continuing his programme of writing 'reminders to ... wholesome teaching' (3:2), he now writes about something we *must understand*, namely that the danger he has warned of is already a living presence in the church.

Peter says that *in the last days* false teachers *will come*. It looks initially as if Peter is talking about the distant future, and some have

---

[1] Spicq, p. 247.
[2] *Prōton*: 'In the first place, above all, especially'. BAGD, p. 726.

even said he is prophesying.[3] But the present tense in verse 5 ('they
... forget') makes it clear that the problem has already infected the
church. Some of those convinced that Peter did not write this letter
call this 'a little unfortunate'[4] stylistic slip; the writer has 'forgotten'
that he is writing as Peter and starts to use the present tense. But
those who hold that position do not notice that the same shift
between future and present tenses took place in 2:1, at a similar
point in an argument (a shift which is masked in the NIV). It is
probable that this is a literary device to underline a warning that is
already being ignored, rather than a mere slip of the pen.[5]

Peter assumes that he is writing in the last days, and that the
existence of the scoffers who mock the idea proves him right. *The
last days* is standard New Testament shorthand for the period
between the first and second comings of Jesus Christ,[6] the period
that, as Peter himself had said, began on the day of Pentecost. 'This
is what was spoken by the prophet Joel: "In the last days, God says,
I will pour out my Spirit on all people." '[7] The last days are not a
date in the future whose arrival will be heralded by the sudden
appearance of *scoffers*. They are today, the church age, the gospel
age, which will always be marked by the presence of scoffers.

When the Old Testament prophets foresaw this age, they said
that it would be accompanied by scoffing and disbelief. Daniel saw
opposition to God taking the form of a ruler who 'will speak against
the Most High and oppress his saints and try to change the set times
and the laws'.[8] This period's hallmark would be a smiling disregard
of God's Word. Peter, with other New Testament writers, says that
those days are now upon us.[9] In a Hebraic phrase, he writes that
scoffers will come, scoffing. But he warns that we must not be taken
in by their high-sounding doubts and cynicism, for they are *following* only *their own evil desires*. That is, they have their own wants
and pleasures, and they justify indulging those desires by raising
queries about those points of theology which condemn them. These
are the people Peter has already described as 'experts in greed',
'mists driven by a storm', 'slaves of depravity' (2:14, 17, 19).
Although these people may present themselves as sophisticated and
knowledgeable, having delicate qualms and posing courageous
questions about the more difficult elements of Christian teaching,
they are in reality driven by their greed and disobedience. It is sin,
not sophistication, which is in the driving-seat, and the false

---

[3] *E.g.* Lenski, p. 338.   [4] Wand, p. 176.
[5] Bauckham (1983) sees it as a stylistic device attached to a testament (p. 288).
Watson, although he is convinced that 2 Peter is a testament, sees the change in tense
as a rhetorical device unconnected to claims to authorship (p. 127).
[6] *E.g.* 2 Tim. 3:1; Heb. 1:2; Jas. 5:3.   [7] Acts 2:16–17.   [8] Dn. 7:25; 11:36–39.
[9] Mt. 24:3–5; Acts 20:29–31; 1 Tim. 4:1; 2 Tim. 3:1–7.

teachers are merely *following*. How do they get away with this extraordinary bluff?

2. Their question and the reason (3:4)

Peter says these people pose a question and then give a thoughtful reason for their question. He responds first to that underlying reason for their question, and then answers the question itself. The question (which he will answer in 3:8–10) is, *Where is this 'coming' he promised?* But the underlying reason is a 'sneering scepticism'[10] which attacks the base of Christian thinking.

> *They will say, 'Where is this "coming" he promised? Ever since our fathers died, everything goes on as it has since the beginning of creation.'*

The question has to do with Christ's coming or *parousia* (see above on 1:16). We know that from the earliest days some Christians found the delay of Jesus Christ's return a problem; Paul had to address the issue in Thessalonica and Corinth.[11] So the fact that its readers are having problems over God's apparent slowness is not necessarily proof that 2 Peter is late. Many centuries before this, Jeremiah had to handle the same issue: 'They keep saying to me, "Where is the word of the LORD? Let it now be fulfilled!"'[12] No doubt the bluntness of Jesus' promises to return had caused some dismay, but only among those who took Jesus to mean that he expected something to happen which did not subsequently occur.[13] Peter's concern here is not the puzzlement of anxious disciples, but the long line of those who have questioned God's ability and willingness to intervene in and judge his world. Their questioning had undoubtedly been sharpened by thinking that the events which surrounded Jesus' life were not all that were to be expected from the visit of God to his people.[14]

That is a perfectly fair question on the surface. But their underlying reason for asking it (which Peter tackles first) shows that they are biblically illiterate. *Ever since our fathers died, everything goes*

---

[10] Kelly, p. 360.   [11] 1 Cor. 15:23; 1 Thes. 2:19; 3:13; 4:15.

[12] Je. 17:15. For similar mocking questions, see Is. 5:19; Ezk. 12:22; Mal. 2:17.

[13] See, helpfully, R. T. France, *Matthew*, Tyndale New Testament Commentary (Leicester: IVP; Grand Rapids: Eerdmans, 1985), pp. 332ff., on the difficulties in Jesus' words towards the end of his life; and B. Witherington, *Jesus, Paul and the End of the World* (Exeter: Paternoster, 1992).

[14] Although it has long been the majority view of scholars that Jesus expected God's reign to break in decisively in his lifetime, and that the later church had to reinterpret those texts, that viewpoint is being radically re-examined. See especially Witherington, *op. cit.*

on as it has since the beginning of creation. Those who regard this letter as late say that the *fathers* here are the first generation of Christians who, it was thought, should not have died, or should have been raised, if the gospel is true.[15] But 'the fathers' is a standard New Testament way of referring to the Old Testament believers. As Hebrews 1:1–2 says, using the same Greek word, 'In the past God spoke to our forefathers through the prophets ... but in these last days he has spoken to us by his Son.'[16] In other words, these people are saying that Jesus Christ has changed nothing; things are just the same as in Old Testament days when *our fathers died.* Going further back, even the Old Testament has not changed anything, because one state of affairs has been in place *since the beginning of creation.* Our world, they would say, is a closed system which has no room for the intervention of God, and any such idea is 'no more than a vulgar myth'.[17] Peter's three biblical examples will show that God stepped in once to create the world, and a second time to flood it; nothing stops him stepping in a third time to judge.

3. The flaw in the reason: God's powerful word (3:5–7)

The flaw in their reasoning is that they have ignored the fact that God relates to his world by means of his *word.*[18] Peter takes three biblical examples to show how vital this is. This is not a new line of argument for Peter, for the false teachers' attack on the integrity of God's word is the reason he has raised and defended the pairing of apostles and prophets. As in 2:4–9, his examples are arranged chronologically.

a. The creation (3:5)

But they deliberately forget that long ago by God's word the heavens existed and the earth was formed out of water and by water.

The first example is where the Bible itself starts, at the creation of the universe. The way God creates is by speaking: 'And God said,

---

[15] *E.g.* Kelly, p. 356. Surprisingly, Lenski, p. 340, goes for this interpretation, although he says Peter is the writer.

[16] See also Peter's speech in Acts 3:13 and Jn. 6:31 (translated 'forefathers'); Rom. 9:5 (translated 'patriarchs').

[17] Elliott, p. 153.

[18] Green (1987) heads these sections, 'Peter argues from history' (5–7), '... from Scripture' (8), '... from the character of God' (9), and '... from the promise of Christ' (10), pp. 140–152. That is neat, but distracts from the central point, which is that Peter argues from Scripture throughout this part of the letter because that is both what his opponents deny and what proves their error.

"Let there be light," and there was light.'[19] Peter is saying that the very continuing existence of our world argues for the dependability of God's word; it is *by God's word* that we exist.[20] Peter is arguing closely from within the Genesis account, where the creation of the *heavens* precedes that of the *earth*. This probably explains his puzzling phrase *the earth was formed out of water and by water*. Commentators differ over the precise nuances of *out of* and *by*, and what influenced Peter's language here. But it is probably sufficient to see the former phrase as a reference to Genesis 1:9: 'And God said, "Let the water . . . be gathered to one place, and let dry ground appear,"' and the latter as a reference to Genesis 1:6: 'And God said, "Let there be an expanse between the waters to separate water from water.'

Peter's finer details may be opaque,[21] but his teaching is clearly that God's means of creation was his word, that his agent of creation was the water, and that the result of his creation was the heavens and the earth. The significance of these three emerges only in the next two examples, but the error of the false teachers is once again evident in that *they deliberately forget* these elementary lessons. We are becoming familiar with Peter's emerging accusation that they are wilfully forgetful (1:9), and he has indicated that he has the task of reminding dangerously forgetful Christians of the truth (1:12–15; 3:1–2). The effort the false teachers make to ensure that they deliberately forget should be surpassed by the effort the Christians make to remember, knowing that they *must understand*.

b. The flood (3:6)

In the Genesis story, the disobedience of Adam and Eve in the garden reaches its climax in the wide-ranging disobedience of mankind at the time of Noah. The water which was the agent of God's creative word now becomes the agent of his judicial word. Peter contradicts the false teachers by this example; everything does *not* go on as it has since the beginning of creation.

> *By these waters also the world of that time was deluged and destroyed.*

All the Bible versions have to make a decision at the beginning of this section. Peter says literally, '. . . by means of which the world of that time . . .' What does 'which' refer to? The word in the Greek is in the plural. An accurate translation therefore looks for something

---

[19] Gn. 1:3; *cf.* 1:6, 9, 11, 14, 20, 24, 26.   [20] See Ps. 33:6; Heb. 11:3.
[21] See Bauckham (1983), p. 298, for a survey of the bewildering range of options for translators.

plural in the previous half-sentence. There are broadly two options. The first is that Peter is referring to the water, which he mentions twice and so can be plural. This is the option the NIV takes (*these waters*). This does link the first two examples (creation and flood) neatly, but it means that there is no one factor common to all three biblical examples.[22]

The second option is that Peter is referring to the water and the word. Blum is among those who commend this translation, saying that 'probably both water and the word are to be understood as the agents for destroying the former world ... as the word and fire will be destructive agents in the future'.[23] This line tidily makes God's word common to all three examples, and God's word also happens to be the major theme of this part of the letter. This interpretation produces the translation, 'By the water and the word also the world of that time was deluged and destroyed.' Peter has already used the flood as a warning of future judgment (2:5), but now he makes an explicit link between the cataclysmic[24] destiny of the people of Noah's day and that of the false teachers. Both head towards destruction (2:1).[25]

This second example – the flood – teaches that if God's creative word is utterly stable and immovable, so is his judicial word. The false teachers argue from the stability of the created order, but, as Scripture shows, that is no bar to God intervening and judging. God is not bound by what we call 'the fixed laws of nature'.

c. The delay (3:7)

Peter is being very careful in his choice of words. God created the *heavens and earth* (*earth* translates the word *gē*), and the earth has remained fixed and stable. What was destroyed at the flood was the human 'world' ('world' in 2:5 translates the word *kosmos*). What lies in the future, though, is the fate of the whole creation, *heavens and earth* (*gē*).[26] Although the flood was an advance warning of what will happen, it was a picture painted on a very small canvas compared to what God has in store.

By the same word the present heavens and earth are reserved for

---

[22] This same criticism applies to taking 'which' to refer the water and the heavens, or indeed just the heavens.

[23] Blum. p. 285.

[24] *Deluged* translates *kataklystheis*. The related noun is *kataklysmos*, which LXX uses throughout the flood narrative.

[25] God's patience is also the theme of Peter's use of Noah in 1 Pet. 3:20.

[26] The NIV meticulously observes this distinction: *kosmos* is always 'world' (1:4; 2:5, 20; 3:6), *gē* is always 'earth' (3:5, 7, 10, 13).

fire, being kept for the day of judgment and destruction of ungodly men.

Again it is *the same word* that Peter is defending, and this time he is saying that the fact that we do not see God actively judging his world is not a sign of his weakness. He is absolutely in control, and his powerful word is being exercised in that creation is *reserved* and *being kept for* its final *judgment.*[27] Then the *present heavens and earth* will be replaced by 'a new heaven and a new earth' (3:13).[28]

In the midst of this wonderful but awful truth, we notice that Peter has changed his imagery from flood to *fire.* Some say he does this under the influence of non-Christian thinking,[29] but that is to miss the biblical controls where fire appears as God's agent of destruction (especially 2:6).[30] Jesus himself said that the flood forewarned of a judgment ending in fire.[31] Even when we remove from our minds the crude cartoons of some medieval artists, and even when we admit that this is imagery which is also drawn as banishment, darkness and punishment,[32] we dare not remove from our Christian thinking what it is that the future holds.

That event will be first of all a *day of judgment*; the standards that Jesus left us will be picked up again and men and women will be measured against them. Those who have lived lives which fail to meet those standards will be declared *ungodly*, the term Peter used to describe the inhabitants of the world of Noah's day and Lot's fellow citizens in Sodom and Gomorrah (2:5–6). Those who are declared ungodly face *destruction.*

It is hard to tackle this theme without a shudder. But Peter's response is to call us to live a godly life in the light of it. As he will show, the reason for God's patience is to lengthen the days during which a change of heart is possible. Clearly, these are terrifying ideas; but we must not find them so threatening and distasteful that we refuse to believe them, for that is the error of the false teachers. Peter is convinced that it is God's right and duty to judge (as he wrote in

---

[27] As Peter has argued in 2:4–9.

[28] The connecting word *de* occurs at the start of this verse but is not translated by the NIV ('inexcusably', says Green [1987], p. 142). Probably to be translated 'and', it links creation, flood and parousia together.

[29] *E.g.* Reicke, p. 175. It is difficult to imagine what use it would be to quote Stoic beliefs about cosmic destruction to the false teachers, when they patently did not believe even the Christian version. See C. P. Thiede, 'A Pagan Reader of 2 Peter', *JSNT* 26 (1986), pp. 79–96.

[30] *E.g.* Ps. 97:3 (and throughout the Psalms); Is. 34:8–9; 66:15–16; Ezk. 15:7; Dn. 7:9–10; Mi. 1:4; Zp. 1:18; 3:8. Kelly says 'the idea that the world will be finally annihilated by fire appears only in 2 Peter in the NT' (p. 360), but see Mt. 3:10–12; 1 Cor. 3:13; 2 Thes. 1:7–8; Heb. 6:7–8; 12:29; 1 Pet. 1:7; Rev. 21:8.

[31] Mt. 24:37–39.   [32] Mt. 25:10–12, 30, 46.

chapter 2), and the wonder of his love is that it offers salvation against this background of destruction.

These three biblical examples have shown that the stability of the created order does not, as the false teachers suppose, argue against the reality of God's judgment. People do still die, just as they have always done, but neither the Old Testament nor the New promised that that would change until there is a completely new creation. The regular ordering of the seasons, the balance and interconnection of the universe from subatomic particle through to interstellar space, all argue for a creator God who is patient. But that does not mean that the world is closed to him. False teachers should realize that the same word that guarantees the stable world they delight in also guarantees the judgment they mock.

2 Peter 3:8–10
12. God's promised patience

Peter now moves to defend the teaching of Jesus' return against the
background of the poisonous scepticism infecting his churches.
Having highlighted the weakness of the scoffers' presuppositions
(3:5–7), Peter returns to their question of verse 4, 'Where is this
"coming" he promised?' He answers that *the Lord is not slow in
keeping his promise*, and that (as he has written in a previous letter)
'the end of all things is near'.[1] His answer continues his theme of
wanting his readers 'to recall the words spoken in the past by the
holy prophets and the command given by our Lord and Saviour
through your apostles' (3:2). He brings out first a promise from the
Old Testament and then a promise from the New. Each text is first
quoted and then explained.

1. The Lord's promised patience demonstrated from the Old Testament (3:8–9)

> *But do not forget this one thing, dear friends: With the Lord a
> day is like a thousand years, and a thousand years are like a day.
> ⁹The Lord is not slow in keeping his promise, as some understand
> slowness. He is patient with you, not wanting anyone to perish,
> but everyone to come to repentance.*

The false teachers' error is rooted in their wilful amnesia; 'they
deliberately forget' (3:5) the promises of the Lord's return. By
contrast, Peter's readers must *not forget this one thing* which he is
about to tell them.[2] Peter has written about the necessity of remembering what the Scriptures teach and the ability of the false teachers to
brainwash themselves. It should therefore be no surprise that what
we must remember is nothing new at all, but the central theme of

---

[1] 1 Pet. 4:7.
[2] Peter uses the same Greek verb, *lanthanō*, in both verses. Here (literally, 'do not
you forget'), the 'you' is an emphatic contrast.

the Old Testament. In 2:4–9, Peter warned that delay in judgment does not mean that God's word is impotent, and also promised that salvation was on offer. He concluded in 2:9 that 'the Lord knows how to rescue godly men from trials'. Here he looks at it from the opposite angle: the pause before the Lord's coming means not so much a delay in judgment as an extension of the time during which men and women may be rescued.

a. Peter's text from the prophets (3:8)

Peter's reference in verse 8 is to Psalm 90:4, 'A thousand years in your sight are like a day that has just gone by, or like a watch in the night.' In line with standard Jewish teaching on the passage,[3] he adds the idea that *a day is like a thousand years*, which means that 'God sees time with a *perspective* we lack . . . [and] with an *intensity* we lack'.[4] He can see the broad sweep of history in a moment, yet he can stretch out a day with patient care.

Whenever the Bible quotes the Bible, it is wise to assume that the writer wants to look at the surrounding passage and not just the words he has quoted. In this case Peter studies Psalm 90, and draws out five points.

First, *God is an eternal God.* Deep in eternity, says the psalm, 'from everlasting to everlasting you are God' (verse 2). This is the perspective from which a millennium can look like a day. The scoffers should have realized that it is fundamental to the Bible's view of God that although he deals with us in our time-span ('you have been our dwelling-place throughout all generations', verse 2), he is himself outside time.[5] And our lives, which look so long in prospect, are 'but trouble and sorrow, for they quickly pass, and we fly away' (verse 10). The scoffers bank everything on their enjoyment here and now, but from the perspective which God teaches us to take here, that is a short-sighted and foolish attitude.

Secondly, *God is a creating God.* 'You brought forth the earth and the world,' says the psalm (verse 2). This too has been a weakness of the scoffers; they do not believe that this world has been created, so they think that it cannot be uncreated. The Bible has a bigger view of God.

Thirdly, *God is a judging God.* 'You turn men back to dust, saying, "Return to dust, O sons of men"' (verse 3). The psalmist has been thinking about the consequences of sin in Genesis 3:19, 'dust you are and to dust you will return'. But he makes us feel the fear of death and judgment on an individual level too, for 'you have

---

[3] Bauckham (1983), pp. 308–310.   [4] Green (1987), p. 146.
[5] Ps. 102:27; Dn. 7:9; 1 Tim. 1:17; Heb. 13:8; Rev. 1:4.

set our iniquities before you, our secret sins in the light of your presence. All our days pass away under your wrath' (verses 8–9). Peter's opponents deny God's right to speak that word of judgment on their secret sins.

Fourthly, *God is a saving God*. The frame of this psalm is God as a covenant God, proclaiming, 'Lord, you have been our dwelling-place' (verse 1), and 'may the favour of the Lord our God rest upon us' (verse 17). Whose 'dwelling-place' and 'God'? Israel's, of course. Therefore, despite God's 'anger', 'indignation' and 'wrath' (7, 9), they can still pray for God to show 'compassion', 'love' and 'favour' (13, 14, 17). The Israelites' only reason for hope was God's covenant promise with them. Peter's opponents were denying God's ability to keep his judging word, and therefore the need for him to exercise his saving word.

Finally, *God is a moral God*. Those who know in advance what behaviour God will judge, and are certain that he will judge, will have a right 'fear' of him (verse 11), and will want to modify their behaviour in the light of that knowledge. So Psalm 90 prays, 'Teach us to number our days aright, that we may gain a heart of wisdom' (verse 12).

These five lessons are central to Psalm 90. Peter's Christians were in danger of being distracted from recalling that God is the eternal Creator, who judges according to his moral law, and saves according to his covenant love.

b. Peter's comment (3.9)

Peter follows his quotation with an explanation. Why had the Christians to remember this? Because God was being accused of *slowness*, or even of being 'slack'.[6] So he stresses in verse 10 that 'the day of the Lord will come' ('will come' is placed first in the original, for emphasis). Whether those who perceive this slowness are the recruiting false teachers, or some Christians who are starting to be swayed, does not affect their accusation. God has clearly promised to judge, so why the lack of action?

The answer, says Peter, lies in correctly understanding that psalm. If Psalm 90:3 ('You turn men back to dust') refers back to Genesis 3:3 (humanity's creation and fall), then the problem is given the widest possible scope. God forbade the man and woman to eat the fruit, saying, 'When you eat of it you will surely die.' Although they did eat, they did not die immediately because the Lord mercifully extended the possibility of salvation.[7] Instead of dying on the day of our disobedience, then, 'the length of our days is seventy

6 Kelly, p. 362. 7 Gn. 2:17; 3:16–24.

years – or eighty, if we have the strength'. But 'all our days pass away under your wrath'.[8] The Old Testament teaches that God is patient.[9]

That, says Peter, is a lesson which the false teachers 'deliberately forget' (3:5), but which we must 'not forget' (3:8). It is not just that, in Bengel's quaint phrase, 'The *age-measurer* (so to speak) of God differs from the *hour-reckoner* of mortals',[10] but that it is for our benefit that God measures time on his timescale rather than on ours. *He is patient with you, not wanting anyone to perish, but everyone to come to repentance.*

Is God then so patient that everyone will be saved? Some have taken this verse in that way, along with a handful of other verses that imply the same.[11] But it is difficult to reconcile that interpretation of these words with what Peter says two verses earlier about the 'destruction of ungodly men' (3:7). It is probably better to say that here is a mystery at the heart of God, where without any contradiction he can will both salvation and judgment. It is because he actively wills both that the obedient death of Jesus saves us from his judgment. In one sense Jesus died for everyone, for 'God so loved the world that he gave his one and only Son'. But it is also true to say that he died only for those who are saved, for 'whoever believes in him shall not perish but have eternal life'.[12] Eternal life is a free option for all, but perishing is the option that will be taken up by many.

In the light of this, Christians must be careful to use the time while God is being *patient*. First, bearing in mind that Peter's direct appeal here is to *you*, we must make sure that we Christians are right with him. Peter speaks here primarily to Christians who are in danger of falling, with the awful warning of the judgment on the false teachers ringing in our ears. It is not enough that we can look back to a past knowledge of Christ. Peter warns us to be on continuous watch lest our lives stretch God's patience to the limit.

Michael Green is surely right to add that 'the logical corollary of this verse is that Christians should use the time before the advent for preaching the gospel',[13] telling others of God's patience with them. Although several parts of the New Testament speak of the apparent delay in Christ's return, and one of the major concerns of the New Testament is how we live in the period before the return, surprisingly few tell us the reasons for the delay. Peter's reason here, that

---

[8] Ps. 90:10, 9.
[9] See Hab. 2:3–4 for the same problem, quoted in Heb. 10:37–38. For God's patience, see Ex. 34:6; Nu. 14:18; Ps. 86:15; Je. 15:15; Jon. 4:2; Rom. 2:4; 9:22; and Peter's comments in 1 Pet. 3:18–22.
[10] Bengel, p. 778.   [11] *E.g.* Ezk. 33:11; 1 Tim. 2:3–4.   [12] Jn. 3:16.
[13] Green (1987), p. 149.

the slowness is caused by God's patience, must mean that we are to use the time left to spread the news about it. Paul echoes this when he asks, 'Do you show contempt for the riches of his kindness, tolerance and patience, not realising that God's kindness leads you towards repentance?'[14] Evangelism leaps to the top of the Christian agenda.

Christians have often responded to the apparent 'problem' of the delay in Christ's return in one of two ways. One reaction has been to become fixated with the minutiae of the Bible's obscurer parts, and obsessed with charts and plans depicting how God is going to fulfil his promises and how the current political crisis only proves its imminence. This inevitably gives rise to inward-looking Christians, who do not see that the reason for God's apparent delay is that he has a task for us in the meantime. It also produces sceptical non-Christians, who see, more clearly than we often do, that we are being duped by people who only want us to buy their books. The second response, more usual among the academic community, has been to interpret the delay as indicating that God's plan is not the personal return of Christ but the extension of his kingdom by other means, whether political, economic, revolutionary or social. Rather than fostering inward-looking Christians, this often produces people who are passionately concerned for issues of justice and mercy in ways that put more traditional Bible-believers to shame. But it requires a radical reworking of the New Testament teaching, and leads to a different kind of scepticism among non-Christians, who see clear biblical doctrines being jettisoned for the sake of a political agenda.

How much wiser we would be if we admitted ignorance over the precise timing of Jesus' return! Even the Lord Jesus himself did not know when it would be.[15] We should therefore keep a level head at times of international conflict and upheaval,[16] and build on the firm information he has given us – that he will return, and that he has tasks for us to work at until he comes.[17] The challenge, then, is to be neither inward-looking obscurantists nor downward-looking secularists, but Christians who are motivated by looking both outward to fulfil the Great Commandment[18] and upward to fulfil the Great Commission.[19] In Peter Lewis's words, 'The delay of Christ's second coming to salvation is not, after all, the failure of God's plan, but rather the condition of its success.'[20]

---

[14] Rom. 2:4.   [15] Mt. 24:36.   [16] Mt. 24:4–8.   [17] Mt. 24:46–51.
[18] Jn. 15:12.   [19] Mt. 28:18–20.
[20] P. Lewis, *The Glory of Christ* (London: Hodder and Stoughton, 1992), p. 405.

2. The Lord's promised return demonstrated from the New Testament (3:10)

Throughout this letter, Peter has been concerned to defend the whole of God's Word from attack. He has consistently made the New Testament apostles and the Old Testament prophets (by which he means the whole Old Testament) an inseparable partnership. Once again here, he shows how they speak with a united voice as he marries the promise of the Lord's patience from Psalm 90 with the frequent New Testament promise of the Lord's return. Again he follows his quotation with an explanation.

> *But the day of the Lord will come like a thief. The heavens will disappear with a roar; the elements will be destroyed by fire, and the earth and everything in it will be laid bare.*

c. Peter's text from the apostles (3:10a)

Peter does not simply quote the apostles, for he is an apostle, and he would have heard from Jesus' own lips the warning, 'Keep watch, because you do not know on what day your Lord will come. But understand this: If the owner of the house had known at what time of night the thief was coming, he would have kept watch and would not have let his house be broken into. So you also must be ready, because the Son of Man will come at an hour when you do not expect him.'[21] It was a promise that John remembered, and one that Paul was also taught, quoting it in his turn.[22] This is the precise counter-balance to what Peter has just argued: that God will be patient, but he will come, and both the patience and the coming have been promised. There will be a day when God says, 'There will be no more delay!'[23] That promised day will be an unwelcome shock to those who thought that it had been postponed indefinitely. The false teachers, of course, would have believed that Jesus expected the kingdom to come fully either in his lifetime or within a few months of his ascension. In the light of that non-event they say that his promises must be reinterpreted in a more poetic, less literal way, and subjected to a more critical examination. To such thinking, Jesus' words only serve to emphasize what an unpleasant shock it will be, for no-one likes to be burgled. The false teachers are like home-owners who casually leave doors and windows open. 'How foolish!' says Peter. Jesus said he will come when we do *not* expect him, not when we *do*,

---

[21] Mt. 24:42–44. [22] Rev. 3:3; 16:15; 1 Thes. 5:2. [23] Rev. 10:6.

141

and that day will be one of unrivalled cosmic destruction.[24]

b. Peter's comment (3:10b)

Peter's words here reflect a variety of backgrounds drawn from the Old Testament, Jewish writings, and other New Testament ideas. He argues in four stages.

First, he says, *the heavens will disappear with a roar*. The single Greek word translated *with a roar*[25] occurs only here in the New Testament, but is common elsewhere. It is a noisy word, used for arrows whizzing, birds' wings rustling, the rushing of a stream in spate, or, as seems to fit best here, the crackling of a fire. With this 'cracking crash'[26] *the heavens will disappear*. In view of the way Peter has thought of the heavens throughout his letter as the spiritual sphere rather than just the sky (1:18; 3:5, 7, 13), he wants us to understand that God is going to judge and remould everything.

Secondly, *the elements will be destroyed by fire*. By *the elements* Peter does not mean the chemical elements listed on the periodic table. Nor does he mean the four elements of fire, earth, air and water which, according to ancient thought, constituted the universe; that would make one element, *fire*, the destroyer of the other three. The word was used of numbers in a series, letters in alphabetical order, or indeed of anything in a row. In time the word came to mean the stars, planets and galaxies; anything, in fact, which was a 'component part of the universe'.[27] If that is right, Peter is in the line of those Old Testament prophets who saw the day of the Lord as one of universal upheaval. In Isaiah's words, 'All the stars of the heavens will be dissolved and the sky rolled up like a scroll; all the starry host will fall like withered leaves from the vine, like shrivelled figs from the fig-tree.'[28]

Peter sees, then, that all the elements of the universe, which in our terms range from subatomic particles through to the vast interstellar emptiness, *will be destroyed by fire*. This blistering destruction is so unimaginably vast that we begin to see how futile it is to think that we can bring about Christ's kingdom by mere revolution or social change, however desirable change may be. Nor could anything as relatively small as a global nuclear holocaust or climate change account for the universal melt-down that Peter envisages.[29] Yet

[24] Much as in his Pentecost text from Joel 2:31 in Acts 2:20.   [25] *Rhoizēdon.*
[26] Lenski, p. 346.
[27] *NIDNTT* 2, p. 452.
[28] Is. 34:4. See also Joel 2:10; Mt. 24:29; Mk. 13:24–31; Rev. 6:12–13; 20:11. This language is of course apocalyptic, but that does not mean that its writers did not intend it in some measure literally as well.
[29] See 1 Pet. 1:7.

nothing less than that will accomplish God's purpose of a new creation.

Thirdly, says Peter, *the earth ... will be laid bare*. If the entire cosmos is to be destroyed, it should not surprise us that our small planet will be included. But Peter is going even further than that. The details of this verse are difficult,[30] but Peter seems to be saying that on that day there will be nowhere to hide. The scoffers who thought that God could not see what they were doing, because he had dropped off, will find that just as they sinned 'in broad daylight' (2:13), now they are judged in God's sight.

Finally, *everything in* the earth *will be laid bare*. That is, everything God has made and done, and everything mankind has made and done, will be laid open and be on full view to him. God will literally judge the works![31] Artists and scientists, insignificant and grand, leader and led, Christian and non-Christian, will all be laid bare to God. This is what Jesus had in mind when he described himself as a master who leaves his servants with work to do and then returns to inspect them.[32]

This terrifying picture (and Peter does mean it to be terrifying) may be difficult for our modern minds to grasp (but no more difficult than for the ancient world). This once-and-for-all end to our space-time home is beyond our imagination. But Peter would want to say that we should not be relying on our imagination. If we rely on that, then we manufacture a God who is too small to be the Creator, Judge and Saviour of the universe – which is precisely what the false teachers have done. Instead, we must rely on the description of God contained in his Word. It might seem that we are taking a massive risk in presenting such a God to our non-Christian friends, and we might fear that they will call us primitive and naïve. But the Bible starts and finishes with a God who creates a universe and then creates a new universe; who makes us in his image and then remakes us in his image; a God who is God, who says, 'Heaven and earth will pass away, but my words will never pass away.'[33]

---

[30] Bauckham (1983) surveys the field, pp. 317–321. He has to decide, among other things, whether the verb is 'laid bare' (as NIV, NRSV) or 'burned up' (AV, RV, and NIV footnote) (he concludes the former); and whether to treat it as a rhetorical question (as Spicq and Kelly suggest). He decides not. So our NIV main text, for all its difficulty, is the best translation. Although Wolters says that 'there seems to be virtually no lexical support for this sense' (p. 407), he has to admit that there is none for his rendering, 'have proved genuine'. A Wolters, 'Worldview and Textual Criticism in 2 Peter 3:10', *Westminster Theological Journal* 49 (1987), pp. 405–413.

[31] *Ta ... erga.*

[32] D. Wenham, 'Being "Found" on the Last Day: New Light on 2 Peter 3:10 and 2 Corinthians 5:3', *NTS* 33 (1987), pp. 477–479.

[33] Mk. 13:31.

2 Peter 3:11–16
13. Looking forward to a new home

'Some say the world will end in fire, Some say in ice.' Robert
Frost's well-known words still sum up the possibilities fairly
accurately . . . Whereas the beginning appears to have been regular and quiescent to a high degree, the final state will be chaotic
and violent . . . All galaxies, stars and atoms will dissolve into
nuclei and radiation. Then the nuclei will be dismembered into
protons and neutrons. They, in turn, will be squeezed until the
quarks confined within them are liberated into a huge cosmic
soup of freely interacting quarks and leptons.[1]

That cosmic collapse may be ten billion years away, but modern
physicists such as Barrow and Silk unanimously predict it with
alarming consistency. The horror of it lies in its scale. If we were
appalled at living on an increasingly polluted planet, we might take
the responsibility for cleaning it up. If we were faced with the
prospect of an exploding sun (another astronomical certainty), we
might cling to the hope that human beings will master interstellar
space travel with enough thoroughness to guarantee the survival of
our species and its cultures. But if what the scientists forecast
beyond that is the destruction of the cosmos itself, then the future is
indeed empty. Nothing survives.

Peering beyond the dust of demolition, Barrow and Silk see that
there is potential for some form of life to survive. 'Where there is
quantum theory there is hope,'[2] is their bleak joke. But it is not a
hope for humankind.

Writers and thinkers have often peered into the future, beyond
the end. Peter's contemporaries would have known of the Stoics,
who thought the world was caught in an endless cycle of life and

---

[1] J. D. Barrow and J. Silk, *The Left Hand of Creation* (London: Unwin, 1983;
New York: Oxford University Press, 1984), p. 224. The opening quotation is from
Robert Frost's poem, 'Fire and Ice'.
[2] *Ibid.*, p. 227.

death, destruction by fire, and rebirth. Some held that the soul survived this process, others that it did not. By Peter's day the pessimists were in the ascendant.

Contrast the Stoics and the scientists, who have an inevitably pessimistic view of the future, with the wonderful, glittering hope that has seized Peter's heart. He has the courage, which neither modern physics nor ancient philosophy shares, to see the destruction of absolutely everything, and yet to believe in its re-creation as something infinitely more wonderful. In line with the hope of the rest of the New Testament, Peter believes in the 'renewal' and 'liberation' of God's created order.[3] Rather than this destruction meaning the end of hope, Peter tells us three times in verses 12–14 to *look forward*, beyond the destruction to a new environment.

1. What does the future hold? (3:11–12a)[4]

Since everything will be destroyed in this way, what kind of people ought you to be? You ought to live holy and godly lives [12]*as you look forward to the day of God and speed its coming.*

A number of puzzling questions leap to our minds. If the prospect of cosmic demolition is true, how can there be hope? How can Peter dare to make the leap between the vast reaches of space and a personal challenge to us? How can an ordinary Christian *speed its coming?* That alone should tell us that this is not the 'Big Crunch' that impersonally and inevitably ends space and time. This is the personal intervention of God the Creator and Saviour. The phrase *will be destroyed* is a present participle in the original, almost as if the process has already started.[5] The person who sees parallels between Peter's vision and that of the scientist should remember that what lies ten billion years ahead for the astrophysicist has already started for the apostle.

If this is how the universe ends, not with an impersonal cosmic implosion but with an encounter with the personal and living God, then our human response does indeed matter. If we can neither fly from him nor be crushed into infinite insignificance, we must face up to our responsibility to *live holy and godly lives.* Peter does not give us a constricting list of do's and don'ts, for the words *holy* and

---

[3] Mt. 19:28; Rom. 8:20–21. There is no discrepancy between Peter's theme of discontinuity and these other themes, as his theology of hope shows. See 1 Cor. 15:42–44.

[4] 2 Pet. 3:11–12a functions in a way parallel to 2:17, introducing the three main themes: 11a→ 12b–13, 11b→ 14, 12a→ 15–16.

[5] So too 'will melt' (12) and 'the home of righteousness' (13) (lit. 'where righteousness *is making its home*').

145

godly are both plural, and literally mean '"in holy forms of behaviour and godly deeds", the plurals implying that there are many ways in which these can be practiced'.[6] Peter wants us to expand these ideas beyond any narrow concept of 'religious things to do'. He wants us to bring the whole of a Christian's life under these two headings so that we are ready to meet the holy God.

How can we *speed* the *day of God*?[7] Partly, Peter seems to say, by not moaning at its apparent slowness, but living in its light. If God is delaying his coming because of our sin (3:8–9), then we encourage him to come by our obedience. Whenever we pray, 'Your kingdom come',[8] we are asking God to intervene in that final climactic way; but we are also committing ourselves to live as his subjects. The prayer for God's return was an early one,[9] and it is a courageous one, for 'only those who are striving after holiness would dare to wish for the coming of the Day of the Lord'.[10]

We also hasten the day by our verbal testimony to Jesus. He taught that 'this gospel of the kingdom will be preached in the whole world as a testimony to all nations, and then the end will come'.[11] He did not intend this statement to reduce our anxiety about his coming (given that the whole world has not yet been reached). Rather, he wanted us to take it as an encouragement to reach the world for him. Certainly, that was the way Peter took these words as he preached in Jerusalem: 'Repent, then, and turn to God, so that your sins may be wiped out, that times of refreshing may come from the Lord, and that he may send the Christ, who has been appointed for you – even Jesus. He must remain in heaven until the time comes for God to restore everything, as he promised long ago through his holy prophets.'[12] The Old Testament prophecies of the hastening of God's return[13] have a new force following the first coming of Jesus, and Jesus underlined that it is within the control of God either to shorten or to lengthen that interim period as he sovereignly wills.[14]

2. How will God keep his promise? (3:12b–13)

That day will bring about the destruction of the heavens by fire, and the elements will melt in the heat. [13]*But in keeping with his promise we are looking forward to a new heaven and a new earth, the home of righteousness.*

---

[6] Hillyer, p. 220.
[7] An unusual phrase for what is usually called 'the day of the Lord'. It also occurs in Rev. 16:14. It is unlikely that Peter means anything theologically different.
[8] Mt. 6:10.   [9] 1 Cor. 16:22; Rev. 22:20.   [10] Wand, p. 182.   [11] Mt. 24:14.
[12] Acts 3:19–21.   [13] *E.g.* Is. 62:11.   [14] Mk. 13:20; Lk. 13:6–9.

Peter more or less repeats his ghastly description from verse 10: 'The heavens will disappear with a roar; the elements will be destroyed by fire.' No doubt he does so partly because 'the mockers will not care to dwell on this feature'.[15] But also it seems that his introduction of the bad news, and his repetition of it before telling us of the way of escape, form a stylistic feature. In the same way, we learnt of the judgment of the angels and the destruction of the world before we learned of Noah's rescue. Once again, we are told that 'the day of God' (verse 12a) will be one of destruction, fire and melting, as the Old Testament had said.[16] The new idea, though, is that this dreadful event is in line with God's salvation *promise*. This promise is clearly set out in Isaiah 65:17:

> Behold, I will create
> new heavens and a new earth.
> The former things will not be remembered,
> nor will they come to mind.

Isaiah's language seems excessive, for on the surface he is talking only about the return of the exiled Jews to their homeland after their exile in Babylon. But he consciously recasts the creation account from Genesis 1:1 to make the returning exiles dissatisfied with their new freedoms and identity, and to lead them to long for a newer, greater future. That is the promise to which Peter and other New Testament writers bear witness – nothing less than a new creation.[17]

Peter has a fresh theme, however, totally consistent with what he has told us already. We know that it is the Christian's destiny to 'participate in the divine nature and escape the corruption in the world caused by evil desires' (1:4), and that we are to look forward to a 'rich welcome' from Jesus Christ (1:11). We know too that against a background of judgment on sin, God rescued 'Noah, a preacher of righteousness', and Lot, who was a 'righteous man' (2:5, 7). Now Peter's final, wonderful truth becomes clear. We are going to have a new home, a *home of righteousness*.[18] We are to be *looking forward* to this brand *new heaven and . . . earth*, and to begin to live a life now that shows how much we are getting ready for it.[19]

We should not misunderstand Peter, as if he were promising

---

[15] Lenski, p. 347.

[16] Most clearly here, as in verse 10, Peter is reflecting Is. 34:4.

[17] Rom. 8:18–23; Eph. 1:9–10; Rev. 21:1.

[18] The NEB misses the connections Peter makes here. Although it describes Noah as 'a preacher of righteousness', it twice calls Lot 'good', and here translates 'the home of justice'. But the same Greek word group (*dikaios*, 'righteous'; *dikaiosynē*, 'righteousness') recurs in all these verses. The REB repeats the NEB's vocabulary, though with slightly different phrasing.

[19] It too was glimpsed in the Old Testament; see Is. 32:16–17.

God's complete abandonment of his creation. That would not match the teaching of the rest of the Bible, nor is it his meaning here. God made a good world,[20] but placed it under a curse of judgment because of human sin.[21] He promised that creation would be renewed and restored,[22] and so even today creation is keenly awaiting that moment when God's people will once again rule God's world in God's way.[23] Christians, too, long for the transformation that has already begun.[24] Peter's word *new* (the Greek word is *kainos*) emphasizes both the radical change that creation will have to undergo, and its continuation. Anthony Hoekema has written, 'The word *neos* means new in time or origin, whereas the word *kainos* means new in nature or in quality.' What Peter teaches here, he continues, is 'not the emergence of a cosmos totally other than the present one, but the creation of a universe which, though it has been gloriously renewed, stands in continuity with the present one'.[25]

3. What kind of people should we be? (3:14)

So then, dear friends, since you are looking forward to this, make every effort to be found spotless, blameless and at peace with him.

Peter's breathtaking link is unavoidable,[26] for in his mind the cosmic re-creation actually involves individual Christians. The NIV's translation, *this*, would be better in the plural (as in the RSV): 'since you wait for these'.[27] It is the hope of both a new heaven and a new earth that should inspire us and drive us on. Peter uses one of his favourite phrases to motivate us: we are to *make every effort* (1:5, 10, 15) to be ready for our new home. This does not mean spending all day dreaming about it or trying to plot its arrival, but being ready in terms of ordinary, standard Christian living.[28]

a. We should be spotless and blameless

Peter is back in the Old Testament again. To be *blameless* was a requirement of both sacrificial animals and the sacrificing priesthood. Anything that was devoted to God was to be absolutely

---

[20] Gn. 1:1 – 2:4. [21] Gn. 3:17–18. [22] Is. 11:6–9; 65:17–25.
[23] Rom. 8:20–23. [24] 2 Cor. 3:18.
[25] A. Hoekema, *The Bible and the Future* (Grand Rapids: Eerdmans, 1979), p. 280.
[26] 'So then' (*dio*) is emphatic.
[27] So too NASB, NRSV, RV.
[28] If *heuriskō* ('be found') is the right reading in 3:10, it forms a stylistic link with the same verb here.

perfect.[29] Although *spotless* is not an Old Testament word, and it is difficult to catch the precise difference between the two words, they became a natural pair; and in the Greek of 1 Peter 1:19 Peter uses them to describe the absolute perfection of Jesus Christ in his death.[30]

Alarmingly, the false teachers have been described by Peter as *blots and blemishes* (2:13, the positive forms of the same two words). Once again we are being told to contrast ourselves with those who face God's judgment, to distance ourselves from them and to be as unlike them as possible. They will have no place in the new *home of righteousness*, for they are 'unrighteous' (2:9).

b. We should be at peace with him

The first prayer Peter made for these Christians was that 'grace and peace' would be theirs (1:2). It has become clear from this letter that we have to understand those ideas as pointing to the future, when Jesus truly acts as our Saviour and the results of his saving death will be plain to see. If we are confident in our relationship with him, we know that he is our Lord whom we obey, and that his 'patience means salvation' (3:15). Trusting him, all is well, because we know that nothing exposed on that day can damage us at all. Our *looking forward* will be over, and we shall receive our 'rich welcome' (1:11).

There is, however, a flip side, for that day will bring 'condemnation' (2:3) and 'destruction' (2:1) for some, especially for the false teachers of whom Peter has been warning us constantly. If our only hope for the future is the 'Lord and Saviour' (2:20), then to deny 'the sovereign Lord who bought' us (2:1) is foolishness indeed. Those who do so are not *at peace* at all; they are 'accursed' (2:14).

4. How can we speed the day of God? (3:15-16)

Bear in mind that our Lord's patience means salvation, just as our dear brother Paul also wrote to you with all the wisdom that God gave him. [16]He writes the same way in all his letters, speaking in them of these matters. His letters contain some things that are hard to understand, which ignorant and unstable people distort, as they do the other Scriptures, to their own destruction.

---

[29] *E.g.* Ex. 29:1; Lv. 1:3, 10; *etc.* The Greek *amōmos* was a standard LXX word for this perfection.
[30] See too Phil. 2:15; Jas. 1:27.

a. We use the time

Peter has already defended God's apparent slowness as really demonstrating his patience (3:9). Now he defines the period of waiting as a time when *salvation* may be offered. He clearly thinks that this will not catch our attention, so he tells us to do the opposite of what the false teachers do. Using the same Greek word,[31] he says that they make a mistake in the way they 'understand' God's patience (3:9), but we are to *bear in mind* that this patience is for our benefit. Since Peter has already told us that this is a time when God is 'not wanting anyone to perish, but everyone to come to repentance' (3:9), he obviously wants us to use the time we have at our disposal for evangelism. The false teachers will naturally have no such concern, for their rampant self-interest will serve only to 'bring the way of truth into disrepute' (2:2).

Christians have enormous difficulty in grasping the two points that although Jesus has left us a number of things to do, there is a clear order of priority in their relative importance. We easily attach greatest importance to the visible and the urgent, such as world hunger and social injustice. Peter has certainly told us that he expects us to demonstrate the Christian characteristics of 'goodness', 'brotherly kindness' and 'love' (1:5, 7). He wants us to be effective and productive in the world (1:8). But it is clear from what Peter has taught that the greatest need our world faces is its need for a Saviour on the day of judgment. That helps us to order our priorities, for everything we do will be laid bare and exposed to God's scrutiny in the cosmic judgment. It may look foolish to assert that evangelism has a higher priority than people's physical needs, and it is true that if we attend only to their souls and never to their bodies, we have misunderstood Peter and Jesus. But Peter wants us to avoid the other danger, which is much more natural; namely, to feed the body while letting the soul starve. The pull will be in that second direction, for we can stand shoulder to shoulder with men and women from the full range of races and beliefs in arranging a food aid programme. To human eyes it looks immensely impressive. But only Christians are able to see not simply the visible and the highly urgent, but also the invisible and the hugely important, and to attach priority to those areas. Only Christians can do God's work of evangelism. Do we share Peter's sense of urgency in our use of time, money, friendships and the things we pray for?

---

[31] *Hēgeomai.* He also uses it in 1:13 ('I think'), and 2:13 ('their idea').

b. We believe the promises

What saps the energy of the Christian who is keen to love in both words and actions is a diminished sense of urgency. Peter therefore underlines for one last time that the promise of Jesus' return is of vital importance in the church today. He gives two reasons, which are variations on what he has written throughout his letter.

First, he wants us to be certain that the whole Bible bears witness to the promise of Jesus' return. It is the message which he shares with *our dear brother Paul.*

For those who believe that this letter is a deliberate forgery, these words are decisive. 'The writer rather ostentatiously stresses his assumed equality with the Apostle.'[32] The reason so many writers feel this problem is the supposed tension between Peter and Paul from the time of their disagreement in Antioch.[33] Yet the idea that this one incident turned into a life-long jealousy is a mere guess. Even the Galatians material shows that each recognized the other as an apostle with a valid ministry.[34] They shared a team member in Silas.[35] It is difficult to conceive of a way in which Peter could have referred to Paul without incurring the critics' displeasure here. There is certainly nothing unusual or anachronistic in any of his terms: *brother* was an accepted term for a fellow Christian worker;[36] *dear* translates *agapētos,* which is once again a standard way of talking about fellow workers.[37] What is ostentatious in this? It would have been much more ostentatious for Peter to talk about Paul as the next generation of Christians did, calling him 'the blessed and glorious Paul' (Polycarp), 'the blessed Paul' (Clement) or 'the sanctified Paul . . . right blessed' (Ignatius).[38]

If this letter is from Peter's hand, then, why should he want to refer to Paul here? Partly to assure his own readers that the most widely read Christian writer *writes the same way in all his letters, speaking in them of these matters.* Perhaps Paul had written especially to this group of Christians (Peter says that Paul *wrote to you*). But attempts to identify which of Paul's letters is being referred to have failed,[39] and in any case Peter's point is that *all* Paul's *letters* argue

---

[32] Sidebottom, p. 125.   [33] Gal. 2:1–21.   [34] Gal. 2:7.
[35] Acts 15:22 – 18:5; 2 Cor. 1:19; 1 Thes. 1:1; 2 Thes. 1:1; 1 Pet. 5:12.
[36] *E.g.* Acts 15:22; Rom. 16:1; 2 Cor. 2:13; Eph. 6:21; Phil. 2:25; Col. 4:7, 9; 1 Thes. 3:2; Phlm. 16; 1 Pet. 5:12; 3 Jn. 3.
[37] *E.g.* Acts 15:25; Rom. 16:12; 1 Cor. 4:17; Eph. 6:21; Col. 1:7; 2 Tim. 1:2; 3 Jn. 1.
[38] Quoted in *NTI*, p. 826.
[39] There are two routes to identification: theologically, the letters which talk of Jesus' return are 1 and 2 Thessalonians; geographically, the letters to Asia Minor are Ephesians and Colossians. But some of Paul's letters were lost (1 Cor. 5:9; Col. 4:16), so we cannot limit the identification to the ones we possess.

that Christians are to live in the light of the Lord's return.[40]

Peter and Paul are not just inspiring and clear-minded Christian leaders; they are inspired and authoritative apostles, and Peter puts Paul's letters in the same category as *the other Scriptures*. Peter is not drawing a distinction between two sorts of writing here. In his mind, Paul's letters are Scripture. This, from the pen of the man who said that 'no prophecy of Scripture came about by the prophet's own interpretation' (1:20), can mean only that he puts them in the same category as the Old Testament. Paul writes with God's authority. This might seem a surprising point for a contemporary to make, but it is the authority that Paul himself claims for his message.[41] Once again, Peter has said that the New Testament apostles and Old Testament prophets bear equally inspired witness to the same promise of Jesus Christ's return (1:16–21).

Secondly, Peter wants us to be certain that the unified biblical promise of Jesus' return is the focus of united attack. Peter is the first to admit that Paul's letters are not easy, for they *contain some things that are hard to understand*. Although they were written *with the wisdom that God gave him*, they seem to have been open to misunderstanding[42] simply because they require hard work.[43] (Perhaps we might feel the same about Peter's letter!)

To misunderstand is one thing; to *distort* is quite another, and that is the problem Peter tackles. He uses a word from twisting rope or torturing on a rack, for people were pulling Paul out of shape in a deliberate desire to make him say something other than his clear intention. They are *ignorant* – which means not that they know nothing, but that they refuse instruction – and *unstable*, people who would lead us away from the 'way of truth', 'the straight way', 'the way of righteousness' (2:2, 15, 21), 'the way which is substantially one and the same in the Old and the New'.[44] The hallmark is not simply an antipathy to Paul but an antipathy to this theme, consistently presented in Scripture, for their abuse of him is merely a symptom of their abuse of the whole Bible.

As we would expect from Peter by now, the end result of mishandling the promise of Jesus' return is *destruction* on the last day

---

[40] Rom. 8:19–21; 13:11–12; 1 Cor. 3:13; 4:5; 15:51–57; 1 Thes. 4:1 – 5:11; 2 Thes. 2:1–14.

[41] Rom. 1:1; Gal. 1:1. The basic picture of God's assembled people in the OT is that of Sinai – they assemble around his word. Paul seems to see his letters functioning in the same way, as the Christians assemble (or are 'in church') to hear them read.

[42] Romans seems constructed in part around possible honest misunderstandings of Paul as he presents his gospel (*e.g.* 3:1, 3, 5; 4:9; 7:1) as well as malicious misrepresentation (*e.g.* 3:8; 6:15), but see too 1 Cor. 6:12–13.

[43] Guthrie says shrewdly, 'Would a pseudepigrapher have adopted the view that Peter did not understand Paul's writings?' *NTI*, p. 827.

[44] Bigg, p. 301.

(*cf.* 2:1); Bible-twisters will not live in the expectation of his return. Peter shows that they shoulder responsibility for their fate, for they mishandle God's promise *to their own destruction*.

There is a note of sober reality for us in all this as we take up the responsibility to handle God's Word with integrity, honesty and a desire to seek out what it says. Parts of it may well be *difficult to understand*, and that is a reason for hard work and thinking, getting to grips with a whole Bible book rather than reading only our favourite verses, and checking what we think with other Christians. Peter wants us to know that serious Bible study requires effort. There is all the difference in the world, though, between finding the Bible difficult, and wilfully twisting it to say only what we find helpful or relevant or reasonable to believe. Where is the voice of God if he says only what we want him to say?

2 Peter 3:17–18
14. The message of 2 Peter

Personal letters tend to wind down at the end, but public correspondence such as we have in the New Testament tends to have a clearer, planned shape. One common feature of the New Testament letters is that the last few sentences often summarize the major themes of the letter as a whole.[1] Here, Peter surveys his major concerns one last time, and sums up for us the message of his second letter.

Therefore, dear friends, since you already know this, be on your guard so that you may not be carried away by the error of lawless men and fall from your secure position. [18]*But grow in the grace and knowledge of our Lord and Saviour Jesus Christ. To him be glory both now and for ever! Amen.*

1. The guarded Christian (3:17)

Forewarned is forearmed, the proverb says, and Peter would presumably agree. He has given us advance information of something we *already know*,[2] namely that the promise of Jesus' return is a doctrine that will come under constant attack. For the third time he refers to the future of the church 'after my departure' (1:15) as being marked by false teachers (2:1–3), scoffers (3:3–4), and now *lawless men*. We must not think Peter saw this as a distant danger,[3] for his

---

[1] *E.g.* Rom. 16:25–27; 1 Cor. 16:22; 2 Cor. 13:7–11; Gal. 6:11–16; 1 Thes. 5:23–24; 1 Tim. 6:20–21; 2 Tim. 4:1–8; Tit. 3:14; 1 Pet. 5:8–9; 1 Jn. 5:18–21; Jude 24–26.

[2] *Proginōskō*, which gives us our word 'prognosis' – what is likely to occur.

[3] Nor is it necessarily a literary device by a disciple of Peter. The changes of tense here cause Bauckham (1983) problems; he says of verse 16 that 'The author's use of the present tense (instead of the future) ... is his most blatant breach of the pseudepigraphical fiction' (p. 324). But that is because he is constraining the letter into a particular genre in which it sits uncomfortably.

constant fear of its eating away at the morale of Christians shows that he is sure of the permanent presence of these people in the church. By contrast, *you* (its position in the sentence is emphatic) must be permanently *on your guard*, alert to the probability that an attack will be mounted.

We must first be sufficiently aware that we know the truth and can recognize an *error* for what it is. Peter has used a wide variety of terms to describe his opponents' position. Having made up 'cleverly invented stories' (1:16; *cf.* 2:3), they are 'false teachers' who 'secretly introduce destructive heresies' (2:1). They may be 'bold and arrogant' (2:10), but they 'blaspheme in matters they do not understand' (2:12) and do untold 'harm' (2:13). 'They mouth empty, boastful words' (2:18), they are 'scoffers' (3:3) who are 'ignorant and unstable' (3:16). It is quite a list of abuse! To us it may seem strong and unnecessary, and R. P. Martin finds a 'rigidity and somewhat mechanical reaction to innovation and theological enterprise'.[4] But Peter can see the damage that results from believing and teaching an *error*. We find it hard to understand how people who seem so amiable can be so harmful, but that can only be because we have not made the effort to be well-taught Christians who are willing to call false teaching false teaching. That puts us in supreme danger, for we are prime targets for those who wish to 'seduce the unstable' (2:14). We should make increasing our knowledge of Christian doctrine a high priority, so that when it is challenged, denied or quietly replaced, we can confidently and accurately affirm the truth.

We must, secondly, be sufficiently aware that we know God's moral expectations and can recognize *lawless* behaviour for what it is. *Lawless* was one of the key words in the description of Sodom and Gomorrah (2:7–8), but it has also been synonymous with 'ungodly', 'unrighteous' and 'corrupt'. This is the 'vomit' to which dogs return and the 'mud' in which pigs love to wallow (2:22). Again, we may find this highly coloured language rather for our delicate taste, but Peter intends to call the refusal of God's right to rule rebellion, and the breaking of God's law lawlessness. If we find his descriptions smelly and repulsive, he would ask us to imagine how lawlessness appears to God.

Thirdly, we must be on guard that we are not *carried away* by the teaching of these people and *fall from* our *secure position*. If these teachers are heading towards destruction, they are not going alone, for they take with them those whom they have managed to 'entice' (2:18) to 'follow' them (2:2). Like grisly Pied Pipers, they

---

[4] Martin, p. 163.

head for hell with a crowd of disciples at their heels.[1] Peter has already reassured us of our *secure position* in Christ (1:12)[2] and assured us that we 'will never fall' (1:10). But he wants us to be alert to those who are 'unstable' (3:16) and who wish to make us 'unstable' in turn (2:14).[3] He sees these false teachers offering us a helping hand, and making us wobble and then fall, which is the dramatic word-picture Luke used to describe a ship 'running aground' and being 'dashed against the rocks'.[4]

We must, then, be alert to those who wish to attract us away from Peter's gospel to another with different teaching and different moral requirements, for on the day of God's judgment that position will be seen to be deeply insecure. If we remain with Jesus Christ and his promises, we shall *never fall*; but if we wander away from him there is quicksand all around.

2. The growing Christian (3:18a)

2 Peter has repeatedly paired the titles of *Lord* and *Saviour* (1:11; 2:20; 3:18),[5] and neither has been redundant. *Lord* has consistently highlighted Jesus Christ's power to judge our world; *Saviour* his willingness to rescue us on that day. Peter has also told us that every Christian has a personal knowledge of Christ, and that we have a responsibility to increase our knowledge of him (1:5). Now he tells us to *grow in the grace and knowledge of our Lord and Saviour*. Why?

Peter has used a wide variety of word-pictures to describe the mental attitude of the false teachers. They are wilfully forgetful (1:9), tale-spinners (2:3) who are painfully self-deluded about their spiritual progress (2:19). In a phrase, 'they deliberately forget' (3:5). By contrast, Peter sees his role as a permanent teacher of the truth. (1:12; 3:1; 3:8). It is as though he is saying that it is impossible to stand still as a Christian, for we all have an in-built tendency to push Jesus Christ to the back of our minds. The only remedy is to make deliberate, constant and frequent efforts to bring him to the front. Had we been first-century Christians, we might have thought that in two thousand years of Christianity a range of exotic errors would have arisen to entice God's people. And indeed they have. Much more striking, though (to confirm Peter's fears), is the fact that those two thousand years have been marked by a struggle to recall

---

[5] The verb 'carried away', *synapagō*, has the idea of being carried away with or alongside someone else.

[6] *Stērigmos* here, with the verb *stērizō* in 1:12, translated 'firmly established'.

[7] *Astēriktos* in each case, from the negative of *stērizō*.

[8] *Ekpiptō* in Acts 27:26, 29.

[9] Peter has also used the titles separately: 'Saviour' (1:1) and 'Lord' (1:16).

what Jesus commanded us to do, without adding anything of our own or subtracting the bits of his teaching we find less acceptable. No matter how long we have been Christians, we cannot rest on years of Sunday School lessons, sermons and quiet times. Every day represents a fresh challenge, when we will be tempted to forget everything we have learned over the years, and trade it in for a novelty item. Peter's solution is to *grow in the grace and knowledge of ... Jesus Christ*. We need to know more about him, to be sure; but we also grow in that knowledge by obeying him, by treating his promises as genuine promises of the *Saviour*, and his commands as genuine commands of the *Lord*.

Peter opened his letter with a prayer for 'grace and peace' (1:2), and we can now see how important those two little words are for him, arching from that opening to these closing words. We are to 'make every effort to be found ... at peace with him' (3:14), and to *grow in ... grace*. In both cases the overwhelming generosity of God is supreme, for peace and grace are ours 'in abundance', and we possess them not through our work but through our 'knowledge of God and of Jesus our Lord' (1:2). But the difference starts now as grace, knowledge and peace become the stuff of our responding obedience, and as we avoid those who deny these central truths, instead holding firmly to them through the battles ahead.

3. The glorious Christ (3:18b)

Peter ends his letter with one of the highest ascriptions of praise to Jesus Christ that we find in the pages of the New Testament. It is quite breathtakingly daring for the New Testament writers to take what was traditionally allowable only as a way of praising God and to use it as a song to the carpenter friend of Peter.[10] Yet all this has been implicit throughout his letter, where both God and Jesus Christ have been described as 'Saviour' or bringing 'salvation' (1:1, *etc.*; 3:15). Both are 'divine' (1:3–4), and the coming day involves the advent of both the Father and the Son.[11] Jesus Christ

---

[10] The only two other similar NT praise songs addressed solely to Jesus Christ are 2 Tim. 4:18 and Rev. 1:3–6, but *cf.* Rev. 5:8–10, 13–14; 7:9–12; and Eph. 5:19, where 'to the Lord' means 'to Christ'. 'It is important to realize that no Jew would listen calmly to a man being described as divine, and it can only have been with the greatest reluctance that Jesus' Jewish followers, however great their love and respect for their leader, could be brought to use such language.' R. T. France, 'The Worship of Jesus, A Neglected Factor in Christological Debate', in H. H. Rowdon (ed.), *Christ the Lord: Essays in Christology Presented to Donald Guthrie* (Leicester: IVP, 1982), p. 25. See too L. Hurtado, *One God, One Lord* (London: SCM, 1988), pp. 93–124.

[11] *Cf.* Blum, pp. 157–158.

has indeed a 'majesty' and a 'glory' which he shares with the 'Majestic Glory' (1:16–17).[12]

Yet even these wonderful closing phrases only reinforce what Peter has been teaching throughout his letter. The words *both now and for ever* attempt to translate a difficult phrase, literally, 'now and for the day of eternity'. How can a day last for ever? Peter has told us, for he urged us to hold on to the prophets' promises 'until the day dawns' (1:19), the 'day of God' (3:12), in whose sight 'a day is like a thousand years, and a thousand years are like a day' (3:8). Peter has returned to that fundamental idea from Psalm 90, and shown us one last glorious and extravagant truth: if the thousands of years which separate us from the first coming of Christ are nothing in God's sight, then the day which sees his return can last for an eternity. Some scholars say that Peter may not have written the last word of this letter, but if that is true, who can blame the unknown scribe who added his awed response in which we can join? *Amen.*

[12] *Cf.* Is. 42:8; Jn. 5:23.

Introduction to Jude

The close correspondence between 2 Peter and Jude is there for any reader to see. It is instructive to spell out some of the more obvious parallel themes and to ask what distinctive contributions, if any, Jude has to make.

1. As in 2 Peter (1:12–21; 3:1–2), so in Jude, *the Christian faith is already in existence as a settled and final body of saving truths.* The Spirit of God led Christ's apostles into 'all truth',[1] and this apostolic faith has now been entrusted to 'the saints', that is, the people of God on earth (Jude 3). This authoritative revelation has been committed to the church 'once for all', not only to proclaim but to protect and safeguard: it is normative as a standard of orthodoxy by which error may be measured and recognized for what it is. Without such a complete rule of faith, or scriptural sufficiency, as Peter has described it,[2] developments of doctrine and tradition will inevitably arise, setting aside the sure foundations.

Jude 3 is of special importance, not because it is a new insight, since a concept of 'the faith' as an authorized gospel message, received by the apostles and delivered to the churches, is recognized in the New Testament from the earliest days.[3] But it is characteristic of Jude to call for action to defend and preserve this gospel. The believers are to 'contend' for the truth, and the verb here is unusually strong. They are to 'fight' for the faith, conscious that there are many enemies ranged against the churches, determined to destroy this sacred deposit. As so often with Jude, one senses his close affinity with the teaching of Paul who 'kept the faith' to the end, and urged his fellow workers to do the same.[4]

Jude, however, is no mere polemicist, spoiling for a fight, seeking any excuse for controversy. He too has a pastor's heart. It is wise to link verse 3 with verse 20a. Jude's ambition is not only to pull down

---

[1] Jn. 16:13.   [2] *Cf.* 2 Pet. 1:19.   [3] *E.g.* Gal. 1:23; 1 Cor. 15:1–8.
[4] *E.g.* 1 Tim. 6:20–21; 2 Tim. 1:13–14.

the strongholds of error, but to see that the loyal believers build up one another in Christ. The only basis on which it is possible to do this is the 'most holy faith', most holy because of its origin in the mind and purposes of God rather than as a product of human inspiration. It is those who shake these foundations who ultimately destroy the knowledge of God within the churches, causing them to lose their distinctive commission and spirituality.

2. As in 2 Peter (2:1), so in Jude (4), *godless teachers have slipped surreptitiously into positions of authority in the churches*. The exposition will show how our understanding of Jude's method of exposing 'these men' has been greatly advanced by the pioneering work of Professor Earle Ellis and Professor Richard Bauckham. Jude has, in fact, written his own 'commentary' on scriptural, apocalyptic and apostolic material to demonstrate that the depravity, activities, and final condemnation of such 'rogue' church leaders have been prophesied from of old (4–15) as well as foretold by the apostles (16–18). This is the main central section of Jude's letter, by which he strives to show his readers just what is the true nature of these popular preachers now breaking up congregations and alienating Christians one from another (19).

If anything, Jude's portrayal of these men and the consequences of their work is more sombre than in 2 Peter. Perhaps the situation has become worse. Certainly verse 5 is a chilling reminder of the tragic happenings in the wilderness, frequently echoed in the early preaching.[5] The people God once delivered, he afterwards destroyed. The severity is almost overwhelming, yet the reason for it is not strange; the people were no longer believers and therefore no longer God's people (5).

In the three selected illustrations of verses 5–7 (for there is opportunity for choice in the use of stock material), Jude is indicating another factor, so easily neglected; *privilege offers no security*. To be a member of the happy multitudes who came out of slavery in Egypt; to possess the highest positions of spiritual authority, comparable to the angels;[6] to live in a 'green and pleasant land' like the Jordan valley ('the garden of the LORD');[7] these are privileges of matchless worth. But the end was far different from the beginning, horrifying even to describe, let alone experience.

There are few warnings more distressing than those concerning grand advantages thrown away. Nor can examples of future suffering compare in severity with verse 7, except from the lips of Jesus when speaking of the godless religious leaders of his day, blind guides and corruptors of the innocent. So we may recognize in Jude a faithful minister of Christ, both through his cautions to the

---

[5] *Cf.* 1 Cor. 10:1–10; Heb. 3:7–19.   [6] *Cf.* Heb. 1:7.   [7] Gn. 13:10.

churches about false teaching, and in his warnings to the false teachers themselves of the divine reckoning that lies ahead of false shepherds whose concern is not to feed the flock but to advance themselves.

3. As in 2 Peter (3:4), so in Jude, *the new teachers are antagonistic, in their mocking way, not merely towards minor matters or isolated articles of the Christian creed, but towards the heart of the gospel itself.* Jude is evidence of this, for 'the grace of God' is synonymous with the gospel of Christ itself. This message they change, or remodel, to their own liking. In its new form, the freedom for which Christ has set us free becomes, as Paul warned the Galatians, a 'yoke of slavery',[8] as the lordship and sovereignty of Christ are disowned and denied.

This is a constant warning in the New Testament. Renounce the authority exercised through his apostles[9] and lawless immorality will, sooner or later, overwhelm the churches. Perversion of the gospel leads to perversion of Christian morality. Thus it becomes evident to the churches, after the damage has been done, that those who led them into this morass, claiming to be led by the Spirit, were in reality led by their own carnal desires (17–19). Jude is a tract for times like our own when many conflicting voices plunge the churches into confusion and unrest, while self-appointed leaders, in Korah's mould (11), are able to gather people around them to champion their authority as pre-eminent.

4. As in 2 Peter (1:5, 10; 3:14), so in Jude, *there is an insistence on the necessity of painstaking effort if the faithful Christian is to stand firm in evil times.* Peter's particular vocabulary is not used by Jude, except, interestingly, with reference to his own determination to write this letter (verse 3, resembling 2 Pet. 1:15). Nevertheless, the message of Jude 21 is clear on the positive activity required of believers who hope to stand firm to the end. Jude also underlines, as apostolic Christianity always does, the keeping power of the risen Christ in which God's true church can have entire confidence. He does this effectively by placing this heartening truth both at the beginning and the end of his letter, that is, in the address (1) as well as in the famous doxology (24–25), 'perhaps the most beautiful of all utterances of this kind in the New Testament'.[10] It is in his first letter, rather than his second, that Peter gives similar assurances,[11] but there is no New Testament Christianity without this promise.[12] Our security is in God's hands, and Christ has promised that his

---

[8] Gal. 5:1.   [9] *Cf.* 2 Pet. 3:2.
[10] E. F. Scott, *Literature of the New Testament, Records of Civilization*, vol. XV (New York: Columbia University Press, 1932), p. 26.
[11] 2 Pet. 1:5; 5:10.   [12] *Cf.* 1 Thes. 5:23.

sheep will never perish.[13] What distorts our confidence in such splendid promises, turning trust into presumption, is *faith without effort*. The 'brief but splendid analysis of Christian living'[14] succinctly given in 20–21 requires application and constant exertion. There will even be struggle and strain in it.

Belief in the precious realities of our 'calling and election'[15] is demonstrated not by complacent faith but by the most diligent attempts to remove from ourselves those ugly blemishes which so disfigured the lives of the new teachers (selfishness, uncleanness, fault-finding, greed, boasting, *etc.*). No-one is more certain than Jude of God's keeping power. This is sufficiently proved by the imperishable words of his doxology which remain an encouragement, often repeated, to the worldwide company of faithful Christians. But no-one more succinctly spells out the practical steps that must be taken if we are to build one another up, keeping ourselves in the love of God, as well as rescuing those in the fellowship who are in imminent danger of apostasy (22–23).

5. As throughout 2 Peter (summarized by 3:18), so in Jude, *their readers are urged to make steady progress in their knowledge of God*. Jude's predilection for groups of three guides us in an understanding of verses 20 and 21, when the trinitarian nature of this exhortation reveals its real significance. Christians are to build on foundations that have already been laid,[16] and they achieve this by responding to the divine activity that, from the start, has been moulding their personal desires, understanding and hopes. If the Holy Spirit is at work in them, the one certainty is that they will pray, hardest of all disciplines to practise consistently and seriously. If they grasp anything of the love of God that has led to their salvation, chastened them, borne with them, and delighted in them, they will determine to keep themselves in that love, daily experience with which nothing else can compare.[17] If their Saviour is coming one day to take them to their eternal home,[18] they will look forward to his return with confidence. As sinful people still, they might anticipate Christ's coming with a very natural apprehension and fearfulness; nevertheless, goodness and mercy have pursued them from the beginning and will not fail them at the end. Truly it is a gospel of grace from start to finish. And as such it leads believing people into a deeper and deeper knowledge of the triune God himself.

6. As in 2 Peter (1:12–15), so in Jude (3), *there is the same sense of urgency that compels both Christian leaders to write letters to their 'dear friends'*. For Jude, the gravity of the situation may be more

---

[13] *Cf.* Jn. 10:28.   [14] Kelly, p. 287.   [15] 2 Pet. 1:10.   [16] *Cf.* 1 Cor. 3:10–15.
[17] *Cf.* Jn. 15:9–10.   [18] *Cf.* Jn. 14:3.

extreme. Divisions in the Christian community are already a fact. The new teachers have captured the allegiance of many, both by claiming great things for themselves and by flattering weak and empty-headed Christians so that they in turn imagine themselves to be 'someone great'.[19] But it is not too late (though in some cases nearly so) to stretch out a helping hand to snatch back those on the brink of disaster. The heart of the true Christian will no doubt leap to take a share in such rescue operations, but Jude offers realistic cautions; in a compassionate zeal to get alongside the wanderers, unwary believers may themselves be contaminated. Only a loathing for polluted things will keep them safe.[20]

7. As in 2 Peter, so in Jude, *the horror of their situation, with present-day 'Cains', 'Balaams' and 'Korahs' causing havoc in the churches, is controlled by their knowledge that it has all happened before.* This is why they bring to the attention of their readers excerpts from the Old Testament record of Israel's story. 'These things happened to them as examples and were written down as a warning *for us*, on whom the fulfilment of the ages has come.'[21]

Today's preacher, likewise, must recapture the Old Testament as an essential part of the Christian Scriptures, since the way we modern Christians can understand what is happening to us in the present is to know what happened to God's people in the past. This will mean taking seriously, as commentaries on the Old Testament, the New Testament writings of a Peter and a Jude. Their evaluation and interpretation of the Old Testament must be ours.

8. As in 2 Peter, so in Jude, *there is an unwavering belief in Jesus as the reigning Lord of the church.* Both writers lay stress on the deity of Christ, partly no doubt in view of the reductionist Christology that characterized the new teaching. Peter is wonderfully eloquent on this theme, as the exposition shows.

But in his short compass, Jude is just as explicit concerning the lordship and sovereignty of Jesus (4). All the later New Testament writings recognize that the church's confession of the fullness of the Godhead, dwelling uniquely in Christ, is under threat from an incipient Gnosticism with its esoteric spirituality. And today the ancient Gnostic belief that human beings are essentially akin to the divine is fast reappearing in popular New Age and cultic preaching.

Is any distinction between 2 Peter and Jude allowable? Possibly it may lie in this, that Peter's special concern is with *individual believers*, in terms of personal growth and responsibilities if they are not to be swept aside by the overwhelmingly popular new teaching. Jude, it seems, is alarmed at the prospect of *whole Christian communities* being destroyed from within. We find a parallel in the

---

[19] *Cf.* Acts 8:9–10. [20] *Cf.* 1 Cor. 10:12–14. [21] 1 Cor. 10:11.

163

pastoral epistles, where the second of Paul's letters to Timothy is taken up with the grievous possibility that a favourite colleague might fail to continue in costly ministry to the end, while in his first letter it is a favourite Christian community which is at risk of losing its gospel standards.

Certainly Peter's special contribution is to show that the Lord 'knows how to rescue godly men from trials'[22] both present and future, and he urges his readers to look to their own personal faith and love in view of the coming destruction of the world. Jude does not neglect this aspect, but his particular interest concerns what the devoted believer can do to build up the Christian fellowships, as well as reclaiming the shaky, the irresolute and the compromised (20–23). It is not the individual alone who will be kept from apostasy and presented before the throne of God without fault, but whole communities of the faithful.[23]

Jude has not been widely valued by modern scholarship until recently, or by most Christian readers. By contrast, it was popular in early times. Origen (c. 185–c. 254), biblical scholar and prolific writer, spoke of it as 'filled with flowing words of heavenly grace'.[24] As the living church recovers its confidence in all the Scriptures, and as we face the same opponents as Jude did, wrestling again with those bogus prophetic revelations that lead to the casting aside within the churches of all moral restraints, we can be sure that Jude's wise warnings and confident faith will be greatly treasured once again by God's people under trial.

---

[22] 2 Pet. 2:9.　　[23] Cf. Eph. 5:25–27.　　[24] Quoted in Charles (1990), p. 109.

Jude 1–2
1. Jude the obscure?

Jude, a servant of Jesus Christ and a brother of James,

To those who have been called, who are loved by God the Father and kept by Jesus Christ:

² *Mercy, peace and love be yours in abundance.*

1. The writer (1a)

No New Testament letter has had a greater battle for acceptance in the history of the church than this short letter of Jude. Luther summed up the feelings of many Christians when he said, 'In it is nothing special except it refers to the Second Epistle of Peter from which it has taken nearly all its words.' He added darkly that 'on the whole it is nothing else than an epistle against our bishops, priests and monks'.[1] Certainly, the letter does show a striking similarity to 2 Peter (although that similarity has been exaggerated and misinterpreted),[2] and it quotes explicitly from two books that are not in any Bible. Many Christians have felt uneasy about Jude's references to 'the archangel Michael, when he was disputing with the devil about the body of Moses' (verse 9) and the prophecy of 'Enoch, the seventh from Adam' (verse 14). It is even claimed that Jude's method involves 'rough-handling and browbeating his opponents with dire threats'.[3] Until relatively recently, it was correct to say that lack of scholarly interest has made Jude 'the most neglected book in the New Testament'.[4]

This obscurity is undeserved. It is true that Christians today are unfamiliar with the material that Jude's Christians were so troubled by, and we may not be able to find the precise problems

---

[1] Luther, p. 298.   [2] See Appendix.   [3] Martin, p. 85.
[4] The title of an article by D. J. Rowston, *NTS* 21 (1974/5), pp. 554–563. Richard Bauckham's commentary and books are recent and important exceptions.

in our churches that Jude is dealing with in his letter. But his analysis of the deeper issues is so clear, and his recommendations so sharp, that the letter has a finer cutting edge and contemporary feel than we might initially think. Even his unusual quotations show a keen mind and a concern for the purity of one small church.

Who was the man who wrote this extraordinary letter?

a. Jude ... a brother of James

There is only one *Jude* in the New Testament who has a brother called *James*, and the two references to him[5] make it clear that the two men were, with Joseph and Simon, the half-brothers of Jesus and the sons of Mary and Joseph.[6] Strictly speaking, Jude is called Judas, but it is easy to see why most Bibles do not confuse him with the notorious Judas Iscariot![7] If Jude and James were among Jesus' half-brothers, then James was not the apostle called James who was one of the twelve, pioneered the church in Jerusalem and was executed by Herod.[8] Instead, he was the James called 'James the Righteous' or 'James the Just', who later led the church in Jerusalem, probably wrote the New Testament letter that bears that name, and was so central to the Council of Jerusalem.[9] It is likely that Jude was one of the first Jewish Christians to leave Jerusalem during the persecution following the death of Stephen,[10] subsequently living and working in the surrounding area.[11] Richard Bauckham's recent work seems to put this letter quite conclusively in an early, Palestinian setting, which would account for its easy references to what are, as far as we are concerned, obscure books.[12] The early Christian writer Eusebius quotes a story that Jude's grandsons appeared before the Emperor Domitian, but, 'despising them as of no account, he let them go, and by a decree put a stop to the persecution of the church. But when they were released they ruled the churches because they were witnesses and were also relatives of the Lord.'[13]

---

[5] Mt. 13:55; Mk. 6:3.

[6] Ellis, p. 229, suggests that Jude is the Judas Barsabbas of Acts 15:22, 32, and that 'brother' here means 'co-worker'; but when there is a Jude who is the natural brother of James, it is unnecessary to make a second, potentially confusing, identification. See comments on 2 Pet. 3:15.

[7] Only the RV calls him Judas.   [8] Acts 1:13 – 12:2.   [9] Acts 15:13–21.

[10] Acts 8:1–2.

[11] This is hinted in Eusebius, *Church History* 3.32.6 (*NPNF* 1, p. 164).

[12] Especially Bauckham (1983), chapter 2.

[13] *Church History* 3.20 (*NPNF* 1, p. 149).

b. Jude, a servant of Jesus Christ

Since Jude was the half-brother of Jesus, and since he and James were happy to be known as such,[14] why does he not refer to his extraordinary family connection here? Possibly the reason might have a root in his reverence for Jesus Christ – an attractive modesty, bearing in mind the doubts and oppositions he had displayed during Jesus' earthly life.[15] This would constitute an 'exquisite example of awestruck humility'.[16] Much more significant, though, is the fact that as he starts his letter, Jude wants to present his claim to write as he does, and for that purpose a knowledge of Jesus as a physical human being is not enough. Even knowledge of Jesus as a close family member is inadequate. That is an extraordinary idea which is hard for us to grasp. We would naturally imagine that his memories of Jesus as an elder brother, and his knowledge of Jesus' habits and manner, would lend weight to his letter. Certainly, it is true that if Jude were writing as a historian, then such information would give him an innate authority. But Jude is writing as a Christian leader, and for that purpose such human knowledge is irrelevant. When Jude became a Christian, he had to change from knowing Jesus as his brother to acknowledging him as the Christ and his Lord (verse 4). The fact that Jude does not refer to his physical relation to Christ, therefore, is no comment on this letter's authorship.[17] Instead, it shows us that no-one is too privileged to be exempt from the need to be converted.

This new relationship to Jesus means that Jude has become Jesus' *servant*. It is a word that other New Testament Christians use of themselves and of one another.[18] It has an overtone of great importance, for Abraham, Moses, David and Daniel are all called 'servants of God'.[19] Jude is therefore a person to be taken with great seriousness. But he confesses to being outside the ring of those who claim to be apostles (verse 17). He happily defers to his brother James as his leader and authority, and will claim no higher right to Christian status than his other 'dear friends' (verses 3, 17, 20), who recognize with him that Jesus is 'our Lord' (verses 4, 17, 21, 25).

---

[14] 1 Cor. 9:5; Gal. 1:19.
[15] Mt. 12:46–50; 13:55–57; Mk. 3:31–35; 6:3–4; Lk. 4:24; 8:19–21; Jn. 7:5.
[16] Wand, p. 195.   [17] *Contra* Kelly, p. 242.
[18] Rom. 1:1; 1 Cor. 7:22; Gal. 1:10; Eph. 6:6; Phil. 1:1; Col. 4:12; 2 Tim. 2:24; Jas. 1:1; 2 Pet. 1:1.
[19] Abraham, Ps. 105:42; Moses, Ne. 9:14; Rev. 15:3; David, Ps. 89:3; Daniel, Dn. 6:20.

2. The readers (1b)

Jude uses the standard letter opening to say three things about his readers. The churches he was writing to cannot be identified precisely, but the letter makes clear that he did not think he was writing a general letter of broad application to an unlimited number of churches. He was writing to a particular group or groups of Christians he knew very well.

a. Christians who are called

Christians are often referred to as people whom God has *called*,[20] and this is an important starting-point for understanding this letter. Every Christian has been called by God to be a Christian, and one of Jude's key ideas is that God will continue to call us home until we join him in heaven.

Yet it goes deeper even than that. A great truth about Israel in the Old Testament was that they too were called by God to be his people.[21] Jude here writes to Christians who stand in a line of succession which stretches back to God's call of Abraham, through today, to a wonderful future in glory. Christians are the people of God, inheriting the promises God made to Israel.

b. Christians who are loved[22]

The second foundation truth is that Christians are *loved*. Jude is saying something more profound than that Christians are loved *by* God (although that is true), for he says, literally, that Christians are 'beloved in God',[23] which is complicated. We are loved by God and we are loved in God. What does Jude mean?[24] It is a wonderfully embracing promise of God's love in an insecure world, for Christians 'are loved by God and ... his love enfolds them'.[25] It is a double guarantee that God's love will not fail us, protecting us from the outside and strengthening us from within. Jude's reason for giving this remarkable reassurance will appear only towards the end

---

[20] *Cf.* Mt. 22:14; Rom. 1:1, 6–7; 8:28; 1 Cor. 1:24, 26; 1 Thes. 5:24; Heb. 3:1.
[21] Especially Is. 42:6; 48:12, 15; 49:1; 54:6.
[22] The AV and NKJV have 'sanctified' here, and many older commentators assume that translation. The reading 'loved' is probably correct, though, and 'sanctified' is possibly an assimilation to 1 Cor. 1:2, which made the Greek flow more easily.
[23] NRSV; SO TOO RV, NASB, NEB, RSV, GNB.
[24] Some say that this is simply where the name of the town to which Jude was writing has dropped out (as at Eph. 1:1), and we should read 'loved by God, in X'. But the Greek here runs more smoothly than the Ephesian hiatus, and the text should be read as it stands.
[25] Kelly, p. 243.

of his letter, as he brings out their responsibility to 'keep' themselves 'in God's love' (verse 21).

Again, this is no novelty for God's people, who have always known that were loved by God.[26] God's love stretches across both the Testaments. But there are a remarkable number of passages in Isaiah where the people who are called are also those who are loved,[27] and perhaps that is where Jude's mind is dwelling. If so, then he is making the identification of Christians with God's ancient people very clear indeed.

c. Christians who are kept

This third grand definition means that Christians are secure for the future when Jesus comes again. This verse (1) does not promise wealth or fame or success; but it promises that when we are poor, despised failures, God has not let go of us, and will not let go of us.[28] In particular, Jude wants us to know that when we see churches flooded with wrong teaching about God, and leaders making money out of peddling quack religion, Christ will keep a firm hold on his people. That was the problem that his churches faced, and the problem he addresses here. The Puritan commentator, Thomas Manton, says quaintly that 'Jesus Christ is the cabinet in which God's jewels are kept; so that if we would stand, we must get out of ourselves and get into him, in whom alone there is safety.'[29] This is obviously a key idea to grasp at the outset of Jude's letter, for he mentions 'keeping' four times in such a short work (here, twice in verse 6 and again in verse 24).

For the third time, Jude uses a term that has deep Old Testament sources, and once again Isaiah has proved important.[30] Jude has chosen three words that deliberately remind us that we are not the first people to hear God's covenant promises. This is his platform to show that God's earlier dealings with Israel lay down a pattern for his dealings with the new Israel.

The three terms also give us a Christian time-frame. We *have been called*, which refers to God's gracious acts in the past; we *are loved*, which describes his gracious attitude to us in the present; and we are being *kept* for a wonderful future with him in endless glory.

3. The prayer (2)

One of the distinctive features of Jude's style is his use of triplets of

---

[26] Dt. 7:7–10; 33:3, 12; 2 Ch. 20:7; Ps. 28:6. [27] *E.g.* Is. 42:6; 43:4; 44:2.
[28] 1 Pet. 1:3–7; 2 Pet. 2:4–9. [29] Manton, p. 43. [30] Is. 49:8.

ideas. We have already seen 'loved', 'called' and 'chosen', and there are many others (5–7, 11, 22–23, and less obvious ones too).[31] Here in verse 2 Jude prays for *mercy, peace and love* to be theirs *in abundance*. Jude is using a standard shape for his greeting,[32] but in common with other New Testament writers he gives it a force which is relevant to his theme.

Mercy is a quite specific word in the context of Jude (*cf.* verses 21–23), referring first to the mercy that God will show us on the day when he judges the world, and secondly to the mercy we are to show those who have slipped away from holding on to this fundamental truth and are believing something else. Jude is thus praying that God will show his readers great mercy now, as they face the danger of slipping away from him, and great mercy too on judgment day.

Peace, the second part of the prayer, also has a future aspect. As we read Jude, we shall encounter those who are 'destroyed' (5), who are 'bound with everlasting chains for judgment on the great Day' (6), and 'who suffer the punishment of eternal fire' (7). For them, 'blackest darkness has been reserved for ever' (13). We discover that such people are in positions of some authority in churches. Clearly, that is enough to disturb any of us, but Jude promises more than God's gift of peace of mind. He means that despite all the difficulties of trying to be a faithful and obedient Christian in a faithless and disobedient church, God has the power to bring us through. We do not need to follow the track taken by so many others whom Jude describes. It is possible to hold firm to God's promises, and on the last day to find ourselves among those who are at peace with him.

Love is a common Christian word, but it has a sharp focus in Jude. God's love is expressed in his plan to bring us into his glorious presence (24). It is like the radar system which provides an aircraft with a safe flight path, for it is certain to guide us to our destination. The warning is that safety can be certain only provided that we keep ourselves in that flight path (21). We cannot rest in the fact that God loves us, as if we could enjoy everything the gospel promises us today. We must keep our eyes on the future, and look forward to the day when we shall see love *in abundance*.

---

[31] Charles (1991) claims to have counted over twenty sets; p. 132.
[32] 1 Pet. 1:2 and 2 Pet. 1:2 are close, substituting 'grace' for 'mercy'.

Jude 3–4
2. Churches in danger

Dear friends, although I was very eager to write to you about the salvation we share, I felt I had to write and urge you to contend for the faith that was once for all entrusted to the saints. [4]For certain men whose condemnation was written about long ago have secretly slipped in among you. They are godless men, who change the grace of our God into a licence for immorality and deny Jesus Christ our only Sovereign and Lord.

Jude has been wanting to write a letter to his *dear friends* in this beloved church for some time, but circumstances have arisen which mean that he has had to put pen to paper with greater urgency than he intended. He has not had to alter his entire plan, however, and it would be too strong to say that 'he changes his mind'.[1] Although he had initially intended to write *about the salvation we share*, his subject has become *the faith that was once for all entrusted to the saints*. But it is probably a mistake to try to tease those two topics apart.[2] Perhaps we should think that where he intended to write a more general letter, the one he actually wrote is more concentrated, dealing with only one aspect of salvation. The new subject for his letter is the action he wants them to take. He not only wants them to have faith, but to *contend for the faith*. The reason is the emergence in the church of a group of people who are having a deadly influence on the lives of the ordinary Christians. In this section, Jude first says how he wants Christians to respond to his letter (because he has written to *urge* them *to contend for the faith*), and then explains the occasion for his letter (*certain men whose condemnation was written about long ago have secretly slipped in among you*).

---

[1] Kistemaker, p. 413.
[2] Green (1987) says that 'our present Jude is not about the salvation we share' (p. 171). But Jude opens and closes on that note of 'salvation'. That indicates a major theme in such a short work, and should in fact control the exegetical line.

1. The salvation we share (3a)

Salvation is a great biblical word, but too often it is allowed to slip from its biblical moorings. We often use the idea of 'being saved' as if it were identical to 'being converted' or 'being a Christian'. But it is much richer than that. Jude's most famous verses (24–25) praise 'God our Saviour', and it is clear from the context there that he means that God will save us in the future. That is the tenor of his entire letter: God 'is able' (24) to save us from the 'condemnation', 'judgment', 'punishment', conviction and destruction (4, 6, 7, 15, 5) that he has 'reserved for ever' (13). In a horrific pairing of images Jude depicts the grim reality of God's wrath; it is 'darkness' but at the same time 'fire' (6–7, 13, 23). To be rescued from that, and to be allowed to change from having 'clothing stained by corrupted flesh' (23) into being 'without fault' (24), is to experience the full scope of God's rescue plan. Until we are in 'his glorious presence' (24), we can only wait for his mercy (21).

Wonderfully, every Christian is qualified to *share* in this salvation. Quite possibly, the people Jude is trying to deal with had an élitist view of their spiritual standing and maturity, and saw themselves as being more free and confident in their morality than other, less mature, law-bound believers. But Jude emphasizes that the offer of salvation is wide open, for it is a 'common faith',[3] and ironically it is open even to the very people who are so scornfully denying it to others.

2. The faith we defend (3b)

Two factors underlie the greater urgency which Jude senses. Circumstances have arisen which ought to call the Christians to a steady defence of the faith, and he is deeply alarmed that they might not have the backbone to conduct that defence. He gives four reasons why we should be uncompromising in our defence of the Christian good news.

a. The faith is closed in its content

By *faith* Jude means those things which we believe, rather than the fact that we believe them; it is objective rather than subjective. To many commentators, this is proof of the lateness of the letter, but there is nothing here to suggest that Jude is talking about a creed or a lengthy doctrinal basis. He means the simple Christian truths

---

[3] Tit. 1:4.

which, from the earliest Christian writings, have been seen as the gospel that saves us.[4]

Disputes over the content of the gospel are common in churches, and the New Testament letters show that this has always been the case and is not necessarily anything to be avoided. Those letters also indicate the form that such disputes take. Sometimes people subtract from the gospel. The clearest New Testament examples of this are a denial of the resurrection (1 Corinthians) or of the return of Christ (2 Peter). On other occasions, the deadly danger is a desire to supplement the message. Thus the New Testament calls on Christians to resist new teaching (Galatians) or new spirituality (Colossians). But the defence against those who want either to supplement or to dilute the Christian message (at those or any other points) must be our rock-solid adherence to the faith, the whole faith, and nothing but the faith.

The same debate continues today. It is commonplace to remove elements of biblical teaching which are culturally embarrassing, on the subjective criterion that they were 'culturally conditioned'. Hence items of belief and patterns of behaviour which were normative for the first Christians are treated as interesting but irrelevant curios. Fortunately, it is relatively easy to spot those who wish to prune the gospel.

The opposite danger is also alive, but much more difficult to isolate. The great twentieth-century theologian Karl Barth was once asked what he thought was the single greatest obstacle to reconciliation between the Reformed churches and the Roman Catholic Church. He replied:

> I think the greatest obstacle could be a very small word which the Roman Church tacks on to every one of our propositions. This very small word 'and'. When we say Jesus, the Catholics say Jesus *and* Mary. We seek to obey our sole Lord, Christ. The Catholics seek to obey Christ *and* his earthly vicar, that is to say the Pope. We believe that the Christian is saved by the merits of Jesus Christ; but the Catholic adds: *and* by his own merits, that is to say, his good works. We think that the only source of Revelation is the Scriptures; the Catholics add: *and* Tradition. We say that knowledge of God comes from faith in his word, as it is expressed in Scripture. The Catholics add: *and* from Reason.[5]

For Jude, the faith has been irrevocably fixed for us. Neither superstitious additions nor secular diminution should shake the

---

[4] Lk. 1:2; Acts 2:42; 20:32; Rom. 6:17; Gal. 1:6–9, 23; 2 Jn. 9.
[5] Karl Barth, 'Prospects for Christian Unity', in J. A. O'Brien (ed.), *Steps to Christian Unity* (London: Collins, 1965), p. 87.

Christian from holding that foundation teaching in its closed entirety.

b. The faith is closed in its authorship

Jude says that the faith was *entrusted* to us. He uses a word that had become almost a technical term in Christian circles to describe how God gave the church the message through the apostles.[6] Jude understands that God is the author of the good news, and the apostles would be among the *saints* who received it. The ultimate responsibility for the gospel lies with God, which is why it is such a terrible thing to change it. 'It is not a thing invented, but given; not found out by us, but delivered by God himself; and delivered to our custody that we may keep it for posterity.'[7]

It is easy to become thoughtless about that, as if it were obvious and to be taken for granted that God would give us an unchangeable gospel. But it is a remarkable privilege. The psalmist says with wonder, 'He has revealed his word to Jacob, his laws and decrees to Israel. He has done this for no other nation; they do not know his laws. Praise the LORD.'[8]

We can begin to see Jude's concern. If God has given us a gospel, and if he is not going to give us another one, we must guard it as highly precious.

c. The faith is closed in its historical setting

The faith was entrusted, Jude says, *once for all*. The word[9] has the meaning of finality and definiteness. So there is no room to think that God grants extra insights and additions down the years of Christian history. Of course, each generation of Christians has had to express that message in the context of fierce arguments, and the Christian creeds and confessions of faith were often geared to answer particular problems in the language of their day. The creeds record not the sum of what Christians believed, but the points which heretics doubted! Those who formulated the creeds knew that they were being forced to crystallize issues in words that were not in the Bible, and did so trembling with fear, solely to defend the authoritative gospel.[10]

---

[6] *Paradidōmi*: Lk. 1:2; Acts 16:4; 1 Cor. 11:2; 15:1–3; 2 Thes. 3:6; 2 Pet. 2:21.
[7] Manton, p. 104.   [8] Ps. 147:19–20.   [9] *Hapax*; *cf.* 1 Pet. 3:18.
[10] This is especially true of the care that was taken over the word *homoousios*, meaning that Jesus is 'of one substance' with the Father. Hilary, a theologian who defended the retention of the term in the Nicene Creed, wrote, 'We are compelled by the error of heretics and blasphemers to do what is unlawful, to scale heights, to express things that are unutterable, to encroach on forbidden matters. And when we

The acid test of our contemporary expression of Christianity is whether it addresses the questions and issues of our day in a relevant manner without losing the distinctive cutting edge of being a 'once for all' faith. That is difficult today, because the relativistic assumption is that all cultures are equally valid, and should share one another's insights. Jude would warn us to take great care at this point, for the people he opposed are still with us. Their hallmark is that they share this relativism. They drift from authentic Christian historical moorings, and see Christianity in terms of a development or process towards an understanding of God, expressed only in contemporary terms. They may well quote the Bible, but they will quote it selectively for illustration, never for authoritative instruction. The successors to Jude's opponents will appear even-handed and generous in their attitude to any religious insight, as long as that insight does not claim finality.

It should therefore be no surprise that Jude has been so long neglected, for he claims that very 'once for all' authority. We have all the more reason to pay attention to him, for the relativism which is at the heart of his opponents is now at the heart of our culture too, and shapes the thinking and viewpoint of even biblically minded Christians. Jude's heretics will seem to make sense to our world, where Jude himself will appear narrow and dangerous. Because we are cultural beings, it will be more natural for us to form alliances with the world than with him.

d. The faith is open to anyone

The faith . . . was once for all entrusted to the saints. Who are *the saints?* All those who are Christians, who have been declared righteous or holy by God. In the New Testament, 'saint' is almost a definition of a Christian,[12] and the writers would have found it strange that we tend to identify sainthood with a few special people. The Christian's name, 'saint', is 'at once an honour, an exhortation, and a reproach. It tells of his high calling, it exhorts him to live up to

---

ought to fulfil the commandments through faith alone, adoring the Father, worshipping the Son together with him, rejoicing in the Holy Spirit, we are forced to stretch the feeble capacity of our language to give expression to indescribable realities. We are constrained by the error of others to err ourselves in the dangerous attempt to set forth in human speech what ought to be kept in the religious awe of our minds . . . Their infidelity drags us into the dubious and dangerous position of having to make a definite statement beyond what heaven has prescribed about matters so sublime and so deeply hidden.' *De Trinitate* 2.2, 5, quoted in T. F. Torrance, *The Trinitarian Faith* (Edinburgh: T. and T. Clark, 1993) pp. 26–27.

[11] *E.g.* Acts 9:13, 32; Rom. 1:7; 2 Cor. 1:1; Eph. 1:1; Rev. 5:8.

it, and it reminds him of his grievous shortcomings.'[12]
The root of the idea lies in Daniel 7.

In my vision at night I looked, and there before me was one like a son of man, coming with the clouds of heaven. He approached the Ancient of Days and was led into his presence. He was given authority, glory and sovereign power; all peoples, nations and men of every language worshipped him. His dominion is an everlasting dominion that will not pass away, and his kingdom is one that will never be destroyed.
... I approached one of those standing there and asked him the true meaning of all this.
So he told me and gave me the interpretation of these things: 'The four great beasts are four kingdoms that will rise from the earth. But the saints of the Most High will receive the kingdom and will possess it for ever – yes, for ever and ever.'[13]

In that important passage, one idea is central for Jude: the saints are those believers who wait for the coming of the Son of Man in power. Once again, Jude has identified the Christians with the people of God, and has told us that our true identity lies in looking for Jesus Christ to return in power. What marks out a 'saint', then, is a desire to live life today in the light of what will happen in the future.

3. The opposition we expect (4)

Jude does not tell us to believe the faith, spread the faith or live the faith, although all those injunctions would be appropriate. Instead, he tells us to *contend for the faith*, a much harder task and an 'exceptionally strong'[14] word. Paul uses a related word to describe his struggle for the gospel.[15] Jude's word implies the ongoing 'wrestling match'[16] that he wants us to become involved in. This will be unpopular, because it is commonly assumed that since Christianity is a faith based on love, it can say only nice, comforting things. The evidence throughout the Bible is that being faithful to God's Word means bringing hard, unpopular warnings as well as bright promises.

Paul's example is instructive here, for he knew when to affirm and when to rebuke. On one occasion, he was being publicly humiliated by a group of evangelists who were apparently trampling on his reputation in order to build their own. In such circumstances, Paul was unfailingly generous, and wrote: 'What does it matter? The

---

[12] Plummer, p. 379. [13] Dn. 7:13–14, 16–18. [14] Kelly, p. 247.
[15] *Agōnizomenos*, 1 Cor. 9:25; Col. 1:29; 4:12.
[16] Blum, p. 388. The word is *epagōnizesthai*.

important thing is that in every way, whether from false motives or true, Christ is preached. And because of this I rejoice.'[17] His own reputation was irrelevant, and he longed only for the furtherance of the gospel. His attitude was quite different when he faced the opposition in Galatia, for there it was Christ's reputation, not his, that was at stake. The generous man gave way to the fighter in him. 'When Peter came to Antioch, I opposed him to his face, because he was clearly in the wrong.'[18] The temptation is to reverse those two reactions, leaping fiercely to the defence of our own reputation, while we let known heretics teach in peace because we do not wish to appear un-Christian! Such a surrender is a tragic reversal of apostolic thinking. Paul's instructions on false teachers are as simple, inescapable and certain as Jude's. Such men, he told Titus, 'must be silenced ... rebuke them ... They are detestable, disobedient and unfit for doing anything good.'[19] Once we have decided that there is a course of action to follow, and that we know that the motives from which we are acting are as pure as they can be, we must *contend*. We must be ready for people to tell us 'not to be so negative', and to face them with Jude's command here. Jude has a reason for his defiant stance, for he has recognized in *certain men* the opposition we face.

a. A predicted opposition

The most important feature about Jude's opponents is that their *condemnation was written about long ago*.[20] Older commentators took the AV's line that Jude is talking about these people's predestination ('who were before of old ordained to this condemnation').[21] But it makes more sense, as we shall see, if Jude is saying that the church should expect false teachers, because there is a long-standing source of written information about them.

For some commentators, that source is 2 Peter. They would point to the way Peter predicts that 'in the last days scoffers will come'.[22] Jude says that they *have secretly slipped in among you*. They would say that by the time of Jude, Peter's prophecy has become a present

---

[17] Phil. 1:18.
[18] Gal. 2:11. He was even less generous with the originators of the false gospel; Gal. 5:12.
[19] Tit. 1:11, 13, 16.
[20] Literally 'this condemnation', which 'refers forward to verses 5–19'. Green (1987), p. 174.
[21] The NIV footnote has 'men who were marked out for condemnation'. Wayne Grudem supports this understanding; *Systematic Theology* (Leicester: IVP; Grand Rapids: Zondervan, 1994), p. 703.
[22] 2 Pet. 3:3.

reality. But the solution may not be that simple. We cannot assume that Peter and Jude were writing to the same church in the same town about the same people, for the heresy in each case is subtly different. It may be that Peter has adapted Jude's message for a more Gentile readership.[23]

Jude says that the source of information on their condemnation was written *long ago*. The word usually means precisely that, but can be translated 'already',[24] so it has some elasticity. The main source of their condemnation is the Old Testament and the teaching that grows from it.[25] But Jude's word could stretch to include 'what the apostles of our Lord Jesus Christ foretold' (verse 17), and yet still go as far back as 'Enoch, the seventh from Adam' (verse 14). Within this great span, Jude selects nine Old Testament examples: unbelieving Israel, fallen angels, Sodom and Gomorrah, Michael, Moses, Cain, Balaam, Korah and Enoch. This series of nine explains the structure of the first part of Jude's letter. Verses 5–19 present a sequence of explanations of biblical teaching. Each section (5–7, 9, 11, 14–15, 17–18) is followed by a Greek word, *houtoi*, literally 'these [men]', which introduces an application (8, 10, 12–13, 16, 19). Richard Bauckham rightly calls this 'a carefully composed ... exegesis'.[26]

The Christians to whom Jude was writing might still say that although they were sure that his warning was prefigured in the Old Testament, it had no possible relevance to them. Jude has already anticipated that response by describing them in terms that make it clear that they (and we) are the new Israel (verses 1–2). If we are, then we must expect the Scriptures that speak to the old Israel to speak to us as well. It should have been obvious to them, because the verb translated *was written about*[27] also means 'to placard in public', with a legal sense of a public accusation.[28] Jude is saying that the Bible speaks clearly on this question, warning that there

---

[23] See Appendix.

[24] *E.g.* Mk. 15:44. The word is *palai*, translated 'past' in 2 Pet. 1:9.

[25] Michael, Moses and Enoch will be discussed in their appropriate sections below.

[26] Bauckham (1983), p. 157. This structure was first suggested by Ellis, and is now generally followed. Jude's exegetical techniques are sometimes called 'midrash', but that is a notoriously slippery term; see *DJG*, pp. 544ff. Jude also uses frequent catchwords to tie his letter together: *asebēs* ('ungodly'), *krisis* ('judgment'), *houtoi* ('these men'), *planē* ('error'), *blasphemeō* ('slander') and *tēreō* ('keep'). But that is merely good style, and does not give the structure. Charles (1990) goes too far in saying that 'they form the links in Jude's polemical argument' (p. 110); see Bauckham (1983), pp. 206–211.

[27] *Prographō*.

[28] For the biblical theme, see Je. 22:30; Mal. 3:16; for the word, BAGD, p. 704. Paul used the same word to describe his preaching: 'Before your very eyes Jesus Christ was *clearly portrayed* as crucified' (Gal. 3:1).

will always be opposition to biblical truths within churches. We have to grasp this before Jude's way of arguing will make any sense to us: our Bible is the whole Bible, and that is where God speaks today.

b. A creeping opposition

Apparently, Jude's readers have been so blind to the perfectly obvious warnings in the Bible that they have not noticed the insidious people who *have secretly slipped in among you.*[29] Presumably these people (Jude talks about them with the disdain displayed by other New Testament writers)[30] were itinerants who 'offered a blend of sophistication and immediacy',[31] and managed to distort an honourable role in the churches into a source of easy income. John had to warn his church about such groups: 'If anyone comes to you and does not bring this teaching, do not take him into your house or welcome him. Anyone who welcomes him shares in his wicked work.'[32] The message had to go out to the churches not to use 'niceness' as an excuse for gullibility. Those who 'have wormed their way in' (NEB) with a different kind of Christianity do not represent a refreshing change or a lost tradition; they come as a serious danger.

c. A godless opposition

Jude says quite bluntly that *they are godless men*, and that is one of the key words he will use throughout his letter to describe them (*cf.* verses 14, 15, 18). It is a word which 'crystallises his view of the heretics'.[33] Although these people no doubt mouthed Christian phrases, quoted the Bible and knew all the new songs, they were not to be taken at face value. No doubt Jude's readers were shocked at the implication of what he was saying. We should be shocked too as we realize that he is talking about people who may write Christian books, speak at Christian conferences and sound very convincing and liberating. Jude was denouncing their friends and their heroes – and therefore perhaps some of our friends and our heroes – as anti-Christian pagans.

---

[29] LS, p. 1333; the word was sometimes used of political infiltration and subversion.
[30] Rom. 3:8; 1 Cor. 4:18; 15:34; 2 Cor. 3:1; 10:12; Gal. 1:7; 1 Tim. 1:3, 19; 2 Pet. 3:9.
[31] Martin, p. 83.   [32] 2 Jn. 10–11.   [33] Kelly, p. 277.

d. A sensual opposition

They *change the grace of our God into a licence for immorality*. One of the first questions the early church had to face was the heady issue: 'Shall we go on sinning, so that grace may increase?'[34] To a sceptical Jew, it looked as if the Christian gospel turned God's generous gift of the law into an opportunity for sin (and that is the attack Paul handled). To a sceptical Greek, the gospel could seem to offer total freedom today on the basis of total forgiveness tomorrow. Throughout the history of the church, there have been those who have taken a position opposed to (Greek *anti*) the idea of law (Greek *nomos*) – the position called 'antinomianism'. Jude uses a word for *immorality* (*aselgeia*) which covers the full range of sensuality, debauchery and sexual permissiveness,[35] all of which were being offered in the name of the gospel of free grace! John Bunyan met a man with antinomian views who 'gave himself up to all manner of filthiness, especially uncleanness . . . and would laugh at exhortations to sobriety. When I laboured to rebuke his wickedness, he would laugh the more.'[36] What antinomians choose to fail to recognize is that if we accept Christ's easier yoke and lighter burden, we are still taking up a yoke and a burden.[37] Christian liberty is not the same as Christian licence.

e. A heretical opposition

'Heretic' is a hard word to use of anyone, but it seems to fit those who are in a church and yet *deny Jesus Christ our only Sovereign and Lord*. Jude is deliberately raising the stakes here. He does so in a way that some early Christians found difficult, and they amended Jude's words. Jude applies to Jesus not only the usual title *Lord* (*kyrios*), but the much stronger term *Sovereign* (*despotēs*), a word the New Testament normally reserves for the sovereignty of God the Father.[38] Jude even says that Jesus is our *only Sovereign*. Although we should honour attempts to be reverential,[39] there is no need to amend the text, or to doubt what Jude is saying about the absolute right of Jesus Christ to our sole loyalty and obedience.[40]

We might expect, then, that the error of 'these men' would be one

---

[34] Rom. 6:1.
[35] Mk. 7:22; Rom. 13:13; 2 Cor. 12:21; Gal. 5:19; Eph. 4:19; 1 Pet. 4:3; 2 Pet. 2:2, 7, 18.
[36] *Grace Abounding*, para. 44. (Everyman edn., London: J. M. Dent, 1928), p. 18.
[37] Mt. 11:28–30.   [38] Lk. 2:29; Acts 4:24; 2 Tim. 2:21; 2 Pet. 2:1; Rev. 6:10.
[39] 'The only Lord God and our Lord Jesus Christ' is how the NKJV phrases it here.
[40] The words 'Sovereign' and 'Lord' are governed by a single definite article in the Greek; only one person is in view.

of theology, perhaps making some blunder over the incarnation or the cross. But instead the error is a wilful rebellion, refusing to submit to *Jesus Christ our only Sovereign and Lord*, and engaging in a 'reckless self-indulgence'.[41] This is both a theological and a moral error; the two are closely tied together. 'These men' have not grasped, or they refuse to grasp, the extent of Jesus Christ's sovereignty, and so they feel free to play fast and loose with it. As Luther says, they 'consider not him as their Lord but themselves as their own Lord'.[42] One of the features of the opposition Jude describes is its inseparable marriage of bad theology and bad morals. If a Christian behaves badly, it must be because he or she has not understood the Bible properly; or, having understood it, refuses to accept its rule.[43]

Jude has now told us why he is writing, and we expect his letter to fulfil that promise. He will first tell us about these predicted dangers (verses 5–19), and then how we can take action (verses 20–25) to 'contend for the faith' – the purpose of his letter.

[41] Green (1987), p. 175.   [42] Luther, p. 300.   [43] 1 Jn. 2:26–27.

Jude 5–8
3. Warnings of judgment: three Old Testament examples

Though you already know all this, I want to remind you that the Lord delivered his people out of Egypt, but later destroyed those who did not believe. ⁶And the angels who did not keep their positions of authority but abandoned their own home – these he has kept in darkness, bound with everlasting chains for judgment on the great Day. ⁷In a similar way, Sodom and Gomorrah and the surrounding towns gave themselves up to sexual immorality and perversion. They serve as an example of those who suffer the punishment of eternal fire.

⁸In the very same way, these dreamers pollute their own bodies, reject authority and slander celestial beings.

The Bible is full of calls to us to remember things. The reason, of course, lies not in our stupidity, but in the importance of memory in biblical terms. We are not told to remember something simply because we might temporarily have forgotten it or because the pressures of the day tempt us to adopt different priorities. Remembering in the Bible is a duty, an act of will; and those who *remind* God's people do so in a tone of solemnity and great moment. God tells Moses to instruct the Israelites to wear tassels on their clothes, 'so you will remember all the commands of the LORD, that you may obey them and not prostitute yourselves by going after the lusts of your own hearts and eyes'.[1] Underneath all the remembering of humans is the wonder that God 'remembers his covenant for ever',[2] and that when he sent Jesus it was because he was 'remembering to be merciful'.[3] There was no danger that God would forget to be merciful, but this kind of language was his way of underlining the seriousness of his commitment to the covenant. When Christians break bread and drink wine together, they do it 'in remembrance'[4] of the Lord Jesus. We are not in danger of forgetting the mere fact of

---

[1] Nu. 15:39.   [2] 1 Ch. 16:15.   [3] Lk. 1:54.   [4] Lk. 22:19.

Jesus' death; but he wants us constantly to recall its significance and remember that he will return. Above all, it is the function of a Christian church leader today to do as Jude did, making sure that Christians understand the gospel and do not budge from it. It is the duty of the teacher to remind the church.

Jude knows perfectly well that his readers *already know* the basic Bible stories he is going to tell them, but it is clear from their behaviour that they have not understood them.[5] Perhaps, like us, they treat Old Testament narratives as good stories for children, that have no message once we become adults. That is bad, and Jude wants to remedy the situation. His words here are not 'an apology',[6] for he is perfectly convinced that he needs to place firmly before us the truths we need so much but are unable to grasp for ourselves.

1. The warnings (5–7)

In line with his plan to show us how the problems we face as churches have always been the problems of God's people, Jude gives us his first series of three Old Testament warnings[7] (the second comes in verses 11–13). These are three examples of the fact that rebellion against God does not succeed. The first one is out of its chronological order, probably to heighten its significance.[8]

a. The people of Israel (5)

Jude's first example is one that struck other New Testament writers[9] for its continuing relevance. Of the many times when God had intervened in Israel's history, two strikingly opposite occasions came to mind. The first was when he *delivered his people out of Egypt*.[10] This was a formative moment for Israel, making a rabble of slaves into God's own people. It came to dominate Old Testament thinking as a pattern of God's saving dealings with his people, and its writers began to use it as a source of hope that God would rescue them from exile in Babylon and save them again.[11] It is not

---

[5] Green (1987) translates this, 'You knew it all once', and says, 'There is no justification for the NIV rendering of *hapax* by *already* and *eidotes* by *know*' (p. 177). 'Already' is weak, but *eidotes*, a perfect active participle, can have a present sense: 'Although you are fully informed' (NSRV). *Pace* GNB, *hapax* belongs here and not with the exodus (see note 13 below).

[6] Kelly, p. 254.

[7] Superficially similar to 2 Pet. 2:4–9, the two passages differ in content (Jude uses the Israelites, Peter the flood), in order (Jude is thematic, Peter chronological) and in purpose (Jude's examples are of judgment, Peter's of judgment and salvation). See comments on 2 Pet. 2:4–9, and the Appendix.

[8] Bauckham (1983), p. 50.   [9] 1 Cor. 10:5–11; Heb. 3:15 – 4:2.

[10] Ex. 1:1 – 14:31.   [11] Is. 63:7–19.

183

surprising, then, that Christians took over this model as a way of teaching about the cross and the salvation Jesus Christ accomplished there. Jesus himself taught us to do that, calling his death an 'exodus'.[12]

The most alarming part of the exodus story for Jude is God's later[13] intervention, when he *destroyed* the generation he had earlier rescued. Moses had sent twelve men on a reconnaissance mission to report on the land which God had promised them and which they were about to invade. They returned with a report of a land which was fertile but well fortified. Despite the encouragement of two expedition members, Joshua and Caleb, the people were dismayed and decided not to enter the land. God's response to their unbelief was that 'not one of the men who saw my glory and the miraculous signs I performed in Egypt and the desert but who disobeyed and tested me ten times – not one of them will ever see the land I promised on oath to their forefathers. No-one who has treated me with contempt will ever see it.' The judgment was that 'they will meet their end in this desert; here they will die'.[14]

The drastic difference between the two divine interventions was caused by one simple factor. In the second, the people of Israel *did not believe*. Despite the numerous promises God had given them, and the numerous proofs of his power, when they were actually faced with the task of acting upon those promises they showed a lack of faith. Here, surely, is where Jude is taking us, for we too lie between two great events in history. Behind us is the cross, which provides the only possible escape from the judgment which lies before us. The only way to gain the benefit from that is to believe it now. But there are people in our churches who look and sound like the people of God, but who will not be saved on the last day, because they rebel against God's promises and rule. Like the Israelites in the desert, they do not believe, and in consequence they will face the Judge. That was the case in the wilderness, it was the case in Jude's day, and it will be the case in ours.

b. The angels of heaven (6)

Jude's second example of an Old Testament judgment is more

---

[12] Lk. 9:31, translated 'departure' by NIV.

[13] Literally, 'a second time'. For that to make sense, *hapax* ('once') would have to refer to the exodus from Egypt. But it should really have a context earlier in the sentence, where it is found. The NIV places the word correctly, at the start of the sentence, but translates the phrase loosely as 'you already know all this'. Jude is subtly contrasting the two acts of God, to save and to judge, with the two comings of Jesus, as Saviour and Judge.

[14] Nu. 13:1 – 14:45.

difficult to untangle. He might be talking about the fall of the angels caused by their rebellion against God, of which Isaiah and Ezekiel give us tantalizing glimpses.[15] But he is more likely to be referring to the strange incident in Genesis 6:1–3: 'When men began to increase in number on the earth and daughters were born to them, the sons of God saw that the daughters of men were beautiful, and they married any of them they chose.' The angels have some *positions of authority*, their areas of God-given responsibility.[16] But they were not satisfied with the role God had given them, and infringed the boundaries by intermarriage with humans. Daryl Charles says, 'The focal point in Jude is not so much the identifying of the exact sin of the angels, rather the fact that the angels *left their domain* and hence are being "reserved" for judgment.'[17]

Jude illuminates this story with a grim pun. The angels, itching with lust, could not *keep* to their place. But God will not be rebelled against, and he has *kept* those same angels until the future judgment. God's judgment, then, is inescapable, even though it may be delayed. The application is clear: the people who infect the churches in the way Jude will describe must not think that they can get away with their rebellious behaviour for ever. If even angels are subject to God's judgment, despite their most strenuous attempts to rebel, what chance do human rebels have?

c. The cities of the plain (7)

Jude's third warning from the Old Testament takes the cities of Sodom and Gomorrah (Gn. 18:1 – 19:29), a well-used biblical example of judgment.[18] There were five cities on the plain, of which Admah and Zeboiim were destroyed along with the other two,[19] and Zoar was spared because of Lot. Jude's focus here is on the two we know best, and on their deserved punishment.

Sodom and Gomorrah were in a beautiful position, 'well watered, like the garden of the LORD',[20] but that did not lead them to be grateful to their Creator, for they were 'arrogant, overfed and unconcerned; they did not help the poor and needy. They were haughty and did detestable things' before God.[21] But Jude focuses

---

[15] Is. 14:12–15; Ezk. 28:11–19.
[16] See, *e.g.*, Ps. 104:4; Dn. 9:21–22; 10:4 – 11:1; Eph. 1:21; 3:10; Col. 2:10, 15; Heb. 1:7. The AV translated the word *archē* ('positions of authority') as 'their first estate', but NKJV has 'proper domain', which is better.
[17] Charles (1991), p. 135.
[18] Dt. 29:23; 32:32; Ps. 107:34; Is. 1:9–10; 3:9; 13:19; Je. 23:14; 49:18; 50:40; La. 4:6; Ezk. 16:46–55; Am. 4:11; Zp. 2:9; Mt. 10:15; 11:24; Lk. 10:12; 17:29; Rom. 9:29; 2 Pet. 2:6; Rev. 11:8.
[19] Dt. 29:23; Ho. 11:8.   [20] Gn. 13:10.   [21] Ezk. 16:49–50.

on the area which the Genesis account highlights too, which is their sexual sin. The words Jude uses are strong, for literally they 'went after other flesh'.[22] This is a highly controversial phrase.

Traditionally, the sin of Sodom has been understood as homosexual activity. This is based on Genesis 19:1–5, in which Lot showed hospitality to two visitors. After the meal, the men of Sodom surrounded the house, demanding to have sex with the guests – who were in fact angels, who had come to warn Lot of the coming destruction of the city. But that theory is currently under two different lines of scrutiny. Richard Bauckham, for example, says that the (human) men of Sodom, in lusting after angels, committed the 'most extravagant of sexual aberrations, which would have transgressed the order of creation as shockingly as the fallen angels did'.[23] The deep root of the sin of Sodom was undoubtedly rebellion against the created order, but it is probably too neat to detect a balance between the two examples, as Bauckham does. The sin intended by the men of Sodom was emphatically not that of lust after angels, since they had no idea of the spiritual significance of their visitors. Their request is simply, 'Where are the men who came to you tonight? Bring them out to us so that we can have sex with them.'[24]

The second attempted revision is to see the sin not as homosexual activity *per se*, but as something more subtle: a breach of courtesy rules. It has been argued that neither the word translated 'have sex with' – literally, 'know' – nor the Old Testament's understanding of Sodom's sin, requires a homosexual interpretation.[25] 'The sin of the men in the street is boorish hostility to foreigners rather than sexual perversion.'[26] But although the word 'know' need not have a sexual connotation, it certainly does have that meaning in the immediate context (*cf.* Gn. 19:8, there translated 'slept with' in NIV). Furthermore, although the Old Testament does not elsewhere refer to any sexual element in Sodom's sin, John Stott correctly says that 'the adjectives "wicked", "vile" and "disgraceful" (Gen. 19:7; Judges 19:23) do not seem appropriate to describe a breach of hospitality'.[27] Despite the attempts of Bailey, which are no doubt well

---

[22] *Sarkos heteras.*   [23] Bauckham (1983), p. 54.   [24] Gn. 19:5.

[25] See D. S. Bailey, *Homosexuality in the Western Christian Tradition* (1955; Hamden: Shoe String, 1975). His views have been criticized by John Stott, *Issues Facing Christians Today* (London: Marshall Pickering; 2nd edn. 1990) = *Decisive Issues Facing Christians Today* (Old Tappan: Revell, 1990), pp. 339–340, and B. G. Webb, *Theological and Pastoral Responses to Homosexuality*, Explorations 8 (Sydney: Openbook Publishers, 1994), pp. 74–78.

[26] Webb's interpretation of Bailey; Webb, *op. cit.*, p. 75.

[27] Stott, *op cit.*, p. 340. The reference to Judges is to a second story that Bailey treats in the same way.

intended pastorally, it seems inescapable that the sin of Sodom was an attempted homosexual gang rape.[28]

Was this the exact situation in Jude's church? Possibly, although it is difficult to say, and an exact correlation is not necessary for Jude's argument. His teaching applies to a wide range of contemporary churches. Sodom was a unique example from biblical history, and it was a notoriously violent and disgraceful city. This example, like the other two warnings here, is a highlighted prototype of God's attitude. It is difficult, however, to ignore the fact that the Bible consistently portrays homosexual practice as rebellion against God's natural order, from which it is both necessary and possible to be saved. Paul reminds the Corinthian Christians: 'Neither the sexually immoral nor idolaters nor adulterers nor male prostitutes nor homosexual offenders nor thieves nor the greedy nor drunkards nor slanderers nor swindlers will inherit the kingdom of God.' But he is able to add: 'And that is what some of you were. But you were washed, you were sanctified, you were justified in the name of the Lord Jesus Christ and by the Spirit of our God.'[29] That means, of course, that homosexual practice is neither better nor worse than any other rebellion against God's law. Jude is not targeting it as the worst imaginable sin. He has already (verse 5) pointed to lack of belief as the ultimate rebellion.[30] He is not telling us to engage in a prurient witch-hunt. His message about obedience will apply to any Christian in any place. Nevertheless, it does seem that the people in his church were expressing their claimed freedom in homosexual sex, and Jude sees that as rebellion.

The horrific fireball of destruction that hit Sodom and the other cities serves *as an example* to us of God's final judgment. 'The angels had the blessings of heaven, the Israelites of the Church and Sodom of the world. But the angels upon their apostasy lost heaven, the murmuring Israelites were shut out of Canaan, and the Sodomites were, together with their fruitful land, destroyed.'[31] These are not just an example; they are a 'warning'[32] of what will happen in the future on a far greater scale. The punishment Sodom and Gomorrah suffered was temporary, and although the volcanic activity of the area constantly reminds tourists of the biblical story, Ezekiel looked forward to their restoration.[33] No such happy

---

[28] Webb's position is close to Bauckham's, but he adds that the 'object was to humiliate the foreigners by subjecting them to homosexual rape, as was often done to prisoners of war in the ancient world' (p. 77, n. 6). It is unclear in his interpretation whether the men of Sodom knew that the messengers were angels.
[29] 1 Cor. 6:9–11.
[30] Jesus used Sodom and Gomorrah to make exactly the same point; Mt. 10:14–15; 11:20–24.
[31] Manton, p. 219.   [32] Kistemaker, p. 382.   [33] Ezk. 16:53–55.

restoration awaits *those who suffer the punishment of eternal fire*, a destiny about which Jesus himself warns us.[34]

Note: eternal fire

There is a sharp division between evangelicals on the destiny of those condemned by God. Some believe that hell is a place of eternal, conscious torment;[35] others that it is a place of irreversible and horrific destruction.[36] Proponents of both views argue on premises far wider than Jude 7, and for neither group is it a main element in their case. The matter must be decided from a complete biblical perspective, for this verse alone is interpreted both ways. Whichever conclusion we reach (and in either case the fate is horrible), Jude has written to warn us of it. Will we take notice?

2. 'These dreamers' (8)

Jude is not presenting us with an abstract theological treatise on the purity of the church, for these Old Testament examples are God's living word to us. It comes as no shock to him that *these dreamers* have arrived and have started to exercise their destructive ministries. In three brief character sketches he reminds us of his examples, summing them up in reverse order, and showing us that they are realities in the church.

a. These dreamers pollute their own bodies[37]

Jude first applies the example of Sodom, a contrast brought out well by the NASB, which says that just as those people 'went after strange flesh', so these people 'defile the flesh'. He broadens out his message here; the problem was obviously a general one, and his phrase covers 'various sexual excesses, doubtless including homosexuality'.[38] A major sign of the presence of these dreamers within

---

[34] Mt. 18:8; 25:41; see too Rev. 19:20; 20:10; 21:8.

[35] *E.g.* J. I. Packer, *The Problem of Eternal Punishment* (Bury St Edmunds: Fellowship of Word and Spirit, Orthos Booklet 10, n.d.), p. 6; *idem*, 'The Problem of Eternal Punishment', *Crux* 26.3 (September 1990), pp. 18–25; J. Blanchard, *Whatever Happened to Hell?* (Welwyn: Evangelical Press, 1993); L. Dixon, *The Other Side of the Good News* (Wheaton: Victor Books, 1992).

[36] Most importantly, E. W. Fudge, *The Fire that Consumes* (Exeter: Paternoster, rev. edn. 1994), but see also J. W. Wenham, 'The Case for Conditional Immortality', in N. M. de S. Cameron (ed.), *Universalism and the Doctrine of Hell* (Grand Rapids: Baker, 1992), pp. 161–191. That volume also includes a critique of Fudge's work by K. S. Harmon (pp. 191–224), which Fudge's revised edition notes.

[37] Jude uses a sentence structure which separates the one sexual sin and the two examples of rebelliousness (*men ... de ... de*).

[38] Blum, p. 391.

our own churches is the loosening of sexual morality and the acceptance of behaviour that other generations of Christians would have found impossible to justify.

b. These dreamers reject authority

More literally, they reject 'lordship' (*kyriotēs*). As the related word 'Lord' (*kyrios*) has already been used in verses 4 and 5, it is clear that Jude is restating his claim that they 'deny ... our only Sovereign and Lord' (4) by their lawless behaviour. If you want to live your own way, he says, you have to adjust your doctrine accordingly, for if you accept Jesus' lordship 'either your doctrine will make your life blush, or your life will make your doctrine blush, and be ashamed'.[39] So a second sign of these dreamers will be a willingness to sit loose to what has normally been understood as the biblical standard, perhaps saying that it is culture-bound and needs reinterpreting.

c. These dreamers slander celestial beings

The *celestial beings* are the angels, literally 'glories'.[40] It is possible that these people were insulting angels or denying their existence, but Jude is more probably referring to the tradition that God's law was given at Sinai by angels.[41] Although the gospel is superior to the law, that is no reason to trample it in the dust, for 'the law is holy, and the commandment is holy, righteous and good'.[42] This third statement thus takes us back to those in verse 5 who wandered in the desert because they did not accept the terms of obedience given them in the covenant. By making this point the first of the three in his initial list (placing it out of chronological order) and now the last in his summary, Jude is underlining that the third and most serious sign of the presence of these dreamers is a rejection of the category of obedience to God's law. We might expect such people to say that the Old and New Testament commands are indefensibly bound to a male-dominated, slave-owning, undemocratic and illiberal society, and have nothing authoritative to say to our own.

---

[39] Manton, p. 113.
[40] *Doxai.* 'Angels' makes more sense here than either civic dignities (Calvin [*Jude*]) or church leaders, although that is the sense in 2 Cor. 8:23, where NIV translates 'honour'.
[41] Acts 7:38, 53; Gal. 3:19; Heb. 2:2.
[42] Rom. 7:12. 'If they were inspired by Paul they represent an exaggerated and seriously distorted Paulinism.' Bauckham (1983), p. 59.

d. But who are these dreamers?

Jude has called them *dreamers*, and that is a clue to a much more serious problem in his church than we would otherwise imagine. These people are not living in a world of their own, nor are they indulging in erotic dreams of angelic orgies.[43] A dreamer, or a dreamer of dreams, in the Old Testament is one who claims to have a message from God. Some dreamers have true words from him,[44] but many more have false ones,[45] and they are dealt with very severely because they tell lies about God. It looks as if the issue facing Jude was that under the cloak of a pretended revelation from God (or even the wrong supposition that it was a true revelation), these dreamers are laying claim to a position of inspired leadership within Jude's church, and the members are too sleepy to notice what is being smuggled in under their noses. Jude has made his position clear: such teachers will have to face the punishment that all rebels against God have faced. He cannot be avoided.

---

[43] *Pace* Kelly, p. 261.   [44] Dn. 2:1; Joel 2:28; Acts 2:16–17.
[45] Dt. 13:1–5; Is. 56:10; Je. 23:16, 32; Zc. 10:2.

Jude 9–10
4. Warnings of judgment: a familiar example

But even the archangel Michael, when he was disputing with the devil about the body of Moses, did not dare to bring a slanderous accusation against him, but said, 'The Lord rebuke you!' [10]*Yet these men speak abusively against whatever they do not understand; and what things they do understand by instinct, like unreasoning animals – these are the very things that destroy them.*

After each group of three Old Testament examples (verses 5–8, 11–13), Jude quotes an episode from the life of an Old Testament character which is not in our Bibles (verses 9–10, 14–16). Many Christians have found this disturbing and difficult; it was one reason for the heated discussion over the letter's inclusion in the Bible. We will look at each example on its own terms, but by way of preparation it is worth examining how we can understand these difficult parts of the Bible.

First, *there is nothing unusual in biblical writers referring to or quoting books that are not in our Bibles.* In the Old Testament we find references to 'the Book of the Wars of the Lord', the records of Nathan the prophet and of Gad the seer, the annals of the kings of Israel and the annals of the kings of Judah.[1] In the New Testament Luke recorded that 'many have undertaken to draw up an account of the things that have been fulfilled among us',[2] and Paul reminded his readers of some words of Jesus that are not recorded in the four gospels: 'It is more blessed to give than to receive.'[3] More strikingly, Paul uses the non-biblical tradition to name Jannes and Jambres, and quotes the pagan Greek writers Cleanthes, Aratus and Menander.[4] He even calls the Cretan poet Epimenides a 'prophet',[5] which should alert us to the fact that the word used here and in Jude 14 is a weak one, 'used on only one occasion in the New Testament

---

[1] Nu. 21:14; 1 Ch. 29:29; 1 Ki. 14:19; *etc.*; 1 Ki. 14:29; *etc.*   [2] Lk. 1:1.
[3] Acts 20:35.   [4] 2 Tim. 3:8; Acts 17:28; 1 Cor. 15:33; Tit. 1:12.
[5] Tit. 1:12.

for a citation from the Old Testament'.[6] If that is right, Jude's readers would not assume that he regarded this material as being on a level with Old Testament Scripture, but as a piece of well-known wisdom.

When Jude quotes books which were in common circulation among his readers at the time he wrote, then, we should not be alarmed. It is like a modern preacher quoting Bunyan or a contemporary song. Jude's quotations mean neither that we should include his sources in our Bibles nor that we should exclude his letter from our Bibles. It is, of course, theoretically possible that Jude knew these stories either from an independent tradition or by direct revelation from God, but it is not necessary to hold either of those positions to believe in the inspiration of Scripture.

Secondly, *Jude carefully adapts his material so that it does not go beyond the bounds of Old Testament teaching.* The words in the mouth of Michael here come from a similar event in Zechariah 3, and the description in Jude 14–15 of what will happen when Jesus returns is based on a long chain of Old Testament prophecies.[7]

Thirdly, *Jude's apocryphal examples follow three Old Testament texts, and each illustrates a point he has previously identified as significant.* The references to apocryphal verses do not add anything to the argument, and we will not misunderstand the main drift of Jude's letter if we do not know the background (the position of most of Jude's readers throughout church history). It looks as if he is deliberately referring to material that he knew his readers read and admired, urging them to see the same lessons there as he has taught them from the Old Testament.

1. Michael, Moses and the devil (9)

The story of Michael, Moses and the devil goes back to Moses' death, recorded in Deuteronomy 34:5–6: 'Moses the servant of the LORD died there in Moab, as the LORD had said. He buried him in Moab, in the valley opposite Beth Peor, but to this day no-one knows where his grave is.' Over time, the moving story of God digging the grave of his servant was elaborated into a story about the rightness of Moses being allowed into heaven. According to the early Christian writer Origen,[8] Jude is here referring to the story told in a book called the

---

[6] Mt. 15:7 and parallels; *NTI*, p. 914.

[7] Bauckham (1983) says: 'The Enoch literature is as important to Jude in this commentary as canonical Scripture is' (p. 226), but this ignores the *reason* for the volume of adapting Jude has done (to make Enoch conform to Scripture), as well as whether he chose the material because his opponents would be using it. See both articles by Charles, and T. R. Wolthius, 'Jude and Jewish Tradition', *Calvin Theological Journal* 22/1 (1987), pp. 21–41.

[8] See Bauckham (1983), p. 48.

Assumption of Moses. It still exists, but unfortunately the part of the book Jude quotes is missing. A number of other early Christian works refer to it, and Richard Bauckham has attempted a reconstruction.[9] Although the story is alien to us, it would have been very familiar to Jude's readers.

In the story, Satan is doing the work for which he is rightly named 'the Accuser',[10] for he is accusing Moses, presumably of the murder of the Egyptian and his later angry disobedience.[11] Moses is being accused of sin, and therefore should not (in Satan's eyes) be allowed into God's holy presence after his death. Michael (a glorious angel whose name means 'who is like God?' and who performs the highest work for God)[12] would be expected to share Satan's view of the impossibility of the presence of sin in heaven, although without Satan's demonic glee. But he refuses to *bring a slanderous accusation against* Moses, and instead allows God to remain the lawgiver and judge. Even the condemnation of Satan is one that he could not make on his own authority. Rather, he *said, 'The Lord rebuke you!'* If God's own law finds Moses guilty, and Satan is able to quote that law against Moses in the presence of God, only God himself has the right to banish the Accuser and remove the curse of the law.

This interpretation takes all the elements of the story in the way Jude's Old Testament reference does. In Zechariah 3:1–2, the prophet reports that an angel 'showed me Joshua the high priest standing before the angel of the LORD, and Satan standing at his right side to accuse him. The LORD said to Satan, "The LORD rebuke you, Satan! The LORD, who has chosen Jerusalem, rebuke you! Is not this man a burning stick snatched from the fire?"' The Joshua here is not the successor to Moses, but the much later high priest who assisted Zerubbabel in the attempt at reform and rebuilding of the temple after the return from exile. The parallels in Jude's mind are clear, for here again a man is being accused by Satan of unfitness to perform God's work (symbolized in the next verse by his wearing 'filthy clothes'). Again, a high-ranking angel stands aside and allows God to decide who is fit to serve him, sinner or not. Only 'the LORD' has the right to banish Satan's legally correct accusation.

This interpretation of the story is more appropriate to Jude's readers than the more usual one, which asserts that it was Satan (not Moses) against whom Michael refuses to bring a slanderous accusation. That interpretation sees Jude as telling his readers to be aware of the authority of even fallen angels, and to avoid treating them

[9] See Bauckham (1983), pp. 65–76. [10] See, *e.g.*, Jb. 1:1 – 2:10; Rev. 12:10.
[11] Ex. 2:11–15; Nu. 20:1–13.
[12] Dn. 10:13, 21; 12:1; Rev. 12:7; he is probably also referred to in 1 Thes. 4:16.

jokingly or abusively. Most interpretations make that assumption,[13] but more literal translations[14] preserve the ambiguity that the NIV brings out well. In Jude's text it is not clear against whom Michael *did not dare to bring a slanderous accusation*, and it is easy but very confusing to think he means Satan. But the Zechariah allusion to Joshua makes it certain. Jude means that Michael refrains from accusing Moses.

The NIV brings out the difficulties of Jude's subtle word-play well. It is important to notice, though, that the phrase translated *bring a slanderous accusation* has nothing to do with being rude or offensive. It is a legal phrase, meaning 'to pass a judgment or decision about slander'.[15] Satan was apparently accusing Moses of slander. Even Michael *did not dare* to make a legal decision about Moses in this case, but handed the decision over to God and rebuked Satan for his presumption. Michael's submissive attitude is quite different from the casual way in which the erring Christians follow Satan's easy model. Like him, they think they prove their spiritual superiority by the way they 'slander celestial beings' (verse 8).

As we read this story through Jude's Old Testament spectacles, it loses its obscurity and gains sharp focus. Jude's antagonists have misunderstood the whole nature of Christian salvation by not realizing what an awesomely great act God performed when he banished the legal charges against us. Not even Michael can declare Moses innocent, and not even Michael can remove the accusations of the law; he simply *did not dare*. Only the sovereignly gracious God can do that, and he will do it on the day of judgment. But by trivializing what God has done, the false teachers dare to 'change the grace of God into a licence for immorality' (verse 4).

2.   'These men' (10)[16]

The problems in Jude's church were coming from people who refused to accept that 'law' and 'obedience' were appropriate ideas for a Christian. 'Surely,' they would say, 'when we were converted we were moved from the sphere where the law controlled and constrained us into one where the themes are freedom and grace.' The stories of Israel, the angels and Sodom and Gomorrah have demonstrated the danger of this. But the story of Moses, Michael and Satan speaks even more directly to them. If anyone knew that he was saved

---

[13] As in GNB, JB, JBP, LB, Moffatt.   [14] AV, NKJV, RV, RSV, NRSV, NEB, NASB.
[15] MM, p. 360.
[16] Kelly calls verse 9 a 'brief digression' (p. 265), but it is difficult to see why a writer of such a short letter would need to digress. Structurally, verse 9 is required before Jude can say 'these men'.

only by God's grace it was Moses, but that did not mean that he was free from obedience to God. We have already seen that Jude would have shared the biblical view that the angels were the guardians of God's moral law, and so if anyone could have brought a legal accusation against Moses it would have been the archangel Michael. *But even* he recognizes that God alone has the right to pardon the guilty. How then can these people in Jude's church claim that because they are forgiven they are no longer required to keep God's good and moral law? Jude's answer is that they are dangerously ignorant.

a. How they respond to things they do not understand

When people are faced with Christian teaching *they do not understand*, some respond by exploring it with interest. The Jews living in Berea heard Paul speak and then 'examined the Scriptures every day to see if what Paul said was true'.[17] Some of the Athenians said, 'We want to hear you again on this subject.'[18] Once someone becomes a Christian, reading and understanding the Bible should become a regular habit, so that we grasp basic truths more clearly and deeply and come to appreciate the greater and richer sweeps of God's salvation plan. John Stott has described evangelical Christians as those who possess 'a submissive spirit, namely their *a priori* resolve to believe and obey whatever Scripture may be found to teach. They are committed to Scripture in advance, whatever it may later be found to say.'[19] That means that when we come across a Christian doctrine that we find difficult to grasp, or a passage of the Bible that we find hard to reconcile with other passages, we assume that there is an intelligent solution to the problem, and when we understand it clearly we shall obey it unconditionally.

This has been the case with the story of Moses, Michael and Satan. For those who find it too alien a story, the way forward is not to cut Jude out of the Bible, or to cut this passage out of Jude, but to put the problem on one side until there is time to explore it more fully.

How very different that attitude is from the sneers of those in Jude's church who were attempting to make other Christians veer off course! Perhaps they had sat under patient explanations of the fact that a Christian is free and yet under God's law, and of the fact that although sin no longer controls our destiny, we still have to do daily battle with it. But they had found this teaching too subtle, and

---

[17] Acts 17:11.   [18] Acts 17:32.

[19] David Edwards and John Stott, *Essentials* (London: Hodder and Stoughton, 1988) = *Evangelical Essentials* (Downers Grove: IVP, 1988), p. 104.

unnecessary. They would proclaim the big, bright slogan, 'Christians are not legalists', and would march off with their plain and simple message. No wonder some Christians were finding their no-nonsense statements appealing, with no need carefully to define precisely what they meant. The false teachers probably thought that orthodox Christian teachers were fudging the issue, and that they were Pharisees at heart.

Jude describes that attitude as *speaking abusively*, translating the word he has previously used to describe their 'slander' (verse 8) against the law-giving angels. We find the same attitude today in claims that Christians should not be concerned for standards of morality that belong to the past, or that it is acceptable for an unmarried Christian couple to sleep together provided they are in love. The examples may change from Jude's day, but the principle is exactly the same. The parts of the Bible we do not understand (or those which are perfectly clear but which we do not want to understand) we toss in the bin so that we can be allowed to indulge ourselves as we want without the inconvenience of God's Word.

b. How they respond to things they do understand

However much Jude's opponents stuck to their favourite few verses, some passages of the Bible would have criticized their position in an utterly unambiguous and powerful way. Jude is digging deep down in their motivation, below the level of rationality and intelligence. In his mind they are *unreasoning animals who understand by instinct*. But even at that low level, they will find the commands of God unavoidable. Jude may even be assuming that they have no Christian knowledge at all, but only the conscience of the most self-indulgent reprobate. Even then, they will still find that their consciences condemn them for their actions. The most basic human experience is that we are not the people we ought to be, and knowledge of that fact contains the germ of an understanding of judgment by God.

This second example of the danger that these people pose, and of our need to beware of them, then, turns out to have little to do with being polite to the devil. Jude wants us to have the utmost respect for God's law, as shown in the attitude of its guardian, Michael, and of the man who brought it to us, Moses.

Jude 11–13
5. Warnings of judgment: three further Old Testament examples

In this passage, Jude pronounces a very solemn judgment on the people who endanger our churches. Using a phrase frequent on the lips of Jesus, but rare elsewhere in the New Testament (outside the depiction of judgment in Revelation), he solemnly pronounces the eternal *woe* to those who mislead God's people.[1] His first set of three Old Testament examples comprised groups (God's people, the angels, and Sodom and Gomorrah; verses 5–7). This second set consists of individuals, who provide an example of leading others in revolt.

1. God judged rebellious leaders (11)

Woe to them! They have taken the way of Cain; they have rushed for profit into Balaam's error; they have been destroyed in Korah's rebellion.

For the second time, Jude mounts an attack using three examples from the Old Testament, with which his readers would have been familiar. Again he dispenses with the chronological order so as to highlight his main example. Korah, who should be the second example, is the third. Jude places him at the end of a series of increasingly strong nouns (*way . . . error . . . rebellion*) and verbs (*taken . . . rushed . . . destroyed*), which means that Korah is the climax. As Jude implicates the erring Christian leaders more and more in the sin of their Old Testament prototypes, he actually makes them participants in Korah's rebellion by using the aorist tense.[2] They have already *been destroyed in Korah's rebellion.* Jude certainly does believe that their 'condemnation was written about long ago' (verse 4).

[1] Mt. 11:21; 18:7; 23:13–29; 26:24; 1 Cor. 9:16; Rev. 8:13; 9:12; 11:14; 12:12; 18:10, 16, 19.
[2] *Apōlonto.*

a. The way of Cain

Cain, the first son of Adam and Eve, killed his brother Abel because of a jealous disagreement over a sacrifice. When Abel sacrificed some of his flock of sheep, Cain offered God some vegetables from his farm; but whereas God accepted Abel's sacrifice, he rejected Cain's. Hence the fratricide.[3]

What becomes clear from the Genesis story is that Cain knowingly and deliberately infringed God's laws. After Cain became angry, but before he committed murder, God asked him, 'Why are you angry? Why is your face downcast? If you do what is right, will you not be accepted? But if you do not do what is right, sin is crouching at your door; it desires to have you, but you must master it.'[4] God's statement could be looking either backwards or forwards – back to the unacceptability of the bloodless sacrifice and the need to reform, or forwards to the danger of Cain's anger. In either case, the next step that Cain takes will be decisive: after such a clear warning from God, his action will demonstrate whether he is willing to submit to God's rules or not. In the event, he is not.

Jewish commentaries on the story regarded Cain as an example of unbelieving cynicism. They are difficult to date with precision,[5] but they do indicate the kind of ideas held by people who taught the Old Testament. One writer put these words in the mind of Cain: 'There is no judgment, no judge, no reward to come; no reward will be given to the righteous, and no destruction for the wicked.'[6] That seems a good insight into the man whom God had warned of the consequences of his action, but who then decided whether he was going to believe God or not. When the writer of Hebrews talks about Abel, he mentions his 'faith' three times, in stark contrast to his unbelieving brother.[7]

As Jude looks at the sadly mistaken Christians in the church who have *taken the way of Cain*, then, he is saying that they understand very clearly the standards that God expects, but that they take it upon themselves to decide whether they are going to accept them or not. Of course, they would not say, 'Those are God's rules and I will reject them.' They are as subtle as the Jewish writer quoted above made Cain out to be, denying that there is such a thing as right and wrong, and that God will ever judge our muddled world by his absolute standards. That is *the way of Cain*.[8]

---

[3] Gn. 4:1–24.   [4] Gn. 4:6–7.   [5] See article 'Targum' in *DJG*, pp. 800–804.
[6] *Targum of Jonathan* on Gn. 4:7; this translation is in Kistemaker, p. 389.
[7] Heb. 11:4; *cf.* 1 Jn. 3:12.
[8] There is no evidence for Reicke's extraordinary thesis that the errorists were revolutionary incendiarists (pp. 210–211).

b. The error of Balaam

Balaam takes the mistake of Cain one step further. He not only knowingly rebels against God; he encourages others to do so as well. The first mention of him occurs in Numbers 22 – 24, where he is hired as a prophet by Balak, king of Moab, to curse Israel. Baalam's answer is: 'Even if Balak gave me his palace filled with silver and gold, I could not do anything great or small to go beyond the command of the LORD my God.'[9] In the unfolding account, his attempts to curse Israel are turned into blessing. He returns to his own town, and we assume that his work is over. But the next episode in Israel's story relates how the Israelite 'men began to indulge in sexual immorality with Moabite women, who invited them to the sacrifices to their gods. The people ate and bowed down before these gods.'[10] The Lord's 'fierce anger'[11] that is now revealed makes a shocking contrast with the blessing in the previous chapter, and the reader wonders how the reversal could have occurred. Only later in Numbers do we discover that Balaam was behind the strategy. Moses refers to the women who 'followed Balaam's advice and were the means of turning the Israelites away from the LORD in what happened at Peor, so that a plague struck the LORD's people'.[12]

In other words, Balaam's greed got the better of him. Balak offered him vast sums of money to subvert the Israelites, and, having been told by God that they were his chosen, blessed people, Balaam mulled the position over in his mind and sought another way to secure the downfall of the people. Just like Cain, he was faced with a clear statement from God about God's intentions, and then decided that God did not mean it.[13] One of the tragedies of his story is that he was one of the best-informed Gentiles about God's plan for Israel, yet his rebelliousness meant that he is last heard of in a list of the slain as the Israelites enter the land.[14]

Jude has already hinted that the people he is worried about are obtaining positions of leadership, and now he makes his concern as clear as he can. Balaam was a biblical warning, an example of a man whose greed led him into rebellion.[15] But his position in this list has as much to do with the second half of his story, when his second design undermines the holiness of the Israelites. The false teachers among Jude's 'dear friends' (verse 3) have heard the promises of God's blessing and warnings of his judgment. They have

[9] Nu. 22:18. [10] Nu. 25:1–2. [11] Nu. 25:4. [12] Nu. 31:16.
[13] Bauckham (1983) overstates his position that 'Jude's reference to Balaam is dependent on the development of tradition about Balaam in post-biblical Judaism' (p. 81). The tradition of Balaam's mutinous behaviour is clearly there in Numbers.
[14] Jos. 13:22. [15] Dt. 23:4; Ne. 13:2, 27: Mi. 6:5.

methodically weighed them and decided that they must, graciously, disagree. They will set up a small group within the church, or perhaps another church, which will examine their newer, alternative teaching. That would mean that they could expect some financial support from their new disciples,[16] and Jude's implication is that it was the *profit* motive that was making them *rush* into this disastrous new error.

c. The rebellion of Korah

Korah's rebellion comes last as the clearest foretelling of the end result of judgment. What started out as freethinking sin (Cain) and turned into an undermining weakness (Balaam) now becomes a full-scale revolt which ends in judgment.

Korah's story is found in Numbers 16:1–35. He, together with other levitical priests, Dathan, Abiram and On, 'became insolent',[17] and instigated a revolt of 250 soldiers against Moses. They obviously hoped that they could mount some kind of *coup* against the small group of leaders with whom Moses worked. Their problem was with the hierarchy of leadership, and they kicked against it. 'The whole community is holy, every one of them … Why then do you set yourselves above the Lord's assembly?' With breathtaking presumption they accused Moses of arrogance: 'You have gone too far!'[18]

Moses replied that, on the contrary, it is 'you Levites' who 'have gone too far'.[19] He called an assembly at which God was to choose between Moses' leadership and the putative leadership of the Levites. God intervened; the earth swallowed up the rebellious leaders, and 'they went down alive into the grave, with everything they owned; the earth closed over them, and they perished and were gone from the community'.[20] The Israelites did not learn from that lesson, and within the next few days they had a further argument with Moses at the same place, Meribah, 'where the Israelites quarrelled with the Lord and where he showed himself holy among them'.[21] The scene at Meribah became a great warning to God's people. Even though Korah's rebellion is not referred to elsewhere in the New Testament, there are echoes of its style.[22]

The lessons we have learned from Cain and Balaam are still in place. Once again, in Korah we have a man who ruminates over

---

[16] The abuse of local churches by itinerants apparently started early: Rom. 16:18; 1 Tim. 6:5; Tit. 1:11.

[17] Nu. 16:1.   [18] Nu. 16:3.   [19] Nu. 16:6.   [20] Nu. 16:33.

[21] Nu. 20:13. Moses and Aaron both quarrelled with God at Meribah too; Nu. 20:24.

[22] 2 Tim. 3:1–9; Heb. 3:7–19; 4:7; 3 Jn. 9–10.

God's order of things and decides that God cannot have meant what he said. So, for reasons of greed, an attempt is made to replace God's laws with another set dreamed up by a man. The new element in Korah's case was the way the rebellion ended. As Richard Bauckham says, 'the sequence of three reaches a climax in the final word *apōlonto*, "were destroyed".'[23]

The crushing parallel must have been even clearer to Jude's readers than to us. The rebellious leaders were occupying the same dangerous position as Korah. God will not allow his people to be snatched from him by a rival claimant, for 'souls are a precious commodity. Christ thought them worthy of his own blood, but seducers count them cheap ware; for their own gain and worldly interests they care not how they betray souls.'[24] As we reach this ghastly climax, it is worth remembering again that the people Jude describes here are not at all easy to spot – if they were, he would not have had to write his letter! This poisonous infiltration, or deadly hijack, is going on under our noses; and if Jude had not warned us that the 'nice people' who want to do this are dangerous rebels, we simply would not know.

2. 'These men' (12–13)

> *These men are blemishes at your love feasts, eating with you without a qualm – shepherds who feed only themselves. They are clouds without rain, blown along by the wind; autumn trees without fruit and uprooted – twice dead.* [13]*They are wild waves of the sea, foaming up their shame; wandering stars, for whom blackest darkness has been reserved for ever.*

Jude's message rolls relentlessly along as if he could not bear to lose our attention for a moment. In a string of six graphic images he shows us that what is going on today is every bit as awesomely rebellious as in the days of Cain, Balaam and Korah.

a. Dirty blemishes

The first Christians sometimes called their meetings 'love feasts' (*agapai*). These would have been ordinary meals at which they shared their problems, prayed, sang, ate bread and drank wine in memory of Jesus' death, and at which there would have been some teaching. It would have felt informal, but, since it would have been loosely based on what happened at the synagogue, it probably followed roughly the same shape each week. 'There is nothing to

---

[23] Bauckham (1983), p. 84.   [24] Manton, p. 271.

suggest that the love feast was a separate kind of meal from the Lord's Supper, and it seems more probable that these were two different names for the same occasion.'[25]

Some wrong-headed Christians were subverting the aim of the meeting, and the 'love feast' was turning into a place of division. It is difficult to know which of two possible meanings Jude intended here:[26] *blemishes*, which became a common meaning only much later, but which would parallel 2 Peter 2:13; or 'reefs', which was the more usual secular meaning. Bauckham, with most commentators, prefers 'reefs', and says that 'close proximity to such people is dangerous, and should be avoided, as a sailor keeps his ship clear of the rocks'.[27] Both translations are attractive, and it is impossible to judge with certainty. In either case, by their presence at the church meetings these people present a severe danger of either wreckage or pollution by their unashamed,[28] unloving activity. What were they doing that was so unhelpful?

b. Greedy shepherds

To be a Christian teacher is to be a pastor or *shepherd*. We expect someone to be on hand at our church meetings to feed us with God's Word. But from the earliest days, Christian leaders had to warn churches against shepherds who wanted only to maltreat the sheep.[29] It was no new problem. The passage that lies behind Jude's reference here is Ezekiel 34:2:[30] 'Woe to the shepherds of Israel who only take care of themselves! Should not shepherds take care of the flock?' Ezekiel warns the rulers of Israel, both priests and kings, that God will end their selfish rule and shepherd his people himself. The point, for Jude, is that the people against whom he is writing were claiming to be teachers, and had convinced everybody that they were good shepherds. But the sheep were starving. Their teaching served only to feed their own egos and self-importance; it did nothing to convert and build up God's people.

c. Empty clouds

In hot, dusty Palestine, a cloud was a signal of much-wanted rain. But a cloud that came with the wind and went with the wind,

---

[25] I. H. Marshall, *Last Supper and Lord's Supper* (Exeter: Paternoster, 1980; Grand Rapids: Eerdmans, 1981), p. 110. Moffat's translation, 'charity suppers', is engagingly eccentric.

[26] The Greek word is *spilas*.   [27] Bauckham (1983), p. 86.

[28] *Aphobos*, 'without the slightest qualm.'

[29] Jn. 10:12–13; Acts 20:28–29; 1 Cor. 9:7–18; 1 Pet 5:2–4.

[30] And possibly Is. 56:11.

casting only its shadow on the dry ground, was useless to the farmer. These shepherds promised a great deal, but it was insubstantial and unproductive. They claimed to be Bible teachers, but did not teach the Bible. 'Like clouds and wind without rain is a man who boasts of gifts he does not give.'[31]

d. Barren trees

Jude is underlining the gap between promise and performance. Go to an apple tree in the season and you expect to find apples. But these trees are fruitless, 'sapless and sterile'.[32] Both John the Baptist and Jesus had encountered and warned of the danger of spiritual barrenness,[33] and here Jude says that churches have started to come up against empty, hollow teachers. To a farmer, 'except as firewood, these trees had no value',[34] but Jude's reference here to their being *twice dead* indicates a worse fate. The phrase probably alludes to the New Testament teaching that those who are condemned on judgment day are condemned to the 'second death', a final, irrevocable separation from God.[35] The people Jude writes about are already marked out for that destiny. Until we die, we all have the opportunity to respond to God's grace; but these men, having heard the gospel, have turned their backs on it. Their future is horribly certain. Just as Jude can implicate them in Korah's rebellion as if they were there in the past, so he can face them with their future as if it were already irrevocably present.[36]

e. Stormy waves

To the desert tribes of Israel, the sea always presented a threat as an image of chaos and danger.[37] As a description of an individual, the sea was an image of a lack of self-control. In a passage Jude alludes to here, Isaiah says, 'The wicked are like the tossing sea, which cannot rest, whose waves cast up mire and mud. "There is no peace," says my God, "for the wicked."'[38] The false teachers are not as barren and unproductive as the previous images alone might suggest, for their storms do produce a lot of booming and crashing. They also leave 'filthy scum'[39] on the beach, *foaming up their shame*. False teachers in our churches will certainly get noticed,

---

[31] Pr. 25:14. [32] Kelly, p. 272.
[33] Mt. 3:10; 7:16–20; 15:13; 21:19; Lk. 13:6–9. 'Uprooting' was a familiar OT model for judgment: Dt. 29:28; Ps. 52:5; Pr. 2:22; Zp. 2:4.
[34] Kistemaker, p. 393. [35] Rev. 2:11; 20:6, 14; 21:8. [36] 1 Tim. 5:6.
[37] Ps. 107:25–28; Ezk. 28:8; Rev. 21:1. [38] Is. 57:20–21.
[39] Green (1987), p. 191.

because they leave a polluted mess behind them as the product of their self-willed ministry.

f. Wandering stars

Before compasses and radar, the only sure guides for a traveller on a dark night were the fixed constellations in the sky. But wandering, apparently erratically, all over the sky were the planets, in orbits that make no sense from the Earth (the Greek word translated *wandering, planētēs*, produces our word 'planet'). So a *wandering star* provides a neat image for a deceptive leadership that promises security and a safe road home, but actually delivers uncertainty and danger. The longer the traveller believed in the certainty of his wandering star, the greater the peril he was in. The ultimate wandering star is the great deceiver himself, the fallen star called Satan.[40] Many New Testament writers warn of the deceptive danger of false teaching,[41] but Jude's warning has a particular power reinforced by a connection hard to see in English. He has warned of 'Balaam's error' (*planē*, verse 11) and now warns of the wandering (*planētēs*) that the error produces.

What is the destiny towards which *these men* are heading? Jude has used a massive breadth of imagery to describe them, and he has drawn his illustrations from the four elements of the ancient world: air (clouds), earth (trees), water (waves) and sky (stars). Others had made similar lists.[42] That broad span narrows down to one single destiny: *blackest darkness is reserved* for them.[43] It is true that Cain's murder, Korah's rebellion and Balaam's subversion received almost instant retribution, whereas the false teachers in Jude's churches and ours often seem to go from strength to strength, gaining in influence and popularity, and growing in credibility. But the position that faith takes is that God is God even over rebels, and if he knew how to judge Cain, Korah and Balaam, he will be able to judge any who oppose him.[44]

---

[40] Is. 14:12–15; Rev. 8:10; 9:1.
[41] Mt. 24:4–5; 1 Tim. 4:1; 2 Tim. 3:13; 1 Jn. 4:6; Rev. 2:20; 13:14.
[42] Bauckham (1983), p. 90, compares the passage with *1 Enoch*, but is much too strong when he says that Jude's use 'is really only significant when this is understood'.
[43] On the eternal nature of the punishment, see above on verse 7.
[44] Mt. 8:12; 22:13.

Jude 14–16
6. Warnings of judgment: a further familiar example

Jude's fourth warning is one of the parts of the letter that have caused thinking Christians some problems. The reader might find it helpful to re-read the introduction to verses 9–10, on Jude's use of extrabiblical material (pp. 191–192).

> *Enoch, the seventh from Adam, prophesied about these men:* '*See, the Lord is coming with thousands upon thousands of his holy ones* [15]*to judge everyone, and to convict all the ungodly of all the ungodly acts they have done in the ungodly way, and of all the harsh words ungodly sinners have spoken against him.*' [16]*These men are grumblers and fault-finders; they follow their own evil desires; they boast about themselves and flatter others for their own advantage.*

1. Enoch (14–15)

Enoch himself is easy to identify, because Jude calls him *the seventh from Adam*. He appears in Genesis 5:21–24: 'When Enoch had lived 65 years, he became the father of Methuselah. And after he became the father of Methuselah, Enoch walked with God 300 years and had other sons and daughters. Altogether, Enoch lived 365 years. Enoch walked with God; then he was no more, because God took him away.' (In this genealogical list he is the seventh from Adam if we include both Adam and him in the list.)[1] He next appears in the Bible as an ancestor of Jesus,[2] and then in Hebrews as a model of faith: 'By faith Enoch was taken from this life, so that he did not experience death; he could not be found, because God had taken him away. For before he was taken, he was commended as one who pleased God.'[3] Although some commentators have insisted that Jude was trying to assign some mystical importance to Enoch by

---

[1] Also in 1 Ch. 1:3 and *1 Enoch* 60:8 (*OTP*, p. 40).   [2] Lk. 3:37.   [3] Heb. 11:5.

referring to the number seven,[4] the simplest explanation remains the best, namely that Jude is distinguishing him from another man of the same name who occurs earlier, in Genesis 4:17.[5]

The problem here is that Jude does not refer to Enoch as a hero of faith, but says that *Enoch prophesied*; and that prophecy is not in our biblical record. Some commentators, following a line taken by some Puritans,[6] say that this simply meant that Jude had access to an account of Enoch's prophecy which is not available to us, either because it is lost or because God told Jude this directly. But the early Church Fathers assumed that Jude is quoting a non-biblical book known as *1 Enoch*,[7] which first appeared in the second century BC. It is heavily influenced by the Old Testament, and opens with a dramatic setting of the day of judgment. Then come a lengthy explanation of the first six chapters of Genesis, which gives a major role to Enoch himself; a series of parables on judgment and the last things; an examination of the sun and the stars in the light of what will happen at the end; and visions about the end times. It closes with a description of what will happen on the earth before the close of its history. It looks as if this book and others like it were common currency in Judaism at the time of the New Testament, and that it formed a normal part of a Jewish Christian's intellectual background, and certainly that of Jude's opponents.[8]

At one point *1 Enoch* says, 'Behold, [God] shall arrive with ten million of the holy ones in order to execute judgment upon all. He will destroy the wicked ones and censure all flesh on account of everything that they have done, that which the sinners and the wicked ones committed against him.'[9] It is immediately obvious that this bears a very noticeable resemblance to what Jude says here. Although it is still possible to say that Jude had access to a direct source and not this book,[10] it looks increasingly likely that Jude was referring to this well-known background material.

Jude is not simply quoting, however, but adapting his material. Just as he drew biblical lessons from the story of Michael, he is

---

[4] According to Reicke, for example, 'Enoch summed up in himself the entire super-holy line'; p. 210.
[5] There is also possible confusion in LXX with the Hanoch of Gn. 25:4 or 46:9.
[6] *E.g.* Manton, p. 289.   [7] *OTP*, pp. 13–89.
[8] Charles (1991) has suggested that this quotation is 'not so much a citation of 1 Enoch due to *Jude's* elevation of the work, as it would be an inclusion adapted for Jude's theological and literary end, an allusion which bears directly due to the *others'* high regard for Enoch'; p. 144.
[9] *1 Enoch* 1:9 (*OTP*, pp. 13–14).
[10] Lenski, for instance, says Jude and *1 Enoch* share the same ancient source. 'Jude quotes Enoch and not some book. How well, and in what manner, the Book of Enoch reproduces Enoch's prophecy is a minor matter and does not affect Jude'; pp. 641–642.

wanting to ensure here that the basic lessons are scriptural in their content. The quotation from Enoch proves to be a handy peg on which he can hang a number of genuine Old Testament quotations.

We would not know, for instance, who Enoch's 'ten million . . . holy ones' were if we did not go back to the passage the book itself is quoting, namely Moses' prayer for Israel as he nears his death:

> The LORD came from Sinai
> and dawned over them from Seir;
> he shone forth from Mount Paran.
> He came with myriads of holy ones
> from the south, from his mountain slopes.
> Surely it is you who love the people;
> all the holy ones are in your hand.
> At your feet they all bow down,
> and from you receive instruction,
> the law that Moses gave us,
> the possession of the assembly of Jacob.[11]

That fits with Jude's themes exactly, because it is yet another Old Testament passage which links the giving of God's law on Sinai to the presence of 'myriads' of angels, the very beings that Jude's opponents 'slander' (verse 8) by their antinomian mindset.

The Old Testament drew on that heart-stopping and magnificent scene, and made it the prototype of God's dreadful judgment in the future.

> See, the LORD is coming with fire,
> and his chariots are like a whirlwind;
> he will bring down his anger with fury,
> and his rebuke with flames of fire.
> For with fire and with his sword
> the LORD will execute judgment upon all men
> and many will be those slain by the LORD.[12]

Once again, the angels accompany the law of the Lord as God comes, this time in judgment and mercy. Because Enoch so accurately crystallizes this strain of Old Testament teaching, Jude says that he *prophesies*.[13] But it is noticeable that he treats both this book and the *Assumption of Moses* with greater caution, and with much

---

[11] Dt. 33:2–4.
[12] Is. 66:15–16. Jude has also drawn on Is. 40:4, 10; Je. 25:31; Mi. 1:3–4; Hab. 3:3–9 and Zc. 14:5 as he has adapted *1 Enoch* to his own end.
[13] Although see Tit. 1:12.

clearer Old Testament controls, than the other examples and texts.[14] Barclay is surely right when he says that 'Jude is simply doing what all the New Testament writers do, and which every writer must do in every age; he is speaking to men in a language which they recognized and understood'.[15] With characteristic verve, Jude says that this old and well-supported testimony *prophesied about these men*. That is, the prophecy refers to the false teachers who were in Jude's churches and are in ours. Thomas Manton says that Jude's principle is that 'what is spoken in the word in general doth as much concern us as if it were spoken to our own persons'.[16] That is a good principle for Jude's reading of the Old Testament, and for our reading of Jude as well. If Jude were writing his letter today to our churches, he would write basically the same letter, because we face the same dangers.

Jude is using this text because of two terms that are each employed four times, and which crystallize what will happen on judgment day. The first is *pantes* ('everyone', 'all'), and the second is *asebeia* ('ungodliness') with its related words.

a. Judgment is universal

Four times in Jude's paraphrase of Enoch, we meet the idea that no-one and nothing escape God's scrutiny. He will judge *everyone*, and convict *all* the ungodly of *all* the ungodly acts and *all* the harsh words they have spoken against him. In order to justify their immoral behaviour, it is quite likely that false teachers here were denying the reality of the force of God's judgment. They were not necessarily denying that God would come (which was the very different error Peter had to answer in 2 Pet. 3:3–13), but simply that when he came, it would mean trouble for them. After all, were they not saved, members of the church, accredited teachers and evidently successful in attracting followers and raising funds? Surely God would reward them rather than judge them when he came? But Jude is adamant that there is no way that we can hide from God either *words* or *acts* which have offended him.

b. Judgment is moral

Four times in this passage Jude uses the word *ungodly*, a strong word describing total moral and spiritual breakdown, 'impiety in

---

[14] It is not the case, as Bauckham (1983) would wish, that this verse from *1 Enoch* is the normative verse which determines the letter as a whole. Charles (1990) has an impressive list of correspondences between Jude, OT and *1 Enoch*, and suggests that both later works consciously reproduce the OT strands here without any innovation; p. 38.

[15] Barclay (*Jude*), p. 231.   [16] Manton, p. 290.

thought and act'.[17] His four uses show how pervasive he thinks the influence is: it is an adjective (*asebeis, the ungodly* [ones], *ungodly sinners*); a noun (*erga asebeias,* literally 'works of ungodliness', *ungodly acts*); and a verb (*asebeō,* act in an *ungodly way*). Jude first introduced the interlopers by calling them *godless men* (verse 4), and he closes his analysis of them by saying that they *follow their own ungodly desires* (verse 18). Clearly, then, this word sums them up with devastating accuracy.

Once people think that they are free from any scrutiny by God, they will feel free to cut themselves loose from his standards. God will be seen as a grumbling but ultimately soft-hearted parent who makes impressive threats but cannot bring himself to act upon them. That is the assumption of many well-intentioned people today, who honestly do not believe that God will act as he has said he will act, and judge according to the moral law he has revealed. Such a view hampers any Christian, because once we cease to believe in the God the Bible reveals, we will feel free to indulge ourselves by making God in our own image. We devise a God who changes his mind about evangelism because we prefer to think that everyone will be saved, or who changes his mind about our obligation as Christians to be involved in society because we would prefer to think that he is concerned only with 'spiritual things'. Jude's opponents had fabricated a God who was not concerned about Christian lifestyle, and the result was a brazen disregard for Christian standards. As Bengel says, 'A *sinner* is bad . . . one who sins *without fear* is worse.'[18]

The word 'ungodliness' has great power, but it would be possible for some of Jude's readers to duck the punch because they would deny that their activity fell into that category. So, using his usual transition phrase, Jude turns his attention to *these men.*

2. 'These men' (16)

Jude's character sketch of these people is becoming more and more specific. Although he is utterly convinced that their 'condemnation was written about long ago' (verse 4) and that they conform to biblical types, he consistently moves into the present tense (*These men are*) as he describes them in enough detail to make them blush.

a. These men are grumblers

Grumblers are always a nuisance, but Jude has in mind a more biblical category than someone who merely makes a constant back-

---

[17] BAGD, p. 114.   [18] Bengel, p. 828.

ground noise of criticism. After Israel had crossed the Red Sea and seen the Egyptian task-force destroyed, only three days elapsed before trouble erupted over the lack of potable water. 'So the people grumbled against Moses, saying, "What are we to drink?"'[19] Shortly after this, it was evidently becoming a sore point for them; at Rephidim 'the people were thirsty for water there, and they grumbled against Moses. They said, "Why did you bring us up out of Egypt to make us and our children and livestock die of thirst?"'[20] The result was God's judgment upon them. 'The LORD said to Moses and Aaron: "How long will this wicked community grumble against me? I have heard the complaints of these grumbling Israelites. So tell them, 'As surely as I live, declares the LORD, I will do to you the very things I heard you say: In this desert your bodies will fall – every one of you twenty years old or more who was counted in the census and who has grumbled against me.'"'[21]

Once again, Jude has shown us a vivid and alarming Old Testament prototype of the kind of resentment towards God that he sees around him. The Israelites grumbled about the conditions in the desert. Since it was obvious that they were going to be there for quite some time, no doubt they wondered whether it might not be wiser to return to Egypt and live there. Jude's concern is Christians who *are grumblers* about conditions on earth. Since we have not been magically whisked off to heaven, but instead face a daily battle against temptations and sins that we do not always want to resist, some might wonder whether we would not be better off living as non-Christians, free to set lower standards for ourselves if we wish. We need not jeopardize our eternal security, they might think, because we are already saved; but the fight to be holy is an unnecessary weight.

Such grumbling against God in the desert, and such *harsh words* ... *against him* in Jude's church, end in the same result: judgment. The Israelites' punishment was that they would not enter their inheritance, the land. Our punishment will be exclusion from the inheritance to which the land pointed, namely heaven itself.[22]

b. These men are fault-finders

Jude's second picture is not an Old Testament one, but comes from among the stock characters of the situation comedies of his day: the moaner who is never satisfied with his lot, a 'malcontent'.[23] One Greek writer summed him up like this:

---

[19] Ex. 15:24. The verb in LXX, as here, is *gongystō*.   [20] Ex. 17:3.
[21] Nu. 14:26–29.
[22] See too 1 Cor. 10:1–13, where the same event teaches the same lesson.

The querulous man will say to him that brings him a portion from his friend's table: 'You begrudged me your soup or your collops [steak], or you would have asked me to dine with you in person.' When his mistress is kissing him he says, 'I wonder whether you kiss me so warmly from your heart.' He is displeased with Zeus, not because he sends no rain, but because he has been so long about sending it. When he finds a purse in the street, it is: 'Ah! but I never found a treasure.' When he bought a slave cheap with much importuning the seller, he cries: 'I wonder if my bargain's too cheap to be good.' When they bring him the good news that he has a son born to him, then it is: 'If you add that I have lost half my fortune, you'll speak the truth.'[23]

Every church contains such people. Jude is focusing on a quite specific characteristic of theirs: they are not happy with being Christians. They are forever gazing over the fence at the non-Christians' greener grass (so they think), at people who are free not only to behave as they wish but to do so with a clear conscience and with as few inhibitions as they choose. Jude would want us to notice the wisdom of Proverbs: 'Do not let your heart envy sinners, but always be zealous for the fear of the LORD. There is surely a future hope for you, and your hope will not be cut off.'[24]

c. These men follow their own evil desires

Becoming a Christian means that a person changes allegiance, and decides to 'follow the Lamb wherever he goes'.[25] These men are going back on their initial commitment to Christ. What is calling them away from him is their past, the way they used to indulge their sinful natures before they became Christians; they have found another master to follow – themselves.

Jude has subtly shown us how these people have undermined themselves. They began as grumblers, unhappy with the discipline of being Christians; then they became fault-finders as they started to envy the lot of the less disciplined non-Christian, and now they have no conviction of their guilt as they follow their own evil desires.

d. These men boast about themselves

The next stage in their spiritual decline is that they mistake their licence for liberty. They think they have achieved a level of

---

[23] NIDNTT 2, p. 145.   [24] Barclay (Jude), pp. 232–233.
[25] Pr. 23:17–18.   [26] Rev. 14:4.

spiritual maturity that has not been achieved by lesser Christians, who are narrow, literal-minded and slavish. They probably *boast about themselves* when other Christians are around, but their heart contains a deeper problem: for those who think they have found a shortcut to spiritual life, 'their big words are uttered against God'.[27]

e. *These men flatter others for their own advantage*

We are all alert to the danger of flattery in theory, but the reality can be very difficult to disentangle and escape. A flatterer has precisely the same evaluation of our talents and abilities that we have always secretly felt, understands our motivations and puts them into words that we would never dare to utter, and promises a future that is, remarkably, centred around the very achievements we have always fantasized about. That person slips under our guard and manages to mislead in the name of telling the truth. No wonder the Bible has to warn us constantly against those who *flatter*.[28] The most dangerous flatterer, of course, is the person who misleads about spiritual status, and who tells lies about God because he wants the hearer on his side. God spoke a word of judgment to the priests of Malachi's day, 'because you have not followed my ways but have shown partiality in matters of the law'.[29] In order to win followers and gain influence, *these men* have deliberately chosen to teach a wrong gospel that will make fewer demands and more promises of instant blessing. That formula proves an attractive danger to any tender-hearted Christian faced with teaching some of the hard parts of the Bible. Every Christian feels tempted from time to time to soften the impact of God's Word, and here are people who have a ready-made alternative to hand. But that, as Jude warns us here, is a treacherous path to follow, and one we must take great care to avoid.

[27] Bauckham (1983), p. 99.
[28] *E.g.* Dt. 10:17; 16:19; 25:13–15; Pr. 18:5; Jas. 2:1–9.
[29] Mal. 2:9. See too Mi. 3:11.

Jude 17–19
7. Signs of the times: a warning from the apostles

> *But, dear friends, remember what the apostles of our Lord Jesus Christ foretold.* [18]*They said to you, 'In the last times there will be scoffers who will follow their own ungodly desires.'* [19]*These are the men who divide you, who follow mere natural instincts and do not have the Spirit.*

If we find it strange that Jude quotes *1 Enoch* or the *Assumption of Moses*, it would have been seen as even stranger in his day that he quotes *the apostles of our Lord Jesus Christ*. What right did a group of twelve contemporary men have to be quoted approvingly alongside the other spiritual giants Jude cites? Jude's answer would be that an apostle was someone who was sent to do something by someone else, and the Twelve had been sent to preach by Jesus Christ. He told them, 'I am sending you out like sheep among wolves.'[1] The apostles stand in relation to the church as the prophets stood in relation to Israel, for they speak God's authoritative word to us. It is therefore right to place the two offices alongside each other, affirming that we are 'built on the foundation of the apostles and prophets, with Christ Jesus himself as the chief cornerstone'.[2] Because he shares this understanding, Jude can easily move from Old Testament references to quoting the apostles without perceiving any incongruity. Perhaps the words *dear friends* do show that he was aware of changing gear slightly, but he is reaching the end of the first part of his letter and will use the same phrase to open up the second part (verse 20).

It was a commonplace of the apostles' teaching that the church would face hard times after their departure because the way would be open for all manner of exotic heresies to emerge. In verse 18, Jude is not directly quoting anything that we have from the

---

[1] Mt. 10:16. For greater detail, see comments on 2 Pet. 1:1.   [2] Eph. 2:20.

apostles' pens (although it is similar to 2 Pet. 2:10), but it accurately summarizes the alarm that they voiced frequently.[3]

1. The signs of the times (17–18)

Jude's readers obviously heard the warning from the lips of several of the apostles themselves,[4] for he not only calls them to remember[5] what the apostles *foretold*, but also what *they said to you*. If they were living in Palestine, a continuous traffic of gifted Christian speakers would have passed through to speak at their meetings. Jude calls them to remember the constant refrain of their messages, rather than to recall one particularly hard-hitting talk: the verb for *said* is in the imperfect tense, and means 'They were in the habit of saying to you'. It does not imply that the apostles were long dead.[6] What then did they keep saying to Jude's readers?

a. The apostles said we live in the last times

When Jesus began his preaching ministry in the synagogue at Nazareth, he opened the scroll at Isaiah 61:1–2:[7]

> The Spirit of the Lord is on me,
>   because he has anointed me
>   to preach good news to the poor.
> He has sent me to proclaim freedom for the prisoners
>   and recovery of sight for the blind,
> to release the oppressed,
>   to proclaim the year of the Lord's favour.

Then he dramatically closed the scroll and announced the fulfilment of this prophecy in his ministry. He deliberately did not include Isaiah's next few words, 'and the day of vengeance of our God'. By that simple omission, Jesus divided the Old Testament hope into two. The Old Testament looked forward to the day of salvation and the day of judgment, the two coming together in one event. Jesus separated them and taught that his first coming as Saviour was different from his second coming as Judge. The period between the two comings of Christ is what the apostles call here *the last times*. They are not teaching what will happen only in the last few weeks

---

[3] Acts 20:17–35; 1 Thes. 4:13; 2 Thes. 2:5; 2 Tim. 4:1–8; 2 Pet. 3:3; 2 Jn. 7–11.
[4] Not necessarily just Peter and Paul, *pace* Kistemaker (p. 401).
[5] See on verse 5.
[6] The *"elegon humin"* would most naturally refer to oral teaching, as in the parallel warning of Phil. 3:18.' Robinson, p. 173.
[7] Lk. 4:16–21. The quotation is in verses 18–19.

and months before Christ returns, but what will mark the whole period of waiting, which is the age Christians live in. Peter explicitly makes it stretch from the first coming of Christ, who 'was revealed in these last times for your sake', to his second coming and 'the coming of the salvation that is ready to be revealed in the last time'.[8] Thus Jude can easily speak of the prophecy being fulfilled in his time, and would expect to find it coming true in ours as well. This is a prophecy for today. What should living in the last times mean?

b. The apostles said there would be scoffers

We have already begun to see the erosion that Jude says is caused by 'harsh words', grumbling and fault-finding (verses 15–16), which originate with those 'shepherds who feed only themselves' (verse 12). The free-thinking and loose theology is already having a perceptibly damaging effect upon their own Christian standards, and it looks as if they are beginning to recruit successfully among Christians who want to fly the nest of the apostles' teaching.

Jude does not tell us what it was that these people were saying,[9] but that means that his warning about scoffers is a general truth which can always find a home. The Bible constantly warns us of the subtle undermining that a sceptical mind can cause,[10] and Jude is keen for us to see how scepticism and an un-Christian lifestyle can be easy partners. He is highly unflattering about it; while the position might seem to start with intellectual questions and lead on to a different idea of obedience, Jude is clear that the *ungodly desires* come first, and the heretical theology to justify them will *follow* later. The fact that someone has a theology, and is able to justify his position by quoting Bible verses, is no guarantee that he is being totally honest with himself in his thinking. The Bible has been used to support a variety of vicious political systems and unsavoury lifestyles, and those caught up in them have found it very hard to see where they were wrong, even though it can be self-evident to Christians outside.

2. 'These are the men' (19)

Jude's final character-sketch of the dangerous people we face is the

---

[8] 1 Pet. 1:20, 5.
[9] In 2 Pet. 3:3 the scoffers have a specific heresy, denying the second coming, but that is not the issue here.
[10] Ps. 1:1; Pr. 1:22; 9:7–8; 13:1; Mt. 7:15; 24:11, 24; Mk. 13:22; Acts 20:29–30; 1 Tim. 1:3–4; 2 Tim. 4:3–4; 1 Jn. 2:18; 4:1–3.

shortest and sharpest of the five. In three stark outlines he makes clear once and for all the consequences of the error they represent.

a. These are the men who divide you

One of their distinguishing hallmarks is a tendency to form small cliques within a church, creating a division between the 'real' Christians, 'the spiritual aristocracy',[11] and the majority. Every church faces the basic distinction between those who are saved and those who are not, but Jude is not criticizing that. His word is a present participle, indicating that these men are habitually divisive, and that they are becoming recognized centres of disagreement and discontent. Some Christians leap to their defence, and others will have nothing to do with them. (As we shall see, both reactions are wrong.) Some swallow their alternative message with gusto and go on special study weekends with them; others are confused because the kind of Christian life they have always lived is being criticized as less than Christian. Although Jesus was absolutely clear that there will be a basic division between two groups of people on judgment day, he was equally clear that we are unable to make that division on the basis of human judgment.[12] We must, of course, be concerned for the purity of the gospel and its teaching. But when people want to set up smaller, 'truer' churches within other churches, using those churches as recruiting-grounds rather than bringing non-Christians to Christ, we can be sure that something is very wrong.

b. These are the men who follow mere natural instincts

Those who regard Jude as a late, second-century letter see his words here as reflecting the problem of Gnosticism in the local church.[13] This later Christian heresy attached central importance to spiritual 'knowledge' (Greek, *gnōsis*) and devalued the material and the physical. While this led some into asceticism, others believed that they could with impunity allow their physical instincts free rein, since the acts of the body had no bearing on the salvation of the spirit. But it is much more likely that Jude is taking some of the key words of the errorists and turning them back on his opponents.

Men . . . who follow mere natural instincts, for example, is a one-word pen-portrait[14] that Jude has already used in verse 10, there translated 'by instinct'. It smacks of people who are less than fully human, living 'life on earth in its external, physical aspects'.[15] In the mouth of the false teachers, the word would of course have

[11] Green (1987), p. 198.   [12] Mt. 13:24–30.   [13] Sidebottom, p. 92.
[14] *Psychikoi.*   [15] BAGD, p. 893.

told Jude's Christians that they were enjoying less than the best, and that there was so much more that they could enjoy if only they were willing to lose their inhibitions. In the mouth of Jude, the word becomes a powerful denunciation of people who, far from being spiritual giants, are being pulled down by the very things over which they claim to have victory. Sin still controls their destiny.

c. These men do not have the Spirit[16]

Jude gives us a horrific glimpse into the twisted theology of these people when he says that they not only justify their behaviour by quoting the Bible, they actually claim that the Holy Spirit is guiding them into their lawless rebellion. Christians who are reluctant to follow them, in their view, do not have the Spirit at all.

By contrast, Jude says that it is these self-proclaimed 'Spirit-led' people who do not have the Spirit, and that their new ideas reflect not openness to the Spirit but openness to their lower desires. It is very easy to claim to be led by the Spirit, and any sensitive Christian will pause when something is taught in the name of the Holy Spirit, and consider whether he might previously have been taught wrongly. But when the Bible is declared outmoded, the resurrection denied, the saving death of Jesus watered down or the biblical guidelines on sex and marriage made amenable to people's greed, and all in the name of 'where the Spirit is leading us', we can be sure that the Spirit is not leading us there at all.

Are these people Christians? We may be rightly reluctant to speak in this forceful way about our contemporaries, but the further extremes of Jude's language leave us in little doubt about this. In verses 22–23, he sets out a number of courses of action to take, depending on the spiritual position of the person concerned. But to apply his logic here, if a person does *not have the Spirit,* that person is no believer.

---

[16] Literally, they do not have (a) spirit. The absence of the definite article does not necessarily mean that Jude is referring to the human rather than the Holy Spirit, *pace* Alford (p. 540). For other examples of the word without a definite article but still referring to the Holy Spirit, see Rom. 8:9, 14; 1 Cor. 2:4; 7:40.

Jude 20–21
8. Contending for the faith:
the Christian

But you, dear friends, build yourselves up in your most holy faith and pray in the Holy Spirit. [21]*Keep yourselves in God's love as you wait for the mercy of our Lord Jesus Christ to bring you to eternal life.*

When Jude began his letter, he said that although his original intention was to write a general letter about 'the salvation we share', he had narrowed down his concern to 'urge you to contend for the faith' (verse 3). By 'salvation' and 'faith' he meant the same Christian message, of course; but his different words and emphases show his apprehension over the disturbances that were occurring in the churches. 'Salvation' is the great future hope of Jesus' return as Saviour, but that hope was being undermined by those who did not 'share' it with Jude or his faithful readers. Similarly, 'the faith' is the fixed Christian gospel, but it was being eroded by those who denied that it was given to the church 'once for all', and instead felt free to 'change the grace of our God into a licence for immorality' (verse 4).

When we are faced with similar pressures today to alter basic Christian doctrine or behaviour, how do we respond? Some are tempted to ignore them and hope they will wither away with time. They would argue that although the church has always been beset by false teachers, God has preserved true teaching, and so we should not be unduly alarmist. Instead, we should concentrate on affirming our fellowship. This is naïve in Jude's eyes, for he says that these people are all too ready to meet in a hollow mockery of fellowship. In the long run, however, they are not loved back into the way of truth, but prove to be 'blemishes at your love feasts, eating with you without the slightest qualm' (verse 12). Evasion will not work.

Others suggest that we need the stress on experience, inner conviction and certainty, married to Jude's passion for truth and structure.[1]

[1] *E.g.* Martin, p. 85.

The difference, they say, is not between truth and heresy, but between personalities and values. But such a warm approach, which would be welcomed by the false teachers, effectively removes any authority from Jude's writing and means that we stand over, not under, his authority.

Yet others find the mere presence of false teaching in a church so alarming that the only course of action is immediate evacuation into other, purer churches. That may solve the problem in the short term; but in this letter Jude is warning that a liberalizing danger will always threaten churches, and the pure church of one generation faces the very real danger of becoming the heretical church of the next. Evasion, even-handedness and evacuation are not answers to error.

That is a hard word for today, as our inter-church philosophy is very often the reverse of Jude's insights. We may say that although we differ in precise points of theology, we aim to meet in unity around the Lord's Supper. The World Council of Churches' *Faith and Order Paper* on *Baptism, Eucharist and Ministry* says: 'The eucharist shows us that our behaviour is inconsistent in face of the reconciling presence of God in human history: we are placed under continual judgment by the persistence of unjust relationships of all kinds in our society, the manifold divisions on account of human pride, material interest and power politics and, above all, the obstinacy of unjustifiable confessional oppositions within the body of Christ.'[2] Jude would not deny that the Lord's Supper is a powerful uniting symbol, for he calls it a 'love feast'; but he would question the assumption that doctrinal differences are by definition unjustifiable, or that such differences must disappear before the more powerful symbol of the shared meal. Jude does not call us to unity at the price of doctrine. He does indeed call us to unity in 'the salvation we share', but also calls us to 'contend for the faith' (verse 3).

So far, Jude has explained only *why* we should 'contend for the faith', the reason being that it is under the attack we should expect. In this final section of six verses, he tells us *how* to contend, setting out the three steps which are necessary if we are to do so. First (verses 20–21), we must take care of ourselves, ensuring that we are correctly centred on God and his gospel. Secondly (verses 22–23), we have certain responsibilities to those who are falling foul of wrong teaching. Thirdly (verses 24–25), we must keep our eyes firmly fixed on the great future which God has promised us. Richard Bauckham properly says that these verses are 'not an appendix to the letter but its climax'.[3]

---

[2] *Baptism, Eucharist and Ministry, Faith and Order Paper* 111 (WCC, 1982), p. 14.
[3] Bauckham (1983), p. 111. He is referring to verses 20–23, but the theme of how we contend for the faith extends to the end of the letter.

This chapter deals with the first of these aspects of contending for the faith. In a series of four pieces of pastoral wisdom which are designed to be an effective remedy against spiritual danger, Jude urges us to keep a watch on ourselves and on one another. They all involve activities for which we are responsible, but they also involve the active work of *God* the Father, *our Lord Jesus Christ* and *the Holy Spirit.*

1. Build yourselves up in your most holy faith (20a)

The *faith*, as we have continually seen in Jude's letter, is that body of doctrine which Christians have believed from the earliest days of the church. Of course, Christians have explored it and expressed it in different ways for different times, but from the outset there has always been a recognizable, defensible gospel. Paul wrote in what is probably the earliest New Testament letter: 'If anybody is preaching to you a gospel other than what you accepted, let him be eternally condemned! ... I want you to know, brothers, that the gospel I preached is not something that man made up.'[4] Because it is not a figment of our collective imaginations, but comes as a direct message from the throne of God himself, it is *most holy* and it has the power to make those who believe it into 'saints' (verse 3; literally 'holy ones'). In the Old Testament, anything which belonged to the holy God was automatically holy, and the punishment for stealing it or maltreating it was the death penalty at God's own hand.[5] Jude has already shown what must happen to those who hijack the most holy faith that God has entrusted to us.

We are not to be so fearful of the awesomeness of this faith that we make the error of treating it like a fragile antique vase, which must be kept locked up and guarded for its own safety. When the Bible urges us to defend the gospel, it tells us to do so by teaching it fearlessly.[6] We are to have a reverent but robust confidence in it and take practical steps to *build* ourselves *up in* it. Growing as Christians, and growing more closely together as Christians, are duties which New Testament writers frequently compare to the constant productive activity of a building site.[7] Jude's desire, then, would not be fulfilled by formulating a short doctrinal basis and then defending it against all comers. Such bases may be useful, but they can be

---

[4] Gal. 1:9, 11.
[5] See, *e.g.*, what happened to Achan when he stole from God (Jos. 7), or Uzzah when the instructions on moving the Ark of the Covenant were ignored (1 Ch. 13:1–14; 15:1–28).
[6] 1 Tim. 6:20 is in the context of 'commanding', which runs from 1:3; 2 Tim. 1:14 is amplified in 2:2, in the context of 'being strong' and 'enduring hardship'.
[7] 1 Cor. 3:9–17; Gal. 2:18; Eph. 2:20–22; 1 Pet. 2:5.

no more than summaries of the wonderful comprehensiveness and interrelatedness of Scripture. Jude wants to see the whole of our lives – that is, our intellects, actions, consciences, motives and imaginations – brought increasingly into conformity to God's Word. This is a life-long activity; he says literally that we are to 'keep on building'.[8] It is also a corporate activity; he instructs his readers to *build yourselves up*, a plural which indicates that we are involved not in a solo spiritual quest but in a common concern and love. The first sign that a Christian is in danger of falling away is a tendency to be a loner, cut off from sources of encouragement and nurture. In a Christian leader, such isolation can mean a dangerous lack of accountability.[9] If we have friends who are physically distant from other Christians, we should make the effort to ensure that they are still spiritually 'plugged in'; and if we have friends who are failing to use the supports that God has provided in the church, we should gently try to win them back. Jude saw Christians drifting away from genuine fellowship into the arms of the heretics, and he wants to warn us that it is dangerous to be a solo Christian. A brick cannot be built into the building unless it is on the building site.

2. Pray in the Holy Spirit (20b)

This is the second time Jude has mentioned the Holy Spirit. He has told us that the counterfeit Christian leaders 'do not have the Spirit' (verse 19), and now he tells the genuine Christians to *pray in the Holy Spirit*. Despite what the counterfeits were probably saying, there is no such person as a Christian who does not have the Holy Spirit, for the Spirit is God's gift to the church at Pentecost and to each of us when we are converted. The false message had spread that there are lower-class Christians, who are saved but still lack the Spirit; and upper-class Christians who have a higher level of spiritual awareness. Jude has turned that argument on its head, for the people who teach that kind of doctrine actually demonstrate that they have not even been converted! Of course, the Bible teaches that we need to be filled with the Spirit,[10] but that is a continual requirement for all Christians. It is not a rebuke to a sub-standard group.

Part of the Holy Spirit's promised work is to make us aware of

---

[8] *Epoikodomountes*, the first of three present participles indicating constant action; the exception is 'keep yourselves' (*tērēsate*, verse 21), which is an aorist imperative, perhaps subtly indicating a rock-like immovability.

[9] Christian leaders are no different from any other Christians, and to the question 'Who pastors the pastor?' we should answer that the local congregation pastors the pastor; Heb. 3:12.

[10] Eph. 5:18.

the gap between the way things should be and the way things are, as understood from the Bible. When we are aware of it on a personal level, we call that experience conviction of sin. When we are aware of it in another person, we may realize that he or she needs to understand a particular Christian truth in order to become a Christian or a better Christian, and we call that experience love. When we are aware of it in a church or an organization, it might take any one of a number of forms.[11] We might want to take a range of actions, but our first and most constant response must be to *pray* for that gap to narrow, especially when the problem is prayerlessness. Calvin comments wisely: 'Such is the coldness of our make-up that none can succeed in praying as he ought without the prompting of the Spirit of God.'[12]

It is important to understand that Jude is not rebuking them for praying in a wrong, fleshly way and encouraging them to a higher mode of praying, as if there was a category of praying 'out of' the Spirit as well as *in the ... Spirit*. J. D. G. Dunn is among those who have argued that case here. He sees that Jude is undermining a two-tier Christianity; Jude 'castigates his opponents as "worldly-minded, lacking the Spirit" ... clearly they have laid claim to be *pneumatichoi* [spiritual], denying the epithet to others. Jude will have none of this.' But then Professor Dunn slips into the same two-tier error that he has just said Jude wants to deny. Jude's 'aim seems to be to achieve the same sort of charismatic balance that Paul strives for in 1 Cor. 14. A reference to charismatic prayer, including glossolalic prayer [prayer in tongues], may therefore be assumed.'[13] But to say that Jude is encouraging speaking in tongues here, and that it 'may be assumed', is to misread him wildly. There is no evidence of that issue being anywhere in Jude's field of vision. Only if we come to this passage having already decided that *pray in the Holy Spirit* means using charismatic gifts will we reach that conclusion. But that is to import into the text a preferred meaning that it cannot be proved to carry. Jude just wants us to pray.

In the context of the issue which Jude says faces us, our prayer for ourselves and one another will be that we may not deviate from our faith and hope. For new Christians we shall pray that they will put down good and healthy roots; for our teachers and leaders, that they will not be led into error and so lead us into

---

[11] Zc. 12:10; Jn. 4:24; Rom. 8:15–16, 26–27; Gal. 4:6; Eph. 6:18.

[12] Calvin (*Jude*), p. 344.

[13] J. D. G. Dunn, *Jesus and the Spirit* (London: SCM; Philadelphia: Westminster, 1975), p. 243; Bauckham (1983), p. 113. But Green (1987) says that if praying in tongues is hinted at 'it is hinted at very obscurely'; p. 200.

error; and for those who have fallen into error, that they may come back – or even be converted.

3. Keep yourselves in God's love (21a)

God's basic attitude towards humankind is his *love*, by which Jude means the strong passion he has to save us from his rightful indignation at our disobedience. He has given us promises of salvation, and the correct response of his covenant people to his covenant love is to echo his love by our obedience.[14] There are always two sides to this. On one side, as Paul found out, 'Christ's love compels us'[15] as an inexorable force, and he prayed that the Ephesians might 'grasp how wide and long and high and deep is the love of Christ'.[16] But on the other side, Jesus warned us to 'remain in my love. If you obey my commands, you will remain in my love, just as I have obeyed my Father's commands and remain in his love.'[17] Although God's love towards us is fixed and promised in his covenant, then, it is possible for us to position ourselves outside it, and instead to face his anger.

Jude has written about both sides of God's love. He opened his letter by telling us that we are 'loved by God the Father and kept by Jesus Christ' (verse 1), and now as he closes he tells us to *keep* ourselves *in God's love*. We know from his letter that the way we do this is by ensuring that we are constantly obeying God. If we want to know what happens to those who do not keep themselves in God's love, we need look no further than the examples of the Israelites in the desert, the angels, the inhabitants of Sodom and Gomorrah, Cain, Balaam and Korah. If we want to see the present counterparts of those people and places, we need only look at those who behave in the same way and share their mocking attitude to God's law

4. Wait for the mercy of our Lord Jesus Christ (21b)

Christianity makes sense only if the promises God makes are kept. God gave the Old Testament believers wonderful promises about what he would do, and they responded to him by patiently and faithfully waiting. Micah saw that all around him the Israelites were deserting the covenant. 'But as for me, I watch in hope for the LORD, I wait for God my Saviour; my God will hear me.'[18] The New Testament opens with the hope being kept alive as Zechariah led the temple worshippers in prayer for the Messiah to come. And when

---

[14] Ex. 24:1–8; Dt. 6:5ff.   [15] 2 Cor. 5:14.   [16] Eph. 3:18.   [17] Jn. 15:9–10.
[18] Mi. 7:7; see also Ps. 130; Dn. 12:13.

223

the baby Jesus was brought to the temple for the first time, he was recognized by Simeon, who had been 'waiting for the consolation of Israel', and by Anna, who 'spoke about the child to all who were looking forward to the redemption of Israel'.[19] Once Jesus had made it clear that he was going back to heaven and would return only later, it became the turn of his disciples to behave 'like men waiting for their master to return from a wedding banquet, so that when he comes and knocks they can immediately open the door for him'.[20]

Jude urges us to *wait for the mercy of our Lord Jesus Christ to bring* us *to eternal life*. This indicates that only God's final intervention in our world will ultimately prove that God's Word is true, and that it is his great gift to those who believe it. We do of course enter into eternal life now as Christians, but what we experience in this life is largely dominated by a battle because we are still waiting for our new resurrection bodies. Paul wrote that 'the whole creation has been groaning ... right up to the present time'. Christians 'groan inwardly as we wait eagerly for our adoption as sons, the redemption of our bodies'. Even the Holy Spirit himself 'intercedes for us with groans that words cannot express'.[21] It is important to realize how supremely right it is that creation, Christians and even God himself 'groan' in this way. God's promises are still waiting for their final fulfilment, and Christians pin their destiny on the future rather than the present.

Jude's prescription has involved the Christians with the living Trinity: they obediently keep themselves in God's love, pray in the Holy Spirit and wait for the mercy of our Lord Jesus Christ. It is a powerful and effective antidote to the poison of the people Jude opposes. For their part, they wilfully 'change the grace of our God into a licence for immorality' (verse 4); they cannot pray because they 'do not have the Spirit' (verse 19); and they rebelliously 'deny Jesus Christ' (verse 4). Jude's opponents would not find themselves 'groaning' as they battle to be holy. Instead, they grumble (verse 16), complaining that God places such heavy demands on them. They long to produce selfish cries of delight as they 'follow their own evil desires' (verse 16). Will they have any hope of *mercy* on that day? Only if we take some action towards them, as Jude is about to tell us.

[19] Lk. 1:10; 2:26, 38.   [20] Lk. 12:36.   [21] Rom. 8:22–23, 26.

Jude 22–23
9. Contending for the faith: the fallen Christian

Once we are firmly established as growing Christians, Jude wants us to become involved in the painful work of helping those who are coming under the influence of dangerous doctrine.

> Be merciful to those who doubt; ²³snatch others from the fire and save them; to others show mercy, mixed with fear – hating even the clothing stained by corrupted flesh.

Although the NIV translation seems clear enough, it is the end result of a lot of hard work on a very difficult piece of Greek. It is a problem to know exactly what Jude wrote. 'It is probably impossible to reach an assured conclusion as to the original text of vv. 22–23a.'[1] There is also difficulty over what Jude meant: principally, whether there are three groups of people (*those who doubt ... others ... others*, as in NIV), or only two (as the NKJV translates it – 'On some have compassion, making a distinction; but others save with fear, pulling them out of the fire, hating even the garment defiled by the flesh').[2] The commentators demonstrate how difficult a passage it is, though most of them prefer the NIV model because of Jude's liking for triplets and triads. His known style suggests that he is more likely to have written about three groups than two, but the likelihood is only marginal. If the threefold grouping is correct, we should be able to trace a gradual progression in the examples Jude gives. He sets out three missions to rescue fallen Christians.

---

[1] Bauckham (1983), p. 108.

[2] AV, NEB and Moffatt translate them as two groups; RV, NASB, GNB, JB, JBP, RSV and NRSV as three; LB, eccentrically, manages to produce four! The most thorough survey, concluding that three groups were in view, is Sakae Kubo, 'Jude 22–23: Two-division Form or Three?' in E. J. Epp and G. D. Fee (eds.), *New Testament Textual Criticism: Its Significance for Exegesis: Essays in Honour of B. M. Metzger* (Oxford: Clarendon, 1981), pp. 239–253.

1. Be merciful to those who doubt (22)

Jude's first group are *those who doubt*, and he uses the same word to describe them as he used to describe Michael 'disputing' with Satan. In that context, the word had a tight legal meaning that helped to explain the scene. Here, it has lost that precision, and probably means 'people who are asking questions', perhaps because they are 'at odds with themselves'.[3] These are the people who are starting to weigh up the claims and arguments on both sides and finding themselves in two minds about the issues.

Our response to such questioning should not be to cast the questioner as a heretical unbeliever! In some Christian settings there is such a zeal for pure doctrine that it is very hard for people to admit that they have questions and misunderstandings, and it is difficult to find a friend who will sit and listen and talk things through. Jude says that our willingness to do that must be characterized by mercy, and the reason lies in verse 21: every Christian recognizes that no-one is good enough to earn God's favour and that the only way to be with him for eternity is to wait for his mercy. What is more natural, then, as we understand that we are objects of God's mercy, than that we should *be merciful* to those who are on the fringes of the church? The fact that the two different objects of mercy should come so closely together must mean that Jude wants us to understand what the hope of mercy is. We are not to go soft on the gospel or to hold out an illusory hope of salvation for everyone, irrespective of their relationship to God. But to those who have questions and who are thinking hard, there must always be a welcome and a patient understanding.

2. Snatch others from the fire and save them (23a)

Jude's second group of falling Christians has gone further than *doubt*; they are actually playing with *fire*. They have begun to engage with the thinking and lifestyle of those 'who change the grace of our God into a licence for immorality' (verse 4), and if people are convinced that some behaviour traditionally denoted immoral is actually acceptable for Christians, they will see no reason to avoid it.

The first part of our action must be to appreciate what a deadly position these people are in. If the prototypes, Sodom and Gomorrah, 'serve as an example of those who suffer the punishment of eternal fire' (verse 7), and our friends are already playing with fire, then we must think hard about what action we can take to help

[3] Blum, p. 395. *Cf.* Mt. 21:21; Mk. 11:23; Rom. 4:20; 14:25.

them. Jude is alluding to Amos 4:11–12, when God said to his
stubborn people:

I overthrew some of you
as I overthrew Sodom and Gomorrah.
You were like a burning stick snatched from the fire,
yet you have not returned to me . . .

Therefore this is what I will do to you, Israel,
and because I will do this to you,
prepare to meet your God, O Israel.

God's judgment on the cities, and his snatching his people from
them, remind us of judgment still to come. The Puritan writer
Thomas Manton wrote: 'When a fire is kindled in a city, we do not
say coldly, Yonder is a great fire, I pray God it do no harm. In times
of public defection we are not to read tame lectures of contemplat-
ive divinity.'[4] That is a healthy corrective for us, especially if we are
in churches which focus intensely on personal spiritual development or the necessity of deep fellowship. Whatever place those
things may have, there is a great fire and it will do great harm, and
some Christians are being taken by the hand and led into it.

Jude referred to Zechariah 3 in verse 9, and now he does so again
as a second Old Testament passage. Zechariah was being shown a
vision of the high priest, Joshua, and was being taught that although
Joshua was unworthy to serve God because of his past, God could
take that past away. 'Then [the angel] showed me Joshua the high
priest standing before the angel of the LORD, and Satan standing at
his right hand to accuse him. The LORD said to Satan, "The LORD
rebuke you, Satan! The LORD, who has chosen Jerusalem, rebuke
you! Is not this man a burning stick snatched from the fire?" '[5] The
'fire' in that case must mean the exile in Babylon, which was God's
judgment upon rebellious Israel. Joshua had been chosen to escape
that judgment and, with a group of returning exiles, to rebuild the
temple.[6]

These two Old Testament examples of judgment by fire and
rescue from it provide an important background to Jude's phrase
here. He is saying that it is still possible for people in peril to escape
God's judgment and to be snatched from the fire. God has proved it
twice already. We need this reassurance because, as we talk to
friends in this position, we will find that they may very well be

[4] Manton, p. 306, commenting on verse 16.   [5] Zc. 3:1–2.
[6] See too Am. 4:11, which might also surface in verse 7. In the memory of that
slavery, Egypt was also remembered as a burning furnace (Dt. 4:20; Je. 11:4), which
makes fire a graphic image of the consequences of undergoing punishment at the
hand of God.

behaving in ways with which they feel quite comfortable. They have grown up with the idea that God's wrath is an antiquated notion in which it is impossible for today's Christian to believe. As we pray for and talk to our friends who think like that, we must keep before ourselves the fact that, without being offensive or insensitive, we are instructed by Jude to *save* them; the *fire* is near and coming closer, and we must watch that we are not sucked into its path as well. *Snatch them*, says Jude.

3. To others show mercy, mixed with fear (23b)

Jude's third rescue mission concerns those who have become fully involved in the false doctrine, perhaps even the ringleaders and teachers. *To others show mercy, mixed with fear – hating even the clothing stained by corrupted flesh.* As with the first group, we are to hold out the *mercy* that is being held out to us, but this time Jude is aware that we will feel very differently.

He says first that the mercy is *mixed with fear*. Once we have seen the reality of the fire, we shall be more clearly aware of the risk that these people are running. Perhaps Jude means we should fear the contamination that involvement with these fallen Christians will bring. Perhaps he means we should fear them because of the way they have managed to persuade so many other Christians to join their movement. Perhaps he means that we should fear God who is a right and holy judge. Any of these would be a good reason to fear, but none would be a good reason for not getting involved, or for staying in a cosy huddle.

Jude says, secondly, that we should hate – initially a shocking word, but one which he uses in a very specific way. We are *hating* not the sinner but *even the clothing stained by corrupted flesh*. Here Jude continues his allusion to Zechariah 3. 'Now Joshua was dressed in filthy clothes as he stood before the angel. The angel said to those who were standing before him, "Take off his filthy clothes." Then he said to Joshua, "See, I have taken away your sin, and I will put rich garments on you."'[7] Joshua's 'filthy clothes' were the result of his exile in Babylon. As he was made to take them off, the angel said he had 'taken away [his] sin'. Jude's reference, then, is above all to the possibility of a full and thorough forgiveness, a complete cleansing and change of clothes that is possible even for the most reprobate. There is no person who is so irredeemably bad that God's forgiveness cannot remove the stain.[8]

What then are we to hate? If the people Jude is describing are repenting, what we must expect of them is a complete reverse of

[7] Zc. 3:3–4.   [8] Lv. 13:47–59; Is. 30:22; Rev. 7:14.

lifestyle and a change of attitude towards their past. For their sake, we cannot afford to require anything less of them; their former lifestyle and attitude are what the gospel is saving them from, and so we must show no compromise. We cannot lower God's standards in the hope that if the terms are easier, more people will repent. That is to love the clothing and to hate the sinners, because it denies the seriousness of their plight.

Jude's three rescue missions have been increasing in range from those who are wondering about falling, through those who are falling, to those who have fallen. Other New Testament writers propose similar ways of handling such issues.[9] We should notice that it is usual in these instances for Christians to act together. A private problem may be solved privately, but public sin of this kind requires concerted and prayerful action.

[9] Mt. 18:15–17; Lk. 17:3; Gal. 6:1–2; 2 Thes. 3:14–15; 1 Tim. 5:19–20; Tit. 3:10; Jas. 5:19–20.

Jude 24–25
10. Contending for the faith: the salvation we share

> *To him who is able to keep you from falling and to present you before his glorious presence without fault and with great joy –* [25]*to the only God our Saviour be glory, majesty, power and authority, through Jesus our Lord, before all ages, now and for evermore! Amen.*

The closing words of Jude's letter are probably the best known. Many people who say and sing this 'magnificent doxology'[1] do so without having travelled the route we have travelled, through Jude's concern for his church. It does make sense as a glorious song in its own right, but put into the context of Jude's argument[2] it leaps into more dramatic life. Jude is closing his letter as he began, with a prayer (*cf.* verses 1–2), and he is still dwelling on the same thoughts. We saw that the statements and concerns there (that we are 'called', 'loved' and 'kept', and that we might know 'mercy', 'peace' and 'love') point us to our future hope. In this closing section, we see how God leads us to that hope; he *is able to keep* us *from falling and to present* us *before his glorious presence*. Jude's letter was intended to prepare us for a long road, and now we look to our journey's end as we prepare to meet our Saviour.

1. He is able to keep you from falling (24a)

Jude says that God *is able*. He is thus introducing two parallel actions of God – one negative (he *is able to keep you from* something) and one positive (he *is able* . . . *to present you* to someone). The little word *able* slightly plays down the magnificent power Jude attributes to God in this verse. God is exercising great power on our behalf.[3]

---

[1] Bauckham (1983), p. 124.
[2] The NIV does not translate *de*, which connects this section with what has gone before. 'Now to him . . .' (NRSV).
[3] Rom. 16:25–27; Eph. 3:20–21.

As marathons become more popular, we are getting used to seeing amateur fun-runners cross the line exhausted and hurting, but exhilarated at having covered so much distance without falling by the way. Having seen what Jude has taught about the dangers that surround even the most ordinary Christian, it is a massive reassurance to discover that God *is able to keep* us *from falling.* Jude has written about the Israelites dying in the desert, angels losing their positions of authority and the cities of the plain being swept from their beautiful setting. All these 'serve as an example' to us (verse 7). We have seen Cain, Balaam and Korah abusing their privileged knowledge about God, and Jude's opponents 'have been destroyed' already in the aftermath of that rebellion (verse 11). Such people in our churches inevitably influence us, and we wonder if we will ever manage to reach the finishing-tape in a race where so many seem to fall along the way. Marathon runners who fall suffer physical injury, but we, if we fall, lose the very prize of salvation.

Jude's reassurance is that God will 'guard you so that you are exempt from stumbling and never trip or make a false step.'[4] We will never fall over our own feet, nor will someone else be able to wrong-foot us. He has urged us to take pains to 'keep' ourselves 'in God's love' (verse 21), and now he gives us God's promise to match that obedience: he will *keep* us *from falling.*[5] As Jude's readers face the challenge of living with the constant pressure to stumble coming even from within the church and among the church's leaders, what a great relief to know that night or day 'He will not let your foot slip – he who watches over you will not slumber; indeed, he who watches over Israel will neither slumber nor sleep'![6]

2. He is able to present you before his presence (24b)

In the Christian marathon, everyone who crosses the line is a winner.[7] The prize is that God brings us *before his glorious presence.* This slightly odd phrase is probably a respectful way for a Jewish writer to talk about the glorious God himself[8] in his 'moral splendour'.[9] This is the final judgment scene, where God's glory is displayed in all its awful purity: 'the glorious appearing

[4] Plummer, p. 464.
[5] The verbal similarity in English is not present in the Greek.
[6] Ps. 121:3–4; *cf.* Ps. 140:4; 141:9.
[7] 1 Cor. 9:27; Gal. 5:7; 2 Tim. 2:5; 4:7–8; Heb. 12:1.
[8] Compare, for example, Matthew's phrase 'the kingdom of heaven' with the other gospels' use of 'the kingdom of God'.
[9] Blum, p. 396.

of our great God and Saviour, Jesus Christ'.[10] The prophet Malachi had imagined that heavenly courtroom scene and asked, 'Who can endure the day of his coming? Who can stand when he appears?'[11] The correct answer is that no-one is able to stand on the basis of the lives we have lived. Yet Jude has seen that a wonderful transformation will have occurred, enabling Christians to face that holiness without flinching.

Jude says that God will be able to present us before his presence *without fault*. That is a most amazing statement. In the tabernacle and temple worship, anything that was presented to God had to be *without fault*: the bulls, rams, lambs, and all the other offerings had to be perfect.[12] In one comprehensive command, God told Moses: 'When any of you brings an offering to the LORD, bring as your offering an animal from either the herd or the flock. If the offering is a burnt offering from the herd, he is to offer a male without defect.'[13] The Israelites had to learn that not only their sacrificial animals had to be faultless; so did they. David saw this with great clarity. 'LORD, who may dwell in your sanctuary? Who may live on your holy hill? He whose walk is blameless and who does what is righteous.'[14] Taken to its logical limit, that would mean that no-one could dwell in the presence of the holy God. That was one of the hard lessons that Israel had to learn from the exile in Babylon.[15] No-one could produce 'the integrity and moral purity which is what [God] really demands from his worshippers'.[16]

Jesus Christ's death changes that, for he died a sacrificial death as 'a lamb without blemish or defect'.[17] The writer to the Hebrews grasped the magnificent difference which that makes. 'The blood of goats and bulls and the ashes of a heifer sprinkled on those who are ceremonially unclean sanctify them so that they are outwardly clean. How much more, then, will the blood of Christ, who through the eternal Spirit offered himself unblemished to God, cleanse our consciences from acts that lead to death, so that we may serve the living God!'[18] It is not surprising, then, that New Testament writers such as Jude use Old Testament sacrificial words to describe the ultimate purity of Christians, for they will share the wonderful purity of Christ.[19]

Jude's 'dear friends' (verses 3, 17, 20) belonged to a church which had prominent members who were 'blemishes' (12) and whose sins

[10] Tit. 2:13 (note that Paul also uses 'Saviour' eschatologically); *cf.* Lk. 9:26; 1 Pet. 4:13.
[11] Mal. 3:2.   [12] See, for example, the descriptions of the offerings in Nu. 28–29.
[13] Lv. 1:2–3.   [14] Ps. 15:1–2.   [15] Lv. 18:24–28.   [16] Kelly, p. 291.
[17] 1 Pet. 1:19.   [18] Heb. 9:13–14.
[19] See, *e.g.*, Eph. 1:4; 5:27; Phil. 2:15; Col. 1:22; 1 Thes. 3:13; notice how they all share Jude's emphasis on our holiness in God's sight in the future.

were like clothing 'stained by corrupted flesh' (23). Perhaps they felt contaminated by being near such people, and worried that some guilt might rub off. Jude holds out to all of them the amazing words that were said to Joshua the high priest, 'See, I have taken away your sin, and I will put rich garments on you.'[20] That scene will surely be characterized by wonderful, exuberant, *great joy* on the part of ourselves,[21] the angels[22] and even Jesus Christ himself.[23]

3. Hallelujah! What a Saviour! (25)

Jude begins to close his letter by bringing together exhilarating words of praise which overflow into one another, and which he probably does not intend us to disentangle too analytically. He wants us to respond with praise to a God whose magnificent dominion is unchallengeable for ever. It cannot be challenged because he has *glory, majesty, power and authority*. Glory (*doxa*) is the public, visible and acclaimed presence of God, the glory of Sinai, in the tabernacle and the temple, which left at the time of the exile. It was again seen on earth only in the face of the Lord Jesus, where the apostles had 'seen his glory, the glory of the One and Only, who came from the Father, full of grace and truth'.[24] We will see it only when he brings us before his glorious presence for ever. His *majesty* is his 'awful transcendence',[25] his eternal right to rule. His *power* underlines his unique claim to his throne (the word it translates, *kratos*, is only ever used of God himself and his work),[26] and he acts in that power when he uses his *authority*.

Jude's timescale is breathtaking too, for he spins us back before the creation of our universe and says that God had this unimaginable power *before all ages*; despite the apparent godlessness of our world, he has it *now*, and nothing will ever replace him *for evermore*.

Jude seems to be echoing the delighted praise of David:

> Praise be to you, O LORD,
> God of our father Israel,
> from everlasting to everlasting.
> Yours, O LORD, is the greatness and the power
> and the glory and the majesty and the splendour,
> for everything in heaven and earth is yours.

[20] Zc. 3:4.   [21] *Cf.* 1 Pet. 1:6; 4:13.   [22] *Cf.* Heb. 12:22.   [23] *Cf.* Jn. 15:11.
[24] Jn. 1:14; *cf.* Ex. 19:16–19; 40:34–38; 1 Ki. 8:10–11; Ezk. 10:1–22.
[25] Kelly, p. 293.
[26] Lk. 1:51; Acts 19:20; Eph. 1:19; 6:10; Col. 1:11; 1 Tim. 6:16; Heb. 2:14; 1 Pet. 4:11; 5:11; Rev. 1:6; 5:13.

> Yours, O LORD, is the kingdom;
>   you are exalted as head over all.
> Wealth and honour come from you;
>   you are the ruler of all things.
> In your hands are strength and power
>   to exalt and give strength to all.
> Now, our God, we give you thanks,
>   and praise your glorious name.[27]

There is, however, a new element in Jude's praise which David could barely see in the distance. All the praise and acknowledgment are offered to God *through Jesus Christ our Lord*. This elevates Jesus to the highest place, for 'words could hardly express more clearly Jude's belief in the pre-existence and eternity of Christ'.[28]

This wonderful heaping up of praise is due to God for one great reason, the reason that has shone through Jude's letter from start to finish, and the only beam of bright light that can offer any glimmer of hope to those who live in a world with a grim present and an even grimmer future under God's judgment. The reason is that he is *the only God our Saviour*.[29] He is the only God there is, which rules out the delusions that Jude's opponents were spreading. In addition, he acts towards us as *Saviour*. It is such a small word, and has been so abused and trivialized in much Christian thinking and praise. But when the mighty day of God comes, more terrible than we can imagine – when we see for the first time who it is we rebel against; how perfect his standards are; how ghastly our sin is; how seriously he meant all the Old Testament warnings of judgment on the grumbling Israelites, the mutinous angels, and Sodom and Gomorrah – then we shall see with fear and wonder what a mighty work the cross of Christ was, and is, and shall be for ever. The fact that God himself[30] has acted on our behalf to rescue us from a judgment which we so thoroughly deserve means that the heavens will echo for ever with our shout of praise: *Amen*.

---

[27] 1 Ch. 29:10–13.   [28] Bigg, p. 344.

[29] 'To the only *wise* God' (AV, followed by NKJV) is probably an assimilation from Rom. 16:27.

[30] Lk. 1:47; 1 Tim. 1:1; 2:3; 4:10; Tit. 1:3; 2:10; 3:4.

Appendix
The authorship of 2 Peter and Jude

This book is an exposition for ordinary Christians rather than a technical commentary, and the aim has not been to interact thoroughly with contemporary scholarship. It has, however, made some major assumptions which go against most current opinion, and these should be explained, albeit briefly. Readers should refer to the much more thorough introductions in the main commentaries, as well as to Guthrie's important essays.[1]

The problems are legion. On the most superficial level, commentators on 2 Peter disagree on where paragraph divisions should fall, and some modern versions present the text in long blocks. This renders it hard for a Bible reader to make sense of 'the most problematical of all the New Testament Epistles'.[2] Then again, even a cursory reading of 2 Peter and Jude together raises the issue of authorship. How are we to account for the obvious similarity between the two letters? Most of Jude appears in 2 Peter in some form, and in a couple of verses there is almost exact correspondence. Are they dependent on each other, and if they are, which is dependent on which? J. A. T. Robinson noted that 'the issues of chronology and authorship are here, more than ever, inextricably connected'.[3]

A glance at 1 Peter raises a third question: could the author of 1 Peter be the author of 2 Peter? The Greek of the first is said to be among the finest in the New Testament, the Greek of the second alleged to be among the worst. After listing other scholars' views of 2 Peter, G. E. Ladd summarizes them as follows: 'It is said to have a degenerate Christology, a sub-Christian eschatology, and an unsatisfactory ethic.'[4]

A little knowledge of church history raises yet a fourth set of

---

[1] *NTI*, pp. 805–857, 901–928.   [2] *NTI*, p. 805.   [3] Robinson, p. 140.
[4] G. E. Ladd. *A Theology of the New Testament* (Grand Rapids: Eerdmans, 1974), p. 603.

difficulties. 2 Peter had an enormous struggle to be included in the New Testament. J. N. D. Kelly says that 'no NT document had a longer and tougher struggle to win acceptance than 2 Peter'.[5] The early historian Eusebius was happy about the canonicity of 1 Peter, but not about that of 2 Peter: 'The so-called second Epistle we have not received as canonical, but nevertheless it has appeared useful to many, and it has been studied with other Scriptures.'[6] Calvin and Luther both expressed doubts about it. Erasmus excluded it. Should it be in our Bibles? If it is by Peter, then it must have been written before his death in AD 68; but if it is not by him, when was it written, and by whom?

A. 2 Peter and Jude: which came first?

Some kind of relationship between 2 Peter and Jude is undeniable, although the similarities are more in terms of their general thrust than precise correlation of words. Ladd overstates the position when he says: 'There is little of theological interest in Jude that is not in 2 Peter.'[7] Donald Guthrie looked at the words that the two letters share and said that 'if 2 Peter is the borrower he has changed 70% of Jude's language and added more of his own'. If, on the other hand, Jude borrowed from 2 Peter, 'the percentage of alteration is slightly higher, combined with a reduction in quantity'.[8] In other words, there is an undeniable link between the two letters, but, whichever author wrote first, both display an originality of style. It follows that the meaning of a word or phrase in one letter is not necessarily a reliable guide to its meaning in the other, and the letters have a right to be treated as separate pieces of work. There are broadly three options.[9]

Option 1:   Jude adapted 2 Peter

This is the standard position of the older scholars. Its strongest argument is that in 2 Peter the danger of false teachers is said to lie in the future ('there will be false teachers among you', 2:1) but in Jude to be in the present ('these men are blemishes at your love feasts', 12). 2 Peter must therefore precede Jude.

But this argument proves nothing of the sort. First, it could be that the churches to which the two letters were written were distant from each other, and that what is a very present danger in one was

---

[5] Kelly, p. 224.   [6] *Church History* 3.3.1.   [7] Ladd, *op. cit.*, p. 607.
[8] *NTI*, p. 925.
[9] Robinson's suggestion that Jude wrote both letters (p. 193) has not convinced other scholars.

still a looming problem in the other. Secondly, this view assumes that the dangers the two letters address are the same, whereas in fact they are subtly different. Jude's errorists do not seem to have reached the point of denying the second coming of Christ. Thirdly, this position fails to acknowledge the assertion of both letters that the infiltration of the false teachers is a mark of the last days (2 Pet. 3:3; Jude 17); they are therefore a continuing presence in the church and can rightly be spoken of in both a present and a future sense. Fourthly, it is said to be difficult to account for Jude's rearranging Peter's material in a less chronological and (apparently) less careful order. Jude's material is equally stylized, however, although that is less immediately obvious. He uses a large number of 'triplets'[10] and 'catchwords'.[11] Each letter has its own style and logic, and these factors do not prove which used which.

Option 2: Jude and 2 Peter adapted a third source

This is the position taken by Bigg, Green and Spicq, among others. It is true that the New Testament refers to lost documents, and that we know that others lie behind the gospels, and so there is no *prima facie* reason why this should not be the case with Jude and 2 Peter. The question is whether we need this theory if one of the other two is more likely to be true. The fact that the decision is finely balanced is no reason to introduce a third explanation. What we need is more evidence, not more hypothetical documents!

Option 3: Peter adapted Jude

This option has the advantage of great neatness, because it simply requires Peter to insert Jude into a larger framework. It would also help to explain the obvious difference between the two, namely that Jude seamlessly weaves in some apocryphal material which is absent from 2 Peter. True, it is hard to think why Jude includes this material. But it is easy to understand why Peter would regard Jude as valuable, but see that it would need to be rewritten, excluding the Jewish apocryphal material, for a wider Gentile readership. Perhaps the first letter, referred to in 2 Peter 3:1, was the original covering note that went out with Jude; now Peter decides to do a more thorough reworking.

Would it be unethical or unapostolic for Peter to adapt Jude? Not necessarily. As Bauckham has recently shown, Jude comes from 'Palestinian Jewish Christian circles',[12] in both its authorship and

---

[10] See Charles (1991).   [11] See Bauckham (1983), p. 5.
[12] Bauckham (1991), p. 280.

intended readership. Possibly Peter felt that although the message of Jude was important for the wider church, his background reading could not be assumed in Gentile churches around the Mediterranean. Hence he took Jude's arrangement of material (which makes perfect logical sense in its setting) and rearranged it to make sense to a wider readership, adding material to give it a different coherence.

B. Who wrote Jude?

There are six men called Jude (or Judas) in the New Testament: Jude the ancestor of Jesus,[13] Judas Iscariot, Judas the son of James,[14] Judas Barsabbas,[15] Judas the Galilean[16] and Jude the Lord's brother.[17] Of these, only the last is recorded as having a brother called James. Assuming that by 'brother of James' (Jude 1) the writer is referring to blood relationship rather than claiming to be a fellow worker, it would make sense if a relatively unknown man were to emphasize his authority to write by mentioning his kinship with a much senior brother. (For the reasons that being a brother of Jesus would not be adequate to confer authority, see the exposition *ad loc.*). It is wholly unnecessary to postulate someone writing in Jude's name, for as far as we can tell, Jude had no authority of his own worth hijacking. Bauckham says that 'Jude, the Lord's brother, a prominent missionary leader in the Palestinian churches of the earliest period, is entirely plausibly the author of this letter'. He concludes provocatively, 'It could easily be among the earliest of the New Testament documents.'[18]

In scholarly circles, the current move towards rhetorical criticism has opened more possibilities. This method examines the forms of argument, presentation, logic and persuasion expected in a literary work of the first century.[19] Its weakness is that it assumes that the New Testament writers would have both known and followed these methods, and it requires a far higher level of sophistication for Jude than we should expect. T. R. Wolthius has speared the tendency with a devastating fictional dialogue between Cicero and Jude. His point is that Jude simply would not have been aware of the complexities in which a philosophical rhetorician was trained.[20]

---

[13] Lk. 3:33.   [14] Lk. 6:16; Acts 1:13; Jn. 14:22.   [15] Acts 15:22–33.
[16] Acts 5:37.   [17] Mt. 13:55; Mk. 6:3.
[18] Bauckham (1991), p. 178.
[19] See G. W. Hansen's article, 'Rhetorical Criticism', in G. F. Hawthorne, R. P. Martin and D. G. Reid (eds.), *Dictionary of Paul and his Letters* (Downers Grove and Leicester: IVP, 1993), pp. 822–826.
[20] T. R. Wolthius, 'Jude and the Rhetorician: A Dialogue on the Rhetorical Nature of the Epistle of Jude', *Calvin Theological Journal* 24/1 (1989), pp. 126–134.

C. Who wrote 2 Peter?

2 Peter claims to be by the apostle Simon Peter, an eye-witness of Jesus' ministry, and no other name has ever been linked with this letter in church tradition. That in itself is important evidence. But although the early Christian writer Origen called 1 and 2 Peter 'the apostle's twin trumpets',[21] his belief that one writer penned both letters has not been universally shared. An international team of Roman Catholic and Lutheran scholars agreed with what they called 'the almost unanimous verdict of critical scholarship that II Peter is not authentically Petrine and that it may have been the last of the New Testament works to be composed'.[22] That odd phrase 'almost unanimous' indicates that there is another view. One scholar who holds this other view is the German commentator Carston Thiede, who says that 'Peter's second letter is a document of undeniable apostolic authority'.[23] Current scholarship usually suggests, not that 2 Peter is a 'forgery' in the derogatory modern sense, but that it is a 'testament' – that is, a document written in the name and with the concerns of a dead hero.

Could the author of 1 Peter have written 2 Peter?

At first sight it seems improbable that one author penned both Petrine letters. The Greek of 1 Peter is 'some of the finest Greek in the whole New Testament ... The person responsible for the poor Greek of 2 Peter could not have written 1 Peter and vice versa.'[24] It is difficult to compare such short works, however, and we should not rely too heavily on the results of such comparisons. But if the differences are there, we may expect early readers to have been even more sensitive to them than modern scholars are. Jerome indeed concluded that the two letters 'are divergent in style, character and structure of words',[25] and his solution was that Peter used a different secretary for each letter.[26] The linguistic problem primarily concerns 1 Peter, of course, because it is unlikely that a fisherman would write in such polished Greek. The incongruity is still probably best accounted for by Jerome's suggestion of a change in amanuensis. 1 Peter 5:12 mentions the involvement of Silas (=Silvanus). He

---

[21] *Homily* on Jos. 7:1. Thiede, pp. 183, 254.
[22] R. E. Brown, K. P. Donfried and J. Reumann (eds.), *Peter in the New Testament* (Minneapolis: Augsburg, 1973; London: Geoffrey Chapman, 1974), p. 17.
[23] Thiede, p. 183.
[24] P. Davids, *1 Peter, New International Commentary on the New Testament* (Grand Rapids: Eerdmans, 1990), p. 4.
[25] Quoted in Kelly, p. 236.   [26] *NTI*, p. 818

was a colleague of Paul,[27] and this might account for the Pauline influence in 1 Peter.

2 Peter, by contrast, lacks elegance of style. It is written in the rough and ready Greek of a 'serious, hastily and urgently devised letter'.[28] There is nothing intrinsically improbable in the idea of Peter knowing Greek; he would, like Jesus and indeed any Jew of his day, have been bilingual. He would have spoken Aramaic at home and Greek when doing business in 'Galilee of the Gentiles'.[29] Quite possibly, he would even have known Hebrew from the synagogue too. According to Bauckham,[30] the Greek of 2 Peter shows that the letter 'belongs to the sphere of Hellenistic Jewish Greek'. But it is difficult to know what that proves, for we do not know what level of Greek a Galilean fisherman would be expected to speak, what fluency and style he might have developed during a long period as a Christian preacher, and how much help he received from a secretary. J. N. Sevenster surveyed the whole question of the knowledge of Greek among the first Christians and concluded: 'Right from the beginning the preaching of the Gospel was not confined to the Jewish land and was directed to non-Jews from beyond the frontiers of Palestine as well as Jews from the diaspora. That is why the Jewish Christians must often have had special occasion to acquire a good knowledge of Greek. Frequently they must have had to speak it in order to maintain regular contact with all the other members of the congregation.'[31] In itself, the style makes no decisive contribution to determining the authorship, although, as Longenecker says, 'perhaps this is how Peter himself wrote when not aided by Silas (1 Peter 5:12), Mark (à la Papias on the composition of Mark's gospel) or Luke (cf. Peter's preaching in Acts)'.[32]

There is also said to be a wide gap between the theologies of 1 and 2 Peter, but that is to make too much of a minor issue. Both letters are brief responses to different problems, and it would be too much to expect a systematic theology to emerge in two such short works.

In his recent commentary on 1 Peter,[33] Peter Davids outlines that letter's position on eschatology and apocalyptic. He suggests two

[27] 2 Cor. 1:19; 1 Thes. 1:1; 2 Thes. 1:1. [28] Thiede, p. 181.
[29] Mt. 4:15. See J. H. Greenlee, 'The Language of the New Testament', *Expositor's Bible Commentary* 1 (Grand Rapids: Zondervan, 1979), pp. 409–416.
[30] Bauckham (1983), pp. 135–136.
[31] J. N. Sevenster, 'Do You Know Greek?' *NovTest* Supplement XIX (Leiden: Brill, 1968), p. 189.
[32] R. N. Longenecker, 'On the Form, Function and Authority of the New Testament Letters', in D. A. Carson and D. J. Woodbridge (eds.), *Scripture and Truth* (Grand Rapids: Baker, 1982; Leicester: IVP, 1983), pp. 101–114.
[33] Davids, *op. cit.*, pp. 15–16.

headings, 'Time' and 'Space', and then analyses the letter. Under 'Time', he concludes that 1 Peter teaches (a) that the early material in Genesis (e.g. the fall) has a universally applicable significance; (b) that the persecution the church experiences today is an eschatological crisis, as focal as Noah's flood; (c) that suffering precedes judgment; and (d) that final judgment is accompanied by final salvation. Under 'Space', he finds that 1 Peter is concerned with (a) other-worldly regions such as heaven and hell, and (b) other-worldly beings, such as angels and evil spirits. Although Davids draws attention to 1 Peter's similarity to James, it is striking how the pattern matches 2 Peter as well. For instance, it can be traced through the following passages in 2 Peter:

1. *Time*	(a) 2:4–8	
	(b) 3:3–7	
	(c) 2:1–3	
2. *Space*	(a) 2:4; 3:12–14	
	(b) 3:4	

Obviously these were topics with which many Christians were concerned. Nevertheless, these passages reveal a substantial overlap of thought between two letters which claim the same author.

What is the evidence outside the New Testament?

Although 2 Peter is rarely quoted by name in the first couple of centuries, scholars' general pessimism about its extrabiblical support is too marked. Thiede says of early writers that 'even those who record doubts expressed by others . . . do not appear to share them wholeheartedly, or even reject them.'.[34] He and Green quote Origen, Clement of Alexandria and Jerome as accepting the authenticity of both letters, although these are late, third-century, evidences for authorship. Green, in his thorough survey, says that 2 Peter 'has incomparably better support for its inclusion than the best attested of the rejected books'.[35]

But how late is 2 Peter? The Dutch theologian Hugo Grotius (1583–1645) was the first to place the letter in the time of the Emperor Trajan.[36] Käsemann[37] famously saw it as very late, written well into the second century. His category of 'early Catholicism' had three main strands: the lack of hope of an imminent return of

---

[34] Thiede, p. 251.   [35] Green (1961), p. 5.   [36] Quoted in *NTI*, p. 822.
[37] Käsemann, pp. 169–195.

Christ, highly organized church leadership, and the regularizing of a body of faith. But it is now widely recognized that even if his picture fits the early church, it certainly does not fit 2 Peter. For this letter has not lost the hope of the imminent return of Christ, makes no reference to any formal church structures, and mentions a formalized body of doctrine only in ways that occur also in other New Testament writings.[38]

The first direct quotation of 2 Peter is in *1 Clement*, a letter written around the end of the first century. Thiede says that once the quotations start appearing, 'the list is as long as for 1 Peter or indeed most other NT letters'.[39] In a more recent article,[40] he has expanded that argument in two important ways. First, he has shown that early writers such as Irenaeus and Origen had very good reasons for not quoting 2 Peter (namely, because of its superficial similarity to non-Christian thinking of the time). The fact that writers do not quote 2 Peter does not mean that they do not know it, but only that it was not relevant to their case. In fact, Thiede suggests that Origen's opponent, Celsus, quotes 2 Peter. Secondly, Thiede shows that 2 Peter has much more in common with other New Testament writings than many scholars admit, and concludes that it 'is firmly established in a scriptural context that makes a first-century date much more plausible than any date *after* the turn of the century'.[41]

The historian Eusebius famously divided the books he knew of into three groups, and 2 Peter and Jude are in the middle grouping of 'disputed books'. However, within that category they are grouped with James and 2 and 3 John as books that were generally accepted, even though the evidence for them was not as strong as for the undisputed books. No books later excluded from the New Testament are grouped with these five, and no New Testament books occur outside these two categories of 'genuine' and 'disputed but accepted'.[42] Guthrie concludes his massive survey with the assertion: 'There is no evidence from any part of the early church that this Epistle was ever regarded as spurious, in spite of the hesitancy which existed over its reception.'[43]

There is a fascinating, though inconclusive, piece of papyrus from the Dead Sea Scrolls at Qumran. A fragment from Qumran Cave 7 (7Q10) has some letters on it which, if they are from the New

---

[38] See the references in Käsemann on 1:12.   [39] Thiede, p. 251.
[40] C. P. Thiede, 'A Pagan Reader of 2 Peter', *JSNT* 26 (1986), pp. 79–96.
[41] *Ibid.*, p. 91.
[42] See D. G. Dunbar, 'The Biblical Canon', in D. A. Carson and J. D. Woodbridge (eds.), *Hermeneutics, Authority and Canon* (Grand Rapids: Zondervan; Leicester: IVP, 1986), pp. 291–360.
[43] *NTI*, p. 811.

Testament at all, come from 2 Peter 1:15. If the identification is correct, then this places the earliest quotation of 2 Peter before AD 68, when the caves were sealed. Even a most enthusiastic supporter, however, says that the identification is 'very tentative'.[44]

The suggestion is, then, that Jude is early and Palestinian, while 2 Peter is later and intended for a broader readership. If the errors that the two letters oppose are related (although they are not quite the same, as the exposition makes clear), then that might help to explain why the present danger in Palestine (Jude) is still a future danger in the wider church (2 Peter).

Could 2 Peter be by someone writing in Peter's name?

As in the cases of Paul, John and other New Testament leaders, a number of works were written after Peter's death and in his name, purporting to come from him. These include the *Gospel of Peter*, the *Acts of Peter* and the *Apocalypse of Peter*. Could 2 Peter have been a further product of a well-meaning disciple?

Many internal pieces of evidence are taken to indicate that this letter is pseudepigraphical, and Meade says that 'no document included in the New Testament gives such thorough evidence of its pseudonymity as does 2 Peter. The arguments against the authenticity are overwhelming.'[45] The claims to be an eye-witness, references to Jesus' teaching, a warm reference to Paul, and even the opening words themselves are taken to prove that the writer is straining too hard at authenticity. Kelly says of the name 'Simeon' (2 Pet. 1:1, in many of the Greek manuscripts) that 'possibly the writer considered that this old-fashioned, Semitic touch would add verisimilitude to the letter's claim to be from Peter himself'.[46] Robinson's point is worth remembering: it is precisely the *absence* of such touches which is often held to prove that 1 Peter is not by Peter![47]

The three main pieces of evidence which are adduced for the pseudepigraphic origin of 2 Peter are as follows.

First, the use of 'knowledge' (*gnōsis*) language is said to indicate the presence of Gnosticism, a second-century phenomenon. On this view, 2 Peter is a response in Peter's name to a problem he could not have foreseen. Mere use of the word 'knowledge', however, does not necessarily demonstrate that the error was present in its full-blown sense. Gnosticism is a notoriously elusive body of

---

[44] Thiede, p. 254.
[45] D. G. Meade, *Pseudonymity and Canon* (Grand Rapids: Eerdmans, 1987), p. 179.
[46] Kelly, p. 296.   [47] Robinson, p. 165.

ideas,[48] and there is no known form of it that shares the profile of the error 2 Peter addresses. Probably the errorists claimed special knowledge that permitted them their freedom, and possibly they were in some loose sense therefore 'gnostic'; but the second-century error is absent from the letter.

Secondly, three factors are said to favour a later rather than an earlier date: the amicable relationship between Peter and Paul, the assertion that Paul wrote Scripture, and the collection of his occasional letters into a canon (see 3:15–16).

The friendliness between Peter and Paul in this letter has been suspect since the nineteenth century. A group of scholars, following Professor F. C. Baur of Tübingen (and therefore known as 'the Tübingen school'), extended the disagreement between the apostles in Galatians 2:11–14 into a lifelong and fundamental antagonism between the 'Petrinists' (Jewish Christians) and the 'Paulinists' (Gentile Christians). Anything which showed them to be willing colleagues – or even made no reference to the division – was to be seen as a late, second-century attempt to rewrite early Christianity in an ideal way.

The effect on New Testament scholarship was stunning, for it left only Romans, Corinthians and Galatians as being by Paul. For our purposes, it inevitably made 2 Peter late and unauthentic.

It is generally thought today that Baur radically overstepped the mark. Neither his secular philosophy nor his elevation of the Galatians crisis has found lasting merit. Although it is true that the disagreement in Galatians was deep and concerned the very essence of the gospel, and although its nature is still a matter of controversy, the evidence for its permanence is not as firm as Baur wished. As far as 2 Peter is concerned, this theory has made a negative rather than a positive contribution. Although its refutation does not prove that 2 Peter is early, the disagreement between Peter and Paul in Galatians is not as great a barrier to accepting the accuracy of 2 Peter 3:15–16 as was once thought, and therefore does not automatically make it late.

The assertion that Paul wrote 'Scripture' is said to be evidence of a late date, because it implies a level of confidence in and respect for Paul's letters which is not found in early Christianity. Yet although the word 'Scripture' is not used of apostolic writings elsewhere in the New Testament, the concept of writing down God's words and being his appointed teacher is clearly found even in early Paul. In 1 Thessalonians, to take but one example, the authority of Paul in speaking the 'word of God' (2:13, 4), writing 'instructions' from God (4:2, 8), and charging the Thessalonians 'before the Lord to

[48] See the article in *NDT*, pp. 272–274.

have this letter read to all the brothers' (5:27) is exactly what we would expect from Peter's view of Paul's letters. An apostle would clearly feel able to write Scripture.

Neither is the idea of a collection of letters proof of a very late date. There is clear evidence that Paul used Paul's letters in that way,[49] and the exposition tries to show that it makes good structural sense for Peter to end with the thought that an apostle wrote Scripture, consistent with the Old Testament's promise of Christ's coming. Peter's words cannot be taken to refer to a complete collection of Paul's letters, and much less a formalized and fixed canon. If Paul's instructions to circulate 1 Thessalonians were taken seriously, it would not have been long before churches were sharing their apostolic writings.

Thirdly, alleged verbal 'slips', such as the reference to 'our fathers' (3:4), the move from future prophecy to present-tense reality (3:3–5), and an over-emphasis on Peter's apostolic office (1:16–18) are said to betray a late, non-apostolic hand. For comments against the first two points, see the exposition of the passages mentioned. Regarding the third, it should be noticed that 1:16–18 does not appeal to Peter's apostolic authority in particular, but to the authority of the apostles as a group. This is a point often missed. Peter's concern is that the witnesses to Jesus' heavenly glory, and of the promise to return, had been denied in totality by the false teachers. His defence is that the apostolic teaching as a body agrees with the Old Testament claims. There is neither an attack on, nor a defence of, Peter's apostleship as an individual. This characteristic of the error supports an argument for an early date, because the collective authority of the apostles later became an unquestionable mark of orthodoxy.

When Meade comments on Green's and Guthrie's defences of a genuine Petrine authorship, he says that 'their defence is really based on a pure and more fundamental objection to pseudo-nymity'.[50] Whether or not that is a fair analysis of their position, it leaves unanswered the question: is there anything inherently *un-Christian* in writing a letter in another's name? Of course, there were secretaries, and possibly they had a large hand in drafting letters; but their work was sent out with the approval and authority of the writer. The question needs to be sharper: is there anything un-Christian in writing a letter in someone else's name without the named author's knowledge and authority?

Christians place a high value on truth, and it is implausible to think that the early Christians would have abandoned that criterion in their writings. On discovering that certain books (such as the *Gospel of*

[49] Col. 4:16.   [50] Meade, *op. cit.*, p. 180.

Peter) were forgeries, early Christians refused to use them. The penalty upon being discovered to be a forger of apostolic material – even a well-meaning one – meant loss of position in the church.[51] Those who wish to defend a pseudonymous authorship for 2 Peter, while wishing to retain it in the canon, therefore have to prove that pseudonymity was a recognized and accepted literary genre, and that a pseudonymous work was not a forgery. Elliott, for instance, says that it was 'a common literary device of the day employed by Jews and Christians alike to link securely the present synagogue and church to the persons with whom such tradition was honestly and fervently believed to have originated'.[52] But that assertion obscures an important distinction.

It was certainly acceptable in a Jewish setting to write material in the name of a long-dead hero of the faith. The exposition has brought us into contact with such material to do with Moses and Enoch. But the phenomenon of pseudepigraphy also involved Adam and Eve, Abraham, Jacob, Elijah, David, Solomon, Isaiah, Daniel and many others.[53] It seems clear, however, that not even the most earnest reader was meant to be taken in by the attributed authorship of such works. They seem to have multiplied over time as pious generations added their own interpretations of what the heroes would have said.

The assertion that it was acceptable to write such material in the name of a recently dead, or even living, hero of the faith, whether Jewish or Christian, is, however, of a different order. Although it is frequently claimed that such practice was common, it has not been proved, and the parallel between the two different kinds of pseudonymity is weak. In the one case, the writings could not possibly be by the named but long-deceased writer, and they would not have been thought genuine. But in the other case, there is a possibility – if not likelihood – of genuine confusion. That is not to say that there were no attempts to write in the name of Christian leaders, for the evidence goes the other way. In addition to the large collection of apocryphal New Testament books,[54] we should notice that early in his ministry Paul encountered the problem of letters which he had not written being circulated in his name.[55] Of course such material was written. The question, however, is whether it was acceptable to write in that form. Despite the strong tide in the other direction, it must be said that there is still no evidence that it was. In fact, there is clear evidence that authors of these works were

[51] *NTI*, pp. 675–683.   [52] Elliott, p. 123.   [53] See Charles (1990) and (1991).
[54] See M. R. James (ed.), *The Apocryphal New Testament* (Oxford: Oxford University Press, 1924).
[55] 2 Thes. 2:2.

punished severely.[56] Every such work bears the mark of a deliberate misuse of a well-known name and would, in modern terms, be called a forgery.

The one claimed exception to this is the literary genre called 'testament'. A testament was a piece written in the name of someone who had recently died, claiming to encapsulate the essence of a lifetime's teaching. It would be written as that person's dying message to his disciples and would include a prediction of the future. The most recent and persuasive adherent of this position for 2 Peter is Richard Bauckham. He produces a number of examples of the genre, identifies the common stylistic features, and says that 2 Peter is both a letter and a testament. Because the work fits into this well-known form, 'the Petrine authorship was intended to be an entirely *transparent* fiction'[57] (his italics), and the recipients would have recognized it. If this is correct, then Bauckham has managed to show that 2 Peter is not by Peter, and that nevertheless there is nothing disreputable in that fact.[58]

It is not certain, however, that Bauckham has cleared the ground as much as he claims.

First, 2 Peter does not fit the normal shape for a 'testament'. Bauckham himself notes, for example, that a testament would normally contain a strong element of prediction, but 2 Peter mentions that the false teachers are a present reality. Bauckham explains that the author 'feels free to break the conventions of the genre he is using for the sake of a literary effect'.[59] He is persuaded that 2 Peter was such an obviously pseudepigraphic work that its writer could abandon the recognized marks of the genre to make a strong point. But in a setting where there was a large amount of pseudepigrapha, with a clear possibility of a high price to pay if the work was thought a forgery, we should expect the author to stay very closely within the genre.

Secondly, the examples of the testament form do not prove that it was possible for 2 Peter to be one: they are either obviously by long-dead heroes (in which case they were not believed to be true anyway) or by contemporaries and rejected by the churches. Bauckham cannot produce an example of a testament openly accepted by the churches as a testament.

Thirdly, following that, none of the discussions of the acceptability of 2 Peter among the early churches makes reference to its

---

[56] Green (1987), p. 35, quotes the stories of what happened to the authors of the *Acts of Paul and Thecla* and the *Gospel of Peter*.

[57] Bauckham (1983), p. 134.

[58] This would also be true of other claimed testaments, such as Acts 20:17–35 and 2 Timothy.

[59] Bauckham (1983), p. 134.

being a testament: they regard it as either by Peter (in which case it would be accepted) or not (in which case it would be rejected). If the work was a piece of *'transparent* fiction', we might expect to see it at least being discussed in those terms; but the early Christians do not seem to have recognized it as such, or even left evidence that there was such a genre to place it in. As Conrad Gempf has noticed, 'If pseudonymous works got into the canon, the church fathers were *fooled* by a transparent literary device that was originally *not* intended to fool anyone.'[60]

Finally, the fact that a work bears a resemblance to a genre is no proof that it belongs to that genre. The genre of 'testament' echoed the way leaders would tend to bid their farewells in real life. The formal similarities between 2 Peter and a testament[61] arise because of the situation, for how else would a departing apostle have written as he faced his death?

The field is very divided, with most commentators assuming that 2 Peter is not by the apostle. The position taken in this exposition is that no sufficient argument or combination of arguments has yet proved that Peter could not be the author, and that the burden of proof must rest with those who wish to deny his authorship. The suggestion that 2 Peter is a testament has not added substantially to the discussion. D. A. Carson's comment on Bauckham's otherwise excellent commentary is sound: 'Why he concluded that 2 Peter is pseudonymous is still not clear to me: his evidence does not strike me as very convincing.'[62]

D. Is 2 Peter one letter?

The first problem many readers encounter is simply that of the 'plot' of 2 Peter. The break between 2:22 and 3:1 is clear even on a first reading, and it was the Dutch theologian Hugo Grotius who first suggested in 1641 that this point marked the start of a second letter.[63] Once readers started to subdivide 2 Peter, there was clear dissatisfaction with the letter as a unit, although no single suggested restructuring holds the field. In 1915, E. I. Robson reached the gloomy conclusion that 2 Peter 'is a thing of shreds and patches; it passes by what seem to be happy-go-lucky sutures, from exhortation to narrative, narrative to prophecy, prophecy to apocalyptic'.[64]

---

[60] C. Gempf, 'Pseudonymity in the New Testament', *Themelios* 17/2 (1992), p. 10.
[61] And between Acts 20:18–35 or 2 Timothy and a testament.
[62] D. A. Carson, *New Testament Commentary Survey* (Leicester: IVP; Grand Rapids: Baker, fourth edn. 1993), p. 83.
[63] Quoted in *NTI*, p. 845
[64] E. I. Robson, *Studies in the Second Epistle of St Peter* (Cambridge: Cambridge University Press, 1915), p. 3.

There are two separate issues: first, is the letter as we have it a coherent unit? Second, if it is a unit, what is its structure?

The unity of 2 Peter

The first question is answered with much greater agreement among scholars today. Although some still want to make 3:1 refer to some other part of 2 Peter,[65] many concur that the letter has a unity of vocabulary and concern. Although the use of Jude's material is unevenly clustered around chapter 2, it is unnecessary to excise it as a later interpolation. As we have seen in the exposition, Peter reworks Jude to give it his own logic.

The difficulty has been to perceive the structure underlying the letter, and the lack of that perception has hindered further moves forward. Bauckham suggests that 2 Peter is a systematic reply to four objections, and this proposal has been developed in an important article by D. F. Watson. He has recently suggested that the structures of both Jude and 2 Peter are highly dependent on the rhetorical systems of their day. His suggestion is certainly welcome for the support it affords to the unity of each letter, but one wonders how accustomed Peter and Jude would have been to such techniques. He says that they 'were familiar with the rhetorical conventions of their time, but it is unknown whether that familiarity is the product of specific training or is the outgrowth of daily interaction with spoken and written culture.'[66] Even if 2 Peter is not by Peter, it is hard to marry that level of sophistication with a letter written in 'poor Greek'.[67]

How does 2 Peter hold together?

In this exposition, we have followed the rule of submitting to the author's 'melodic line', rather than imposing our own. For those readers who might be interested in discovering the structure that has thus become evident, this section pulls together the comments made at various earlier points and shows how the letter can be viewed as a tightly argued unit.

The main step is to perceive that *chapter 2 and chapter 3 each*

---

[65] *E.g.* M. McNamara, who suggests that chapter 1 is the letter. 'The Unity of Second Peter: A Reconsideration', *Scripture* 12 (1960), pp. 13–19. See Green (1987), p. 47, for a brief survey of other proposals.

[66] Watson, p. 189. See the witty reaction to this in T. R. Wolthius, 'Jude and the Rhetorician: A Dialogue on the Rhetorical Nature of the Epistle of Jude', *Calvin Theological Journal* 24/1 (1989), pp. 126–134.

[67] P. Davids, *The First Epistle of Peter, New International Commentary on the New Testament* (Grand Rapids: Eerdmans, 1990), p. 4.

contain two introductory headlines: 2:10 (paralleled in 3:4) and 2:17 (paralleled in 3:11–12a). If the two chapters have similar shapes, the fact that chapter 3 does not follow on from chapter 2 is not a problem. It was not intended to do so. Rather, both chapters equally derive from 1:16–21. That section has as its twin subjects 'the power' and 'the coming', and both receive authenticity from the prophets and the apostles. Chapter 2 then takes up the theme of 'power', and chapter 3 the theme of 'coming'. Each chapter explains the Old Testament antecedents of Peter's position (2:4–9; 3:5–7) and its confirmation through the apostles (2:21; 3:15–16). The problem the false teachers raise by their very existence is the apparent inability of God to do what he has promised (2:9; 3:4). The exposition suggests that the subject of chapter 2 is 'the power of the Lord Jesus to judge (despite appearances to the contrary)', and that of chapter 3 is 'the promise of the Lord Jesus to come (despite appearances to the contrary)'.

If we turn to the beginning of the letter, the shape of 2 Peter as a whole becomes more evident. The section 1:3–4 acts as a heading over the entire letter, and in many ways encapsulates it: God's power enables us to live in a manner that he will not condemn, through our personal knowledge of him worked out in a holy life. That is the theme of chapter 2, applied to Christians who believe rather than false teachers who question. God's promises will enable us to escape the final conflagration and to take our place in the new home rather than the old one. That is the theme of chapter 3. The concluding verses of the letter (3:17–18) match this opening, emphasizing the danger of those who encourage us to follow them into lawless disobedience – the behaviour that, as chapter 2 teaches us, God will judge. Such behaviour has no place in our new home – the teaching of chapter 3. We therefore need to grow in our knowledge of the one who will be our Saviour.

The next verses, 1:5–7, follow on from these opening words: 'for this very reason' we need to live lives now that demonstrate our future values and our faith in a Judge who will judge, a King who will come and a Saviour who will save.

The section 1:8–11 then falls into place. It seems odd at first that Peter argues so negatively: he says that God will keep us from being 'ineffective and unproductive' rather than that God will make us effective and productive. But if chapters 2 and 3 balance each other, then we might expect this section to anticipate the application of both chapters. The negative warning of 1:8–10 prefigures the negative warning of chapter 2's application (2:17–22; note the 'falling away' motif in each). The positive encouragement of 1:10–11 prefigures the positive encouragement of chapter 3's application (3:11–16; note the hope in a new created order in each).

Then, in 1:12–15, we have the reasons for Peter's writing. This paragraph stands as a formal gateway to the coming section as Peter solemnly urges his readers never to move from what he is about to tell them.

2 Peter, then, coheres much more tightly as a literary unit than is normally thought. The twin themes of power and coming dominate both the shape and content of the letter, and 1:16–21 becomes the key passage for a correct understanding of the whole.

Such a deeply structured way of writing is alien to us. But we should not think of 2 Peter, or indeed most of the New Testament, as primarily written pieces of work. They were written to be listened to in public rather than read privately, and therefore the writers had to give aural clues to the progress of an argument. The original manuscripts lacked our modern indicators of structure – punctuation, paragraphs and variety of typefaces – and it should not surprise us that the authors developed methods of laying out the text that would make the meaning clear.

Study guide

The aim of this study guide is to help you to get to the heart of what the authors have written and to challenge you to apply what you learn to your own life. The questions have been designed for use by individuals or by small groups of Christians meeting, perhaps for an hour or two each week, to study, discuss and pray together.

The guide provides material for each of the sections in the book. When used by a group with limited time, the leader should decide beforehand which questions are most appropriate for the group to discuss during the meeting, and which should perhaps be left for group members to work through by themselves or in smaller groups during the week.

In order to be able to contribute fully and learn from the group meetings, each member of the group needs to read through the section or sections under discussion, together with the passages in each letter to which they refer.

It is important not to let these studies become merely academic exercises. Guard against this by making time to think through and discuss how what you discover *works out in practice* for you. Make sure you begin and end each study by focusing on God in praise and prayer. Ask the Holy Spirit to speak to you through your discussion together.

2 Peter

2 Peter 1:1–2
1. The genuine article (pp. 28–42)

1   What lies 'at the heart of Peter's concern in this letter' (p. 28)? What experience have you had of this?
2   How do you know that the Christianity you 'have received, believed, lived and passed on to others' (p. 29) is authentic? Do you think this really matters? Why?

1. The genuine apostle: the gospel's origin (1:1a)

3 What double significance is there in Peter's description of himself as *a servant . . . of Jesus Christ* (p. 31)?

4 How does a Christian leader merit the description 'apostolic'? Why should we avoid calling such leaders 'apostles' today (pp. 31ff.)?

'The reason for Peter's importance and authority today lies not in his intellect or personality, but in the one who sent [him] to us' (p. 33).

---

2. The genuine Christian: the gospel's quality (1:1b)

5 How would you answer someone who cast doubt on the relevance for us today of what happened to Jesus two thousand years ago (p. 34)?

6 What aspects of being a Christian does Peter stress here which are as true for us now as they were for the first Christians (pp. 34f.)?

3. The genuine experience: the gospel's results (1:2)

7 What does Peter mean by *grace and peace*? In what ways do you experience these (pp. 35ff.)?

8 'It is dangerously easy to be a well-informed non-Christian who misses the key ingredient' (p. 37). What key ingredient is this? Where does it come from?

4. The genuine Christ: the gospel's content (1:1b–2)

9 What are the four titles that Peter uses 'as indicators of the purity of our message's content' (p. 38)? What does each of these mean?

10 'There is a constant temptation to separate these four titles' (p. 41). In what ways do you face this temptation? Why?

2 Peter 1:3–4
2. The power and the promises (pp. 43–54)

1 How do you react when you see people who are 'enjoying things which the Bible clearly forbids' (p. 43)? How does what Peter says here help?

1. The power of Jesus Christ (1:3)

2 What is the power of Jesus intended to achieve in us (pp. 45ff.)? Does it do this in your life? How?

3 'There will always be people who want to supplement the work of Christ with extra teaching' (p. 48). What experience have you had of this tendency? How is it to be resisted?

2. The promises of Jesus Christ (1:4)

4 Why do some commentators object to the claim that Christians *may participate in the divine nature* (pp. 51f.)? What do you think? Why?

5 What does Christopher Green mean by 'under-realized' and 'over-realized' eschatology (p. 52)? In which direction do you tend to err? What is the answer to these distortions?

2 Peter 1:5–11
3. The productive Christian (pp. 55–64)

1 'If we are justified by God's irrevocable grace, we enjoy a new kind of relationship with God where ideas of law and obedience are inappropriate' (p. 55). How would you answer this claim in the light of what Peter says here?

1. The effective Christian (1:5–9)

2 If Jesus has given us 'everything we need for life and godliness' (1:3), why do we need to *make every effort* (1:5) to supplement our faith (p. 57)?

'Personal and private assent to Jesus' lordship, if it is authentic, must work itself out in public and practical ways' (p. 57).

---

3 Peter sets out a number of ingredients that make up the Christian character (pp. 58ff.). Why does he select these in particular? Which do you find you need to work on? How will you set about it?

4 What happens to those who do not have these qualities (pp. 61f.)? Why?

2. The eternal Christian (1:10–11)

5 What is 'the acid test of the genuineness of our faith' (p. 63)? On this basis, how genuine is yours?

6 What two eternal blessings does Peter mention here (pp. 63f.)? What does he mean by them?

2 Peter 1:12–15
4. Remember, remember (pp. 65–72)

1. Reminding (1:12)

1 Why does Peter need to keep reminding his readers about what he has just told them (pp. 66ff.)?

2 How can those who teach the Bible resist the 'temptation to hold people's attention with something new' (p. 67)? Why is it so important that they do so?

'Returning continually to the core truths of Christianity is part of a growing Christian self-understanding' (p. 68).

---

3 What lesson does Peter apply here from his own experience (p. 68)? Can you apply the same lesson from yours?

2. Refreshing (1:13–14)

4 How has Peter come to terms with the imminence of his death (pp. 68f.)? What is his priority at this time?

5 If you knew you had only, say, a week left to live, what do you think you would do? Why?

3. Remembering (1:15)

6 What suggestions have been made as to what Peter is referring to in this verse (pp. 70f.)? Which do you think is more likely?

7 What is the basic underlying point from which the scholarly discussions about this verse might distract us (p. 71)? How does this point apply to you?

4. The danger of spiritual absent-mindedness

8 'Although two thousand years of church history have elapsed, there is a sense in which every generation of Christians is only the second generation' (p. 71). What practical implications of this observation can you think of?

'The business of the church and of preaching is not to present us with new and interesting ideas, it is rather to go on reminding us of certain fundamental and eternal truths' (Martyn Lloyd-Jones, quoted on p. 71).

---

2 Peter 1:16–21
5. The witnesses (pp. 73–84)

1. The apostles' evidence (1:16–18)

1 Which particular doctrine was Peter and his fellow apostles accused of inventing (pp. 74f.)? How does he defend his position?
2 What significance is there in the allusions to Psalm 2 in verse 17 (pp. 77ff.)?

2. The prophets' evidence (1:19–21)

3 What two reasons does Peter give for reading the Old Testament (pp. 82f.)?
4 What does Peter want his readers to understand *above all* about the Old Testament (pp. 83f.)? Why is this so important?
5 How does what Peter writes here help us to understand the relationship between the Old and New Testaments (p. 84)?

2 Peter 2:1–3
6. The fifth column (pp. 85–93)

1. The ever-present danger (2:1a)

1 Why do you think that 'false teaching is an ever-present and inevitable danger in any church or denomination' (p. 87)? Why does God allow this?

2. The ever-gullible church (2:1b–3a)

2   What five warning signs does Peter identify to help his readers spot false teachers (pp. 87ff.)?
3   What light do these verses shed on the question whether it is possible for a Christian to lose salvation (pp. 88f.)?

'It is an inevitable hallmark of no longer believing in the second coming that ethics becomes a matter of private choice and taste' (p. 90).

---

4   Why are false teachers so popular (p. 90)? To what extent do you let people's popularity determine whether or not what they say is true?
5   Do you face the temptation to let 'the bank balance rule the church's priorities' (p. 92)? What does this lead to? What steps can be taken to avoid this?

3. The ever-wakeful God (2:3b)

6   How would you answer someone who suggested that, given the way false teachers seem to get away with it, the idea of divine judgment is clearly illusory (pp. 92f.)?

2 Peter 2:4–9
7. Putting the world on hold (pp. 94–102)

1. Three biblical examples of God's wise judgment (2:4–8)

1   What two points does Peter make from the example of the angels who sinned (pp. 95ff.)?
2   What further points emerge from the example of the ungodly people in the time of Noah (p. 98)?
3   Two other points come from the example of Sodom and Gomorrah. What are they (pp. 100f.)?
4   How does what Peter says here challenge our attitude to the world around us? How might this work out in practice for you?

2. God is in control (2:9)

5   What is the 'hard topic' (p. 101) which Peter now deals with? What is his answer?

> 'The temptation is to think that because the unright-
> eous seem to run the world, and sometimes the
> churches too, God has ceased to rule. He has not'
> (p. 102).

6   '... The alert Christian will find it a painful business to be
faithful surrounded by filth' (p. 102). To what extent are you
actually rather comfortable with the world around you? Why is
this a dangerous state to be in?

2 Peter 2:10–22, Part I (2:10–16)
8. Profile of a deadly minister (pp. 103–114)

> 'What twentieth-century Christians might well notice
> is the sharp difference between the respect paid to false
> teachers today and the treatment they received from
> the apostles' (G. H. Clark, quoted on p. 103).

1. What happened then still happens today (2:10a)

1   Can you think of any examples of false teachers known to you?
How have you recognized them?
2   What two characteristics of false teachers does Peter focus on
here (pp. 104f.)?

2. False teachers despise legitimate spiritual authority
(2:10b–13a)

3   What underlying error is Peter dealing with in these verses
(pp. 106ff.)?
4   'Well-explained rationalism and modern reinterpretations of
Christian ethics are an excuse for people to get away with what
they want' (p. 109). What examples of this can you think of?
What will be the result for those who teach such things?

3. False teachers follow the corrupt desire of the sinful nature (2:13b–16)

5 What effects of following 'the corrupt desire of the sinful nature' (2:10) does Peter mention here (pp. 110ff.)?

6 How does the story of Balaam illustrate Peter's argument (pp. 112ff.)?

7 Can you think of any situations in which perhaps you need to be prepared to be like the donkey who confronted Balaam (p. 114)?

2 Peter 2:10–22, Part II (2:17–22)
9. Profile of a deadly ministry (pp. 115–123)

1. How to spot the problem (2:17)

1 Does false teaching make you angry (p. 115)? Why?

2. Dry springs: they have nothing of value to say (2:18)

2 What does Peter lead us to expect of false teachers here (pp. 116f.)? Can you think of any examples?

3. Driven mists: they are powerless in the face of sin (2:19)

'We must beware of people whose promises differ from God's' (p. 118).

---

3 What is wrong with the promise of freedom made by the false teachers Peter has in mind here (pp. 118f.)?

4 'Closer examination will reveal a gap between (on the one hand) what these people claim publicly for their relationship with God, and (on the other) their private self-indulgence' (p. 119). Are there any such gaps between your public and private life? From what Peter has said so far, what can such hypocrisy lead to?

4. Darkness is reserved: they are destined for judgment (2:20–22)

5 Why do these verses cause 'great anxiety' to some Christians (p. 120)? How may such concerns be allayed?

6 What classic diagnostic features of unbelief does Christopher Green identify (pp. 121f)? How would you help someone who discovers these things in his or her own life?

7 Were the false teachers Peter is writing about *ever* Christians (pp. 122f.)? How do you reach your conclusion?

2 Peter 3:1–2
10. Have you forgotten anything? (pp. 124–127)

1. The connection with 2 Peter 2

1 'This section starts with a sudden jolt' (p. 124). How may this be explained (p. 125)? Which solution seems most satisfactory to you? Why?

2. The connection with 2 Peter 1

2 What links are there between the beginning of chapter 3 and chapter 1 (p. 125)? What does this underline about Peter's strategy in the letter as a whole?

3. The connection with the past

3 If this is Peter's second letter, which was his first (pp. 125f.)? How do you evaluate the suggestions that have been made?

4. The connections

4 'What these verses confirm is that Peter is still...' (p. 126). What does Christopher Green have in mind? How do these verses do this?

2 Peter 3:3–7
11. God's powerful Word (pp. 128–135)

1 What is the 'key question' that Peter now has to face (p. 128)? Why is it such an important one for the way we live our lives?

1. Scoffers will come (3:3)

2 What does Peter mean by *the last days* (p. 129)? What are we to expect during this time?

2. Their question and the reason (3:4)

3 What is the underlying reason for the question asked by the scoffers (p. 130)?

3. The flaw in the reason: God's powerful word (3:5–7)

4 How have the scoffers gone wrong in the reasoning behind their question (pp. 131f.)? Why have they made this mistake?

2 Peter 3:8–10
12. God's promised patience (pp. 136–143)

1. The Lord's promised patience demonstrated from the Old Testament (3:8–9)

1 How do the scoffers choose to interpret God's apparent failure to judge (pp. 136f.)? What is the correct interpretation of this fact? How does Peter demonstrate this?

2 How does the context of Psalm 90 help to broaden our understanding of what Peter is saying here (pp. 138ff.)?

3 Do these verses mean that, in the end, everyone will be saved (p. 139)? How do you arrive at your conclusion?

4 What 'logical corollary' (p. 139) of verse 9 does Christopher Green mention here? How are you going about this?

2. The Lord's promised return demonstrated from the New Testament (3:10)

5 What are the four stages of Peter's description of the day of judgment (pp. 142f.)?

6 What risk might we seem to be taking 'in presenting such a God to our non-Christian friends' (p. 143)? Do you hesitate at this point? What do you think Peter would say to you?

2 Peter 3:11–16
13. Looking forward to a new home
(pp. 144–153)

1. What does the future hold? (3:11–12a)

1 According to Peter, why does our human response to the future destruction of the cosmos matter so much (pp. 145f.)?

2 What can we do to speed the coming of the day of God (p. 146)? To what extent are you doing these things?

'Only those who are striving after holiness would dare to wish for the coming of the Day of the Lord'
(J. W. C. Wand, quoted on p. 146).

---

2. How will God keep his promise? (3:12b–13)

3 What 'new idea' about divine judgment is contained in these verses (pp. 147f.)? How should this affect the way we live now?

3. What kind of people should we be? (3:14)

4 Why is it so important for us to *make every effort* to live holy lives, as Peter indicates here (pp. 148f.)?

5 Does anything prevent you from being *found spotless, blameless and at peace with him*? What can you do about it?

4. How can we speed the day of God? (3:15–16)

6 What do 'Christians have enormous difficulty in grasping' (p. 150)? Why is this? How does what Peter says help?

7 How does Peter underline the urgency of his appeal concerning the return of Jesus (pp. 151ff.)?

8 How can we learn to 'handle God's Word with integrity, honesty and a desire to seek out what it says' (p. 153)?

2 Peter 3:17–18
14. The message of 2 Peter (pp. 154–158)

1. The guarded Christian (3:17)

1 What three areas in which Christians need to be guarded does Christopher Green draw to our attention (pp. 155f.)? How can we remain firm?

2. The growing Christian (3:18a)

2 Why is it so important for us to *grow in the grace and knowledge of . . . Christ* (pp. 156f.)? How can we do this?

> *'Every day represents a fresh challenge, when we will be tempted to forget everything we have learned over the years, and trade it in for a novelty item' (p. 157).*

3. The glorious Christ (3:18b)

3 What is 'quite breathtakingly daring' about this final verse (pp. 157f.)?

Jude

Jude 1–2
1. Jude the obscure? (pp. 165–170)

1. The writer (1a)

1 Why has this letter had such a 'battle for acceptance in the history of the church' (pp. 165f.)?

2 What do we know about Jude (pp. 166f.)? If he really was Jesus' brother, why does he not mention the fact?

2. The readers (1b)

3 What three things does Jude say about his readers (pp. 169f.)? Why does he stress aspects which hark back to the Old Testament?

> *'Jesus Christ is the cabinet in which God's jewels are kept; so that if we would stand, we must get out of ourselves and get into him, in whom alone there is safety' (Thomas Manton, quoted on p. 169).*

3. The prayer (2)

4 In what ways do the topics in Jude's prayer have 'a force which is relevant to his theme' (p. 170)?

263

Jude 3–4
2. Churches in danger (pp. 171–181)

1. The salvation we share (3a)

1 What do you understand by the word 'salvation' (p. 172)? What specifically does Jude say about it here?

2. The faith we defend (3b)

2 In what senses does 'the faith' need defending (pp. 172ff.)? Why?

3 What does Christopher Green describe as 'the acid test of our contemporary expression of Christianity' (p. 175)? Do you find this difficult? Why?

4 Are you comfortable applying the label 'saint' to yourself (pp. 175f.)? In what ways is this for you 'at once an honour, an exhortation, and a reproach'?

3. The opposition we expect (4)

5 What does (or would) it mean for you to 'contend for the faith' in your situation (pp. 176f.)?

'The evidence throughout the Bible is that being faithful to God's Word means bringing hard, unpopular warnings as well as bright promises' (p. 176).

---

6 How are we to determine when it is right to affirm and when to rebuke those who think differently from us (p. 176f.)?

7 How do you react to the warning that 'there will always be opposition to biblical truths within churches' (pp. 178f)?

8 How does Jude characterize those against whom his readers are to contend for the faith (pp. 179ff.)? How can we recognize similar people today?

Jude 5–8
3. Warnings of judgment:
three Old Testament examples (pp. 182–190)

1 What is 'the importance of memory in biblical terms' (pp. 182f)? What is the test of a good memory? How good is yours?

1 The warnings (5–7)

2 What three examples of warnings from the Old Testament does Jude bring in at this point (pp. 183ff.)? What lessons does he intend us to learn?

3 Why is the traditional understanding of the identity of the sin of Sodom 'currently under ... scrutiny' (p. 186)? What do you think? Why?

2 'These dreamers' (8)

4 How does Jude characterize those he warns his readers about here (pp. 188ff.)? How are their modern counterparts likely to express themselves?

'If you accept Jesus' lordship "either your doctrine will make your life blush, or your life will make your doctrine blush, and be ashamed"' (Thomas Manton, quoted on p. 189).

---

5 Why does Jude call them *dreamers* (p. 190)? In what ways is this 'a clue to a much more serious problem in his church than we would otherwise imagine'? Is this a problem in your church?

Jude 9–10
4. Warnings of judgment:
a familiar example (pp. 191–196)

1 Why have some Christians had difficulty with the episodes alluded to in verses 9–10 and 14–16 (pp. 191f.)? How does what Christopher Green says here help?

265

1. Michael, Moses and the devil (9)

2 What point is Jude making by recounting this story (p. 194)?

2. 'These men' (10)

3 'The problems in Jude's church were coming from people who ... (p. 194).' What? How does Jude further characterize them? How can we avoid falling into the same errors?
4 'The examples may change from Jude's day, but the principle is exactly the same' (p. 196). What principle? What modern examples can you think of?

Jude 11–13
5. Warnings of judgment: three further Old Testament examples (pp. 197–204)

1. God judged rebellious leaders (11)

1 What truths are illustrated by the mention of Cain, Balaam and Korah (pp. 197ff.)? In what way is this list a sequence?
2 What is 'worth remembering' (p. 201) as we reach 'this ghastly climax'?

2. 'These men' (12–13)

3 How does Jude describe the equivalents of Cain, Balaam and Korah in his own day (pp. 201ff.)? What are these images intended to convey?
4 What evidence of such activity are you aware of in their modern counterparts?

Jude 14–16
6. Warnings of judgment: a further familiar example (pp. 205–212)

1. Enoch (14–15)

1 What problem is raised for some by the fact that Enoch's prophecy 'is not in our biblical record' (p. 206)? How may it be resolved?
2 What two points about God's judgment are underlined by these verses (pp. 208f.)?

> '*Once we cease to believe in the God the Bible reveals,*
> *we will feel free to indulge ourselves by making God in*
> *our own image' (pp. 209).*

2. 'These men' (16)

3 What does Jude intend us to understand by the word *grumblers* (pp. 209f.)?
4 How would you answer someone who suggested that 'the fight to be holy is an unnecessary weight' (p. 210)?
5 How else does Jude describe *these men* (pp. 210ff.)? Why is what they do so dangerous?

Jude 17–19
7. Signs of the times:
a warning from the apostles (pp. 213–217)

1 What might have been strange to Jude's original readers about his quoting of the apostles (p. 213)? How does this help us in evaluating the relationship between Old and New Testaments?

1. The signs of the times (17–18)

2 What do these verses indicate as having been the 'constant refrain' of the apostles (pp. 214f.)? Why is this still so important today?

> '*Jude is keen for us to see how scepticism and an*
> *un-Christian lifestyle can be easy partners' (p. 215).*

2. 'These are the men' (19)

3 What threefold description does Jude now give of the false teachers (pp. 216f.)? What experience have you had of these things?
4 In what practical ways should we demonstrate concern for 'the purity of the gospel' (p. 216)? Which suggested routes to such purity would Jude encourage us to avoid?

5 'It is very easy to claim to be led by the Spirit' (p. 217). How can
   we be sure that we really are being led by the Spirit?

Jude 20–21
8. Contending for the faith:
the Christian (pp. 218–224)

1 Christopher Green suggests two wrong responses to the activity
   of false teachers. What are these (pp. 218f.)? In what ways are
   you tempted to adopt them yourself?

---

*'The pure church of one generation faces the very real
danger of becoming the heretical church of the next'
(p. 219).*

---

2 What examples of 'unity at the price of doctrine' can you think
   of (p. 219)? What could you do to put this right?

1. Build yourselves up in your most holy faith (20a)

3 Why does Jude call our faith *most holy* (p. 220)? What implications of this can you think of?
4 What is 'the first sign that a Christian is in danger of falling
   away' (p. 221)? Do you know anyone in this position? How
   could you help?

2. Pray in the Holy Spirit (20b)

5 What do you think it means to *pray in the Holy Spirit*
   (pp. 221ff.)? How far can your conclusions be justified from
   what Jude writes in this letter?

3. Keep yourselves in God's love (21a)

6 How might we 'position ourselves outside' the love of God
   (p. 223)? What steps can we take to avoid this?

4. Wait for the mercy of our Lord Jesus Christ (21b)

7 In what senses do you enjoy eternal life now (p. 224)? What
   awaits you in the future? Why is it so important to get this
   distinction right?

Jude 22–23
9. Contending for the faith:
the fallen Christian (pp. 225–229)

1. Be merciful to those who doubt (22)

1 What is your attitude to those with doubts about their faith? What would it mean in practice for you to give more help to such people (p. 226)?

2. Snatch others from the fire and save them (23a)

2 What does Jude mean here by *fire* (pp. 226f.)? How can people be snatched from it?

3. To others show mercy, mixed with fear (23b)

3 How does the episode described in Zechariah 3 help in understanding these verses (p. 228)?

4 'There is no person who is so irredeemably bad that God's forgiveness cannot remove the stain' (p. 228). What are the implications of this statement for us in our attitude to false teachers?

'We cannot lower God's standards in the hope that if the terms are easier, more people will repent' (p. 229).

Jude 24–25
10. Contending for the faith:
the salvation we share (pp. 230–234)

1. He is able to keep you from falling (24a)

1 What 'massive reassurance' do these verses contain (p. 231)? How does this apply to you?

2. He is able to present you before his presence (24b)

2 What 'wonderful transformation' is Jude looking forward to (p. 232)? How will God achieve this?

3. Hallelujah! What a Saviour! (25)

3 What 'new element in Jude's praise' is underlined here (p. 234)?
4 What is the 'one great reason' behind Jude's expression of praise (p. 234)? To what extent can you share in what he says? How?